The South:
A Concise History

Volume II

The South:
A Concise History

Jeanette Keith

Prentice
Hall

Upper Saddle River, New Jersey 07458

Library of Congress Cataloging-in-Publication Data
KEITH, JEANETTE.
    The South: a concise history / Jeanette Keith.
        p.   cm.
    Includes bibliographical references and index.
    ISBN 0-13-022056-6 (vol. 1) — ISBN 0-13-094198-0 (vol. 2)
    1. Southern States—History. 2. Southern States—Social conditions. I. Title.
F209 .K44 2002
975—dc21

                                                                            2001034599

Editorial Director: *Charlyce Jones Owen*
Acquisitions Editor: *Emsal Hasan*
AVP, Director of Production and Manufacturing: *Barbara Kittle*
Editorial Production/Supervision and Interior Design: *Judith Winthrop*
Cover Design: *Kiwi Design*
Prepress and Manufacturing Buyer: *Tricia Kenny*
Supervisor of Production Services: *Guy Ruggiero*
Cartographers: *Carto-Graphics, Mirella Signoretto*
Copy editor: *Jamie Fuller*

This book was set in 10.5/13 New Baskerville by The Composing Room
of Michigan, Inc. and was printed and bound by Courier-Stoughton
The cover was printed by Phoenix Color Corporation.

© 2002 by Pearson Education
Upper Saddle River, New Jersey 07458

Printed in the United States of America
10 9 8 7 6 5 4 3 2 1

ISBN 0-13-094198-0

PEARSON EDUCATION LTD., *London*
PEARSON EDUCATION AUSTRALIA PTY, Limited, *Sydney*
PEARSON EDUCATION SINGAPORE, Pte. Ltd.
PEARSON EDUCATION NORTH ASIA LTD., *Hong Kong*
PEARSON EDUCATION CANADA, LTD, *Toronto*
PEARSON EDUCACIÓN DE MEXICO, S.A. DE C.V.
PEARSON EDUCATION– –JAPAN, *Tokyo*
PEARSON EDUCATION MALAYSIA, Pte. Ltd.
PEARSON EDUCATION, Upper Saddle River, *New Jersey*

Contents

3

Modern Times:
The South 1900–1930 *88*

4

The South and the Nation,
1930–1946 *124*

Preface

Although I am a native Southerner, born and raised in rural Tennessee, I teach southern history at Bloomsburg University of Pennsylvania, a small state college in the North. My students think southern history is dramatic, full of exotic characters and exciting events. They are fascinated by the Old South and the Civil War, moved by the Civil Rights Movement, and curious about southern culture and folkways. Their interest is partly practical: many of them will be moving south in search of work after graduation.

For my southern history class, I wanted to assign a series of primary texts, essays, scholarly articles, and fiction pieces, but I knew that my students would need a textbook for background. Unable to find the sort of concise narrative history I wanted, I wrote this book.

The South: A Concise History is one extended story, or history, of the nation's most distinctive region from colonial settlement to the present. In composing this story, I have tried to incorporate new scholarship about race, class, and gender. This is another way of saying that the characters in this story are not just members of the political elite, but also include dirt farmers, Indians, plantation mistresses, slaves, factory workers, civil rights leaders, and all the motley collection of personages that make southern history one of the best stories around.

I have concentrated more on what happened than on detailed explanations of why, in the belief that the route into history comes through narrative: knowledge of the basic outline of events is a necessary precursor to analysis. In that spirit, I urge students of southern history to use this book as an avenue into further exploration of southern history and culture.

The field of southern history is fiercely political and deeply contested. I am sure that southern historians of all political stripes will find things here that offend them. I am also positive that my fellow historians will wish I had done more with this or supplied more information on that. The book is intentionally short. Far from wanting the last word, I hope that readers of this book will be intrigued by the stories they find here and look for more history and analysis, starting with the suggestions for further reading and viewing appended to each chapter.

For their help with and judicious criticism of this project, I wish to thank Tony Allen, Michael Hickey, Susan Stemont, Scott Nelson, Cindy Hahamovitch, Mark Quintanilla, Jeff Davis, Tim Tyson, Mel McKiven, Anastatia Sims, David Carlton, members of the Southern Humanities Council (who heard about the project in a presentation in 1999) and the readers who critiqued the manuscript for Prentice Hall: Eric H. Walther, University of Houston; Tommy R. Thompson, University of Nebraska at Omaha; Richard L. Hume, Washington State University; Norman G. Raiford, Greenville Technical College; Christopher Waldrep, East Illinois University; Robert Thurston, Miami University. All sins of commission and omission in this work are my own.

Most of all, I wish to thank my students at Bloomsburg University of Pennsylvania, where I have taught American history for the past twelve years. Over the years, their comments and questions have enlightened me as to what students can be expected to know, and not to know, about the history of the South. They have also been very forthright about what they would like to know more about, and what they would not. If this book proves readable and entertaining as well as useful, much credit is due to them.

Introduction

Why Study the South?

In the summer of the first year of the new millennium, the state of South Carolina removed from its statehouse the Confederate flag, a symbol of a nation that had been dead for 135 years. Raised above the capitol in 1962 in commemoration of the centennial of the Civil War, the flag of the defeated rebellion had other meanings as well. For some South Carolinians, the flag symbolized "southern heritage," a complex of emotions and ideas including loyalty to home and honor to ancestors, particularly those who fought for southern independence against the federal government in the 1860s. For others, the flag symbolized slavery, and they consid-ered it a shameful reminder of past racial injustice and present-day racism.

When the National Association for the Advancement of Colored People (NAACP) called on tourists to boycott South Carolina until the flag was removed, the battle lines were drawn. Southern heritage advocates, overwhelmingly white people, insisted that the flag had nothing to do with racism, while the NAACP and its supporters, both black and white, retorted that the flag signified both slavery and white supremacy. Meanwhile, the tourism boycott hurt businesses in the state, and businessmen of all races began pressuring the state government to take the flag down.

Finally, the state's governor worked out a compromise: the flag would be removed from the capitol spire but placed above a Confederate memorial on the grounds nearby. In July, cadets from the Citadel, a state-funded military school located in Charleston, ceremoniously removed the flag and, accompanied by an honor guard dressed in gray uniforms, carried it to its new location. At the event, crowds representing both sides waved flags and picket signs and shouted at each other. Unsatisfied, the president of the NAACP called for the continuation of the boycott and bitterly criticized the black South Carolina legislators who had voted for the compromise.

Two other southern states, Georgia and Mississippi, had replicas of the Confederate flag built into their state flags. Students of the issue expected the controversy to continue for years to come.

.   .   .

Why study the South? In this time of global markets and international business, when Americans from Maine to California share the same popular culture with people all over the planet, shouldn't we concentrate on the big national picture? Aren't all Americans pretty much alike anyway, regardless of which region they live in?

As the saga of the continuing controversy over the Confederate flag indicates, the answer is—not exactly. While southerners of all races today are more like other Americans than they are different, the differences can still be striking. Where else in this country do people get so mad over history? But of course, no other region in the United States has a history like the South's.

At the core of that history is the Civil War, a major turning point not only in regional but in national history. The war grew out of decades of sectional conflict revolving around the issue of slavery. Prevalent in all the states when the nation was founded, slavery was abolished in the northern states after the Revolution, thus becoming the South's "peculiar institution." By the 1850s slavery seemed the essential cornerstone of southern life to most of the region's political leaders. They viewed the creation of the Republican Party as a threat, since the Republicans built their politics around promises to prevent the spread of slavery into newly acquired western territories. Many southern leaders believed that the Republicans, once in power, would not be content with stopping the spread of slavery but would move to abolish the institution in the South. The election of Republican Abraham Lincoln in 1860 provoked the crisis: convinced that their peculiar institution was no longer safe in the federal union, the Deep South states seceded to form the Confederate States of America. When Lincoln called for troops to put down the rebellion, most of the upper tier of the South joined the Confederacy. The ensuing war lasted for four years (1861–65) and still heads the list of the nation's most deadly conflicts, having claimed the lives of 600,000 American men.

The war established the United States as a nation, not just a conglomerate of affiliated states. It settled the question of states' rights: the federal government is sovereign over the states. Beginning as a war of national unification, the Civil War ended as a war of liberation, setting free millions of Americans of African descent. Although the Union did not fight the war to free the slaves—ending slavery did not become federal policy until two years into the conflict and was then prompted by military necessity—generations of Americans have chosen to gloss over that fact, creating a mythology of the nation as crusader for freedom. Socially, politically, and economically, the United States as we know it today was born through the destruction of the Old South.

But within the region old times were not forgotten. The nation's designated defeated, the only Americans (until Vietnam) to lose a war, white southerners built a cult of loss and remembrance that reverberates in political conflicts today. However, their unwillingness to let go of the Old South also reflected the dearth of economic choices available in the region after the Civil War.

During the late nineteenth and early twentieth centuries, the South was the nation's poorest region, with the vast majority of the population, regardless of race, working in low-wage jobs or in agriculture. The region's states anchored the bottom of every statistical list measuring progress, having the nation's worst schools, poorest health, lowest incomes, and so on. It was a full century after the Civil War before the southern economy began to draw even with the rest of the nation.

During this time of poverty and defeat, white southerners created a system of legal structures that cut blacks out of the political system and denied them equal access to public facilities and state-funded services. The "Jim Crow" system, as it was called, segregated blacks from whites in all public places. Middle-aged southern whites and blacks today can still remember segregated schools and water fountains labeled "White" or "Colored." When black southerners began to struggle for their rights, sometimes with the somewhat reluctant help of the federal government, many white southerners resisted defiantly; it was during that period, in the 1960s, that the Confederate flag appeared again over the South Carolina capitol.

Today the South is as officially racially integrated as any other part of the nation. Legal segregation having ended almost forty years ago, black professionals have created a small market in the memorabilia of Jim Crow, buying up the "Whites Only" and "Colored Only" signs as antiques. After decades of leaving the region for better jobs and living conditions in the North, African-Americans began in the 1970s to move back to the South, a trend that continues. Black politicians serve as mayors of major southern cities, sheriffs of southern counties, and legislators throughout the region.

But southern memories are long. The South's greatest writer, Nobel Prize-winning novelist William Faulkner, once had a character say that the past was not dead: "Hell, it isn't even past." As the flag controversy shows, southerners sometimes act as if Faulkner was right. In the South, history matters, and bad history—history that tells lies about the past— can have serious contemporary political consequences. For people living in the region, a sense of history can be an essential social, cultural and political skill. Those contemplating moving south would do well to at least familiarize themselves with the outlines of southern history, to avoid costly social and business faux pas.

However, historians think studying the South can be useful for other reasons as well. One group of historians says that we should study the region because the South is historically separate, or "distinctive," from the rest of the nation. Therefore, studying southern history allows us to make comparisons that help us understand national or world history. Other historians argue just the opposite: that the American South is "America squared," in the words of historian Steven Stowe. This is another way of saying that you cannot understand America without understanding the South: southern history *is* American history. Dominant themes in national history can be seen most clearly in the history of the South.

Southern Heritage Politics

"We, the founders of the Southern party, acting in the spirit of our Southern colonial and Confederate forefathers, believing American civilization derives its greatest strength from its historic Christian faith and its fidelity to limited constitutional government . . ." Thus begins the "Asheville Declaration" of a new political party, founded in 1999.

The Southern Party's Declaration (which can be found on its web site, http://www.southernparty.org/) provides a useful summary of distilled "southern heritage" rhetoric. The Southern Party insists that the Constitution created a government with limited powers, delegated to it by the states. States reserved the right to withdraw from the compact if needed to protect their liberties. But when the Southern states withdrew from the Union in 1861, they were "illegally invaded and conquered," before being subjugated, "the effects of which are still being felt today in the form of predatory taxation, an imperial presidency, and a tyrannical judiciary." Currently, the declaration says, the culture of the South is under threat from political correctness, as purveyed in schools, churches, and media, all designed to destroy southern culture.

In other publications, leaders of the Southern Party deny any intention to reestablish white supremacy and protest the use of the Confederate flag and other Old South symbols by hate groups.

This tiny political party has big plans. The Southern Party's goal is to increase local and state autonomy, ultimately leading to southern independence. It states that the process may take a long time but holds out as examples successes scored by nationalist movements in Quebec and, especially, Scotland, which recently convened its first independent parliament in almost 300 years.

But history is not just for professional historians. History buffs—those who study history because they love it—seem especially attracted to the history of the South, perhaps because it contains some of the most dramatic stories around. Those who study history because they are fascinated by human character find southern history to be full of examples of people exhibiting the worst, and the best, qualities found in human nature. Whatever else it may be, southern history is never boring, and it is studied in colleges from Atlanta to Tokyo.

Where is the South?

It depends on whom you ask: linguists, historians, sociologists, and geographers tend to have different answers. Linguists point out that various forms of the southern accent can be found from Maryland to central Florida, west through Texas, and north into southern Indiana and Illinois, which were originally settled by

Map of southern states

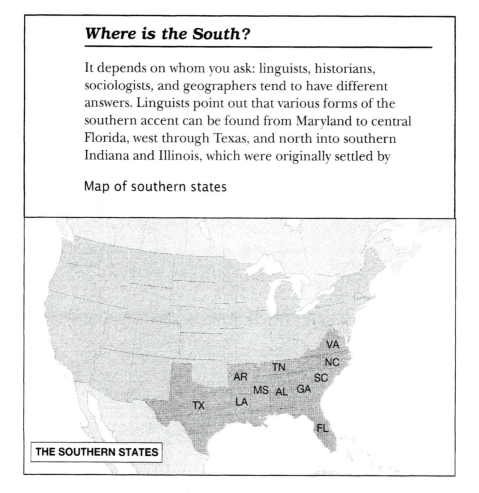

THE SOUTHERN STATES

southerners. Sociologists suggest that the South can be defined as that place where people think they are southerners; by this definition, places like northern Virginia and southern Florida are not in the South. Geographers might define the South by growing season and rainfall, thereby eliminating northern Kentucky and Virginia by temperature and western Texas for lack of rain. Historians have generally used two other factors to define the South: slavery and the Civil War. Historians argue that since slavery as a labor system is the most important difference between North and South, the South can be defined as composed of those states that still had slaves in 1860. By that definition, the South includes Delaware, Maryland, Kentucky, and Missouri. Other historians argue that the South can best be defined by the experience of the Civil War: the southern states are the ones that seceded, went to war, and were defeated. This book uses the last of these definitions. For our purposes, the South is composed of the states of the former Confederacy: Virginia, North and South Carolina, Florida, Georgia, Alabama, Mississippi, Louisiana, Texas, Arkansas, and Tennessee. However, students will find occasional references to events in the border states as well.

Separating History from Legend

For almost as long as there has been a United States, Americans have told stories about the distinctive qualities of the South. Much of what Americans think they know about the region falls under the category of myths and legends, both positive and negative.

Southern historians sometimes refer to the legend of the prewar Old South as the "moonlight and magnolias myth." Created by songwriters and novelists, enshrined in movies like *Gone with the Wind*, the mythological romantic Old South of gallant white men, spirited belles, and happy slaves is still attractive to a large portion of the American public. People with no ancestral connection to the South dress up as Confederates to reenact Civil War battles, take tours of antebellum mansions, and watch *North and South* every time the miniseries plays on television. Very few people, however, choose to reenact the role of plantation slave.

Nonsoutherners helped create the myth. Stephen Foster, the man who wrote the moonlight-and-magnolias music—those songs about Susannah, the Old Kentucky Home, Camptown Races, and all that doodah—was born in Pittsburgh and worked out of New York City. *Gone with the Wind,* the film that fixed the Old South myth in the public mind, was of course a Hollywood creation, although based on a novel written by a Georgian. White southerners have also been enthusiastic molders of the legend, creating their own myth of the Old South that both justifies and memorializes the Southern men who fought for independence in the Civil War. Many white southerners express pride in the South's distinctive past and loyalty to southern ways, including traditional notions of hospitality, courtesy, courage, and honor.

On the other hand, many Americans despise the myth of the romantic South. For them, the region is America's heart of darkness. This attitude dates to the 1830s, when antislavery writers, attempting to convince a northern audience that slavery was evil, depicted white southerners overwhelmingly as morally depraved, sexually predatory, and ferociously violent, not to mention ignorant, backward, and lazy. This stereotype has been too useful to die: even today it allows people in other regions of the country to cherish their own moral superiority and to congratulate themselves on the progress shown by their own institutions, without ever putting those assumptions to a reality check.

Historians find some truth, and a lot of nonsense, in both mythologies. Yet we must be aware that myths, however historically inaccurate, condition the way that people look at southern history and at the South today, and take that into account when studying regional history.

Regional Stereotypes

Sociologist John Shelton Reed has been studying the South for decades, with interesting and often amusing results. He began by studying self-identification, asking people if they thought they were southern. Among his findings from the 1970s was the following: the more education and money a white southerner had, the more important was southern identity. While less educated and sophisticated whites identified most with their own community, more educated and traveled southerners surveyed identified with "the South." What did being southern mean? In 1987 Reed polled self-identified white southern students at the University of North Carolina, gave them a list of terms, and asked them which applied to white southerners, which to white northerners, and which to Americans in general. Southern traits picked by the students included tradition-loving, very religious, courteous, and loyal to family ties; they labeled white northerners industrious, materialistic, progressive, aggressive, arrogant, loud, and rude.

Themes

Although there are many ways to look at the history of the South, in this book we will trace several interrelated themes. Look for the following topics to come up, with variations, in each chapter:

Race, Class, and Gender

For many Americans, the major theme of southern history is race. Those who know little about the region are still likely to remember that the Old South's society and economy depended on racially based slavery. Others remember the Jim Crow South. To some Americans, southern history is about white supremacy in the region that was home to the overwhelming majority of the nation's African-American population until well into the twentieth century.

Recently, however, historians have begun to look at the issue of race in southern history in a new light. Guided by the insistence of biologists that race has no scientific meaning, historians and social scientists have

Courtesy of Bruce Plante, *Chattanooga Times*.

This cartoon appeared during the Confederate flag controversy. What stereotypes does it reflect?

come to see race as socially constructed. That is, human beings chose to see some differences, and to ignore others, to create categories of difference that often serve the ends of the people in power. In the United States, most of the work of socially constructing race was done in the South, beginning in the colonial period: it was there that constructs of blackness and whiteness still influential upon American life first emerged. Today historians study the role of race in the South to see how the concept evolved, changed, and was used by various groups in the region's history.

Throughout most of southern history, white racial solidarity required that all white men be considered equal and equally responsible for keeping black men subordinate. All white men gained status by keeping blacks down. That was the way the southern system worked—in theory. However, white southerners understood quite well that all white men were not truly equal. The southern white upper class considered itself an aristocracy and expected deference from those with less money, status, and power. Poor whites often resented the power of the elite and expressed that resentment through politics. African-Americans, well aware of class differences among whites, looked down on very poor whites, whom they labeled "trash," and even within slavery developed their own system of rank. With emancipation, class differences sometimes led to conflicts within the black community. Among southerners of all races, class divisions led to bitter cultural and political struggles, some of which continue to shape southern politics to this day.

The traditional power of white men derived from their gender as well as their color. When southerners said that the South was a white *man's* country, they were not kidding. In the Old South, being a man meant being a master. White men demonstrated masculinity through their control of their households, including their slaves. Black men understood that in the South, gender intersected with race: to be denied equal rights with white men was to be denied manhood, and to assert equality was to assert masculinity. Southern gender roles for women were also shaped by race. White men justified slavery and segregation on the basis of gender, claiming that they did what they did to blacks to protect "white womanhood." On the other hand, one of the perks of white masculinity was sexual access to black women, with or without their consent. The history of southern gender roles has meant that struggles for racial justice always had gender implications, while attempts by women of both races to attain equality have been complicated by racial issues.

Religion

Today the South is as much distinguished by religion as by race. Yet the region sometimes called the "Bible Belt" was not always so. Colonial New England was settled in part by religious zealots, but the white leaders of the southern colonies came to America to make money. How the South got religion, and what black and white southerners did with their religious beliefs, is a major theme of southern history. The region is dominated by evangelical Protestants, Christians who believe that being "saved" is the most important event in a person's life. Southern blacks and whites share religious fervor, although they still mostly worship in separate congregations. To secular Americans, the force of southern religion is almost incomprehensible, and those who move into the region are astonished to be asked, "What church do you go to?" right after questions about name and occupation. Yet in southern history, religion has played a role in everything from slavery to the Civil Rights Movement to present-day politics.

Politics and Government: The Defense of Liberty

In 1784 Thomas Jefferson, the American revolutionary from Virginia, wrote to a French acquaintance that his fellow southerners were "zealous for their own liberties, but trampling on those of others." This contradiction is central to southern history: the slave society of the Old South produced many of the nation's most ardent proponents of freedom. Over the last 400 years, white southerners have defended liberty, as they understood it. Sometimes they believed that the greatest threat to their liberties was in the very organizations designed to defend them: governments, whether local or national. Since antebellum days, some white southerners have felt either that other Americans were hostile toward the South's institutions (especially slavery and segregation) or that the rest of the nation treated them as second-class citizens. On the local level, white southerners have been resistant to government regulation of private property, with impact on matters ranging from gun laws to zoning. Ironically, white southerners have often combined suspicion toward the government with willingness to grab as much government largess as possible: southern politicians have long been masters of pork-barrel politics, ensuring that their districts get ample shares of federal appropriations. Distrust of government, defense of liberty, and pork-barrel politics provide three interlocking themes of southern political history.

This volume takes up the history of the "New South," following the region's development from postwar Reconstruction to the present. On the face of it, this sweep of history lacks the drama afforded by an event as grand as the Civil War. Yet understanding the history of the New South is essential for insights into the region today. New South history can be grim, as befits the history of a defeated would-be nation. Students accustomed to the South's present booming economy should remember that the "old" New South, from the 1880s through the 1930s, was the United States' poorest region, a place characterized by hard work and poverty, occasionally spiced with disease, hunger, lynchings, and race riots.

During World War II, defense plant employment brought prosperity to southerners of both races, while the experience of fighting a war against the overtly racist Nazis helped underscore the evils of America's own racial systems. After the war, as the South experienced a period of economic prosperity, black southerners began a movement for racial equality. Sometimes called the black Freedom Movement, sometimes the Civil Rights Movement, the events that transformed the South were also called "Second Reconstruction." As the name indicates, the history of the recent South grows out of its past.

Suggestions for Further Reading

PETER APPLEBOME, *Dixie Rising: How the South is Shaping American Values, Politics, and Culture* (1997)

JOHN BOLES, *The South Through Time* (1995)

ROY BLOUNT, ED., *Roy Blount's Book of Southern Humor* (1994)

W. J. CASH, *The Mind of the South* (1941)

WILLIAM J. COOPER AND THOMAS E. TERRILL, *The American South* (1991)

CARL N. DEGLER, *Place over Time: The Continuity of South Distinctiveness* (1977)

LARRY J. GRIFFIN AND DON H. DOYLE, EDS., *The South as an American Problem* (1995)

TONY HORWITZ, *Confederates in the Attic: Dispatches from the Unfinished Civil War* (1998)

JACK TEMPLE KIRBY, *Media-Made Dixie* (1978)

JOHN SHELTON REED, *One South: An Ethnic Approach to Regional Culture* (1982)

————, *1001 Things Everyone Should Know About the South* (1996)

WILLIAM R. TAYLOR, *Cavalier and Yankee* (1961)

CHARLES REAGAN WILSON AND WILLIAM FERRIS, EDS., *Encyclopedia of Southern Culture* (1989)

C. VANN WOODWARD, *The Burden of Southern History*, 3d ed. (1993)

chapter

1

Reconstruction, 1862–1877

The Civil War has become a hobby for many Americans. People enjoy reading about campaigns, visiting battlefields on summer vacations, and even dressing up as Civil War soldiers to reenact battles. For many people, the war is deeply romantic, an American epic. No one feels that way about Reconstruction, the period from 1862 to 1877 during which the shattered nation attempted to reunify and reconstruct itself. After the sweeping narrative and fascinating characters of the Civil War, Reconstruction is a historical letdown. Reconstruction is about politics, economics, and law, not items easy to dramatize in period costumes. Even worse, Reconstruction is not a story with a happy ending.

The major players in Reconstruction all wanted different things. Having lost the war, white southerners accepted defeat but wanted to come back into the Union without making serious changes in the South's social system. Black southerners, now free, wanted the accoutrements of true freedom under the American system: political and property rights. The federal government, then under the control of the victorious Republican Party, wanted the South to become more like its idealized vision of the North, a haven of free labor and entrepreneurial capitalism. These were not compatible goals. Understandably, then, Reconstruction was a time of intense political conflict in the South and in the national government. Reconstruction lasted three times as long as the Civil War itself. When the period came to an end, none of the major players had completely achieved their goals, and all had become disillusioned and tired of the entire process.

No period in American history has been the subject of more debate than Reconstruction. Even the people who participated in Reconstruction disagreed about what happened then. For generations after 1877, white southerners learned from their parents and grandparents that Reconstruction represented the wicked revenge of the victorious North upon the prostrate, defeated South. White southerners insisted that Reconstruction, not the Civil War, left a legacy of bitterness between North and South. Meanwhile, black southerners remembered Reconstruction as a brief, shining moment when true political, social, and economic opportunities seemed possible for them; after Reconstruction, that hope had to be deferred for a hundred years.

The Historiography of Reconstruction

History does not change: what happened in the past happened. However, the way that historians interpret events often does change. Historians are influenced by the times in which they live, and they pick up on new ideas and concepts. Moreover, historians learn to use new techniques and technologies of research, thus changing the way they see the past. The way historians wrote about Reconstruction in 1920 is not the way they write about it today. The study of the evolution of historical writing is called *historiography*. Students working on doctorates in history spend at least as much time studying historiography as history, and sometimes more.

No field in American history offers a more dramatic historiography than that of Reconstruction, or one more revealing of American regional and racial attitudes. In the late nineteenth and early twentieth centuries, Columbia

University professor William Dunning and his students created a "school" of history that condemned Reconstruction as harsh, punitive, and a tragic error. This interpretation held sway for fifty years and became part of American popular culture: it is the version of history found in films like *Gone with the Wind,* for example.

The members of the Dunning school wrote as they did in part because they accepted without much question concepts about race held by most educated white Americans of the time. They assumed that blacks really were inferior, incapable of governing themselves, and they pictured black politicians as the pitiful dupes of carpetbaggers and scalawags. Understandably, the first challenges to the Dunning school came from black historians, led by W. E. B. DuBois, who in 1935 published *Black Reconstruction in America, 1860–1880.* However, the racial climate in the nation as a whole meant that DuBois and his followers did not receive much of a hearing.

In the 1950s, as the Civil Rights Movement heated up, the idea that blacks did not deserve citizenship rights seemed less and less defensible. Historians began to look again at Reconstruction. They produced a series of works that now comprise the revisionist school of Reconstruction historiography. The revisionists insisted that Reconstruction had produced much that was good in southern life, including the region's first public school systems. They pointed out that corruption in the South was no worse than elsewhere in the nation at the time. They rehabilitated the reputations of carpetbagger leaders, noting that many were motivated by principle, not profit. They showed how whites had terrorized politically active blacks. Most of all, revisionists showed blacks as political actors in their own right, not puppets.

Since the 1970s, a new postrevisionist school of Reconstruction historiography has developed. Taking for granted the right of black people to participate in politics, this new school instead focuses more on the Republican

> Party's mistakes during Reconstruction, both nationally and in the South.

Historians continue to debate the meaning of Reconstruction's modest successes and great failures, aware that within Reconstruction history lie the roots of the nation's current racial problems. Did the federal government fail at Reconstruction because it tried too hard to transform the South's social system? Conversely, did Reconstruction fail because the federal government lost its nerve and gave up on reforming the South? Did Reconstruction go too far, or not far enough?

If we see the Civil War and Reconstruction period as one long struggle from secession to reunification, then who won? Did white southerners lose the war but win the peace?

Reconstruction as National Policy

Reconstruction tied together in one tangled knot a number of difficult questions. First, the constitutional issues: Were the Confederate states really out of the Union, and if so, how could they be brought back in? Were white southerners citizens of the United States with constitutional rights that had to be respected, or were they defeated enemies with no rights that victors had to respect? Then, the racial issues: Under the Thirteenth Amendment, blacks had been permanently set free, but did freedom mean equality? What was the status of the freedpeople to be? Would black men be given the rights of white male citizens, including the right to vote, or would they be relegated to partial citizenship, like white women? Finally, the social and economic issues: Did the end of slavery mean that black southerners and whites would meet as social equals? Would black and white children attend the same schools? Would black men and women be paid wages for the labor they had hitherto done as slaves? Or would the planters' lands be confiscated and given to their former slaves?

Although most of these questions would be settled in the South, all of them had great relevance to the nation as a whole. Most important of all were the issues revolving around the postwar racial settlement. By making decisions about race in the South, the federal government effectively created a national racial policy that remained in effect until the 1960s.

Reconstruction during the War

In a very real sense Reconstruction began as soon as Union armies occupied southern states. By 1862 Louisiana and large parts of the upper South were under federal control. Lincoln appointed military governors for those states. Then in 1863 Lincoln announced his own plans for postwar Reconstruction in his Proclamation of Amnesty and Reconstruction. Any Confederate supporter who swore future loyalty and promised to accept abolition would be pardoned of his treason. (Lincoln exempted top-ranked Confederate military and political leaders from the offer.) When 10 percent of the men who had voted in 1860 took the loyalty oath, they could then proceed to form a new state government. Lincoln required that the state governments formed under this plan write into their new state constitutions provisions abolishing slavery.

Significantly, Lincoln did not demand that the newly reconstructed states give freedmen any sort of political power. When representatives of Louisiana's sizable population of free people of color petitioned the president for the right to vote, Lincoln suggested to the governor of Louisiana that it might be appropriate to let African-American property owners and/or Union veterans participate in the upcoming state constitutional convention. As mild as this suggestion was, it was ignored; the new state governments formed under Lincoln's plan were for white men only. Indeed, many southern Unionists expressed with equal vehemence hatred for the "aristocrats" who had led the South into war and disdain for the former slaves.

Lincoln's 1863 Reconstruction plans should be seen as a part of his overall strategy for Union victory. His extreme leniency was designed to encourage southerners to give up the fight and rejoin the Union; he asked only that they agree to give up slavery. His plans also reflected his own interpretation of the Constitution. From the start of the war, Lincoln had denied that the Confederate states were, or even could be, out of the Union. If southerners were not out of the Union, then they had the same rights as all American citizens and could not be treated as conquered enemies. Finally, Lincoln's plan was based upon his acute understanding of American party politics. Himself a former Whig, Lincoln had friends and political acquaintances in the South, and he knew that many of them only half-heartedly supported the Confederacy. Through leniency, Lincoln hoped to encourage these men to support the Union, and, not coincidentally, the Republican Party.

In 1864, concerned that Lincoln's plan did too little to protect the former slaves, Congress passed the Wade-Davis Bill. This legislation would have required that a majority of the state's white males swear a loyalty oath to the Union before readmittance. In addition, the Wade-Davis Bill restricted voting for the new state constitutional conventions to men who could take an "Ironclad Oath" that they had never supported the Confederacy. Finally, the Bill promised blacks equality under the law but not the right to vote. Lincoln refused to sign the bill, so it never became law. This angered some members of Congress, including the authors of the bill, who accused Lincoln of trying to dominate the Reconstruction process. Congress refused to seat the representatives of Lincoln's reconstructed southern governments, thus effectively keeping them out of the Union.

The controversy over the Wade-Davis Bill highlighted conflicts between Lincoln and some members of his own party over Reconstruction policy. While Lincoln favored reconciliation, some Republicans in Congress advocated punishment. Of that faction, the most outspoken was Pennsylvania Congressman Thaddeus Stevens, who argued that defeated and occupied areas of the South were "conquered territories," and that southerners were defeated enemies to whom the Constitution no longer applied. Congressmen who took this position argued that Reconstruction should do more than bring the southern states back into the Union. Instead, the victorious Union should sweep away the racial, social, and economic systems of the Old South and replace them with new institutions modeled on those of the North.

Like Lincoln, most Republican congressmen were not willing to go that far. Instead, they agreed with Massachusetts Senator Charles Sumner that the Confederate states had committed "state suicide" in seceding. Having destroyed their legitimate state governments, Sumner said, the Confederate states had reverted to territorial status and would have to be readmitted to the Union. According to the Constitution, the federal government could admit only those states with properly republican governments. Sumner and other Republicans took that to mean that the federal government had the right to reform southern state governments before readmitting the states to the Union. In 1864, this meant that all the readmitted states would have to agree to abolish slavery.

The Freedmen's Bureau

In March 1865, Congress passed and Lincoln signed the first major Reconstruction legislation, an act authorizing the creation of the Bureau of Refugees, Freedmen, and Abandoned Lands. The Freedmen's Bureau, as it was commonly called, was a new thing in American history, an agency whose functions included emergency relief management, welfare, and mediation. Between 1865 and 1870, bureau workers distributed approximately 22 million meals and provided shelter for thousands of refugees, many of them white. The Bureau also acted as a welfare agency. To help the 4 million former slaves adjust to liberty, the Freedmen's Bureau ran schools. Having been denied literacy during slavery, freedmen, women, and children flocked to these schools, often cosponsored by northern religious or philanthropic organizations. In addition, the bureau urged freedmen and their former masters to work out labor contracts and arbitrated conflicts between landowners and workers.

The bureau was also charged with settling former slaves on "abandoned" lands. Some members of Congress wanted to confiscate the lands of Confederate leaders and redistribute them to the former slaves. Although the Lincoln administration and Congress as a whole were not willing to go that far, the bureau and the army did sponsor some land redistribution, making it possible for a few former slaves to gain title to lands confiscated for back taxes. In addition, Sherman, encumbered by thousands of contrabands following his march through Georgia, had settled them on plots of land along the coast, with a promise to clear up the titles later. These resettlement efforts, taking place as they did in the last days of the war, convinced many freedmen that the federal government was going to give each family "forty acres and a mule," the requisites for self-sufficiency.

Reconstruction policy had not been finalized by the time of Lincoln's death in April 1865. Some historians, noting Lincoln's personal tendencies toward compassion and leniency, have suggested that Reconstruc-

Richmond ladies going to receive government rations. The Freedman's Bureau fed thousands of refugees, regardless of color or politics. This drawing, which appeared in 1865 in *Harper's Weekly,* captures the disdain of upper-class Confederate women for the occupying Union army. The original caption reads, "Don't you think that Yankee must feel like shrinking into his boots before such high-toned Southern ladies as we!" Library of Congress.

tion history would have taken a very different course had Lincoln lived. Others have scoffed at this, pointing out that Lincoln's kindly nature had not prevented him from authorizing total war against Confederate civilians, or, indeed, from presiding over the bloodiest war in American history. These historians believe that Lincoln would have exhibited in Reconstruction the same characteristics he did as war leader: tough-mindedness, flexibility, and a shrewd sense of the politically feasible. Whether Lincoln's leadership would have made Reconstruction easier, or harder, for freed-people and for defeated white southerners is a question that can never be answered. What is certain is that Lincoln had much better political skills than his successor.

Johnson, Congress, and Reconstruction

Andrew Johnson was a southern Democrat, a Jacksonian from upper East Tennessee. Like Lincoln, Johnson had been a poor boy, raised without advantages or education in the backwoods. A small-town tailor before he became a professional politician, by the late 1850s Johnson had risen to the U.S. Senate, where he defended slavery, states' rights, and Jacksonian Democracy, southern style. True to the heritage of Old Hickory, in 1861 Johnson denounced secession as treason and refused to follow Tennessee out of the Union. When Tennessee fell to Union occupation, Lincoln appointed Johnson military governor. Running for reelection in 1864, Lincoln wanted his campaign to represent national unity. As a southerner and a Democrat loyal to the Union, Johnson made an attractive running mate. He also appealed to radical Republicans, who liked his disdain for the planter aristocracy and his repeated statement, "treason must be made odious and traitors punished." Radicals overlooked another facet of Johnson's politics. Like many southern Unionists, Johnson hated the region's slaveholding elite, but he also hated the slaves. Firmly committed to white supremacy, Johnson was determined to keep the South a white man's country.

Johnson became president in April 1865, upon Lincoln's assassination. Congress was then out of session and would not reconvene until December, leaving Johnson in sole control of Reconstruction policy. Following Lincoln's plan, Johnson promised amnesty to southerners who would take loyalty oaths. (He exempted high Confederate officials and persons owning property worth more than $20,000. These members of the Confederate elite would have to apply directly to the president for a pardon. As it turned out, Johnson handed out pardons like candy to almost anyone who asked.) Johnson urged the former Confederate states to hold conventions to draw up new state constitutions, which he insisted must include provisions to abolish slavery, nullify secession, and repudiate the Confederate debt. Like Lincoln, Johnson suggested that the new state constitutions might include provisions allowing black male property owners to vote.

The Republicans and Black Suffrage

Republican Party leaders realized that their victory in the war had actually injured the party itself. Under the Constitution, each southern slave had been counted as three-fifths of a person for representation in the House. With the end of slavery, former slaves would be counted the same as whites, and the South would gain a dozen new congressional seats. Republican leaders expected that most of those seats would be filled by Democrats, since few white southerners would vote for members of the party of Lincoln. However, Republicans had reason to believe that former slaves would.

Giving black men the right to vote was a radical move in 1865. Only a few years previously the Supreme Court, in the *Dred Scott* decision, had ruled that blacks were not citizens. Moreover, most northern states did not allow blacks the right to vote. To give African-Americans suffrage in Mississippi without doing so in Minnesota would be a difficult trick to pull off. In the fall of 1865 Republicans took the issue of black suffrage to three northern states, Connecticut, Minnesota, and Wisconsin. In all three cases, voters rejected proposals to let black men vote. Republican leaders realized that they lacked support for African-American suffrage and put aside the issue for the time being.

Good Old Rebels

During the summer and fall of 1865 former Confederates took oaths of new loyalty, created new state constitutions and state governments, and elected representatives to send to the U.S. Congress in December. In doing so, southerners signaled that their version of the meaning of the Civil War differed in significant ways from that of the Republican Party and of many northerners. Defeated but not humbled, southerners did not consider their losses a negative verdict against their entire society. Instead, they clung to their traditional beliefs in white supremacy, states' rights, and the personal liberty of white men. They expected the Reconstructed South to be very much like the Old South, but without slavery.

Southerners accepted the demise of slavery. Indeed, anyone who reads southern letters and diaries from the period will be struck by how often people—particularly women—express relief at being delivered from the burden of slavery and the care and maintenance of slaves. However, planters still needed to control black labor, and southerners of all classes continued to support white supremacy. In 1865, many southern states enacted Black Codes designed to codify the status of all blacks as less than full citizens. In some states, blacks were forbidden to buy property in towns; in others, forbidden to work at anything but agricultural labor. Most of the states' Black Codes restricted gun ownership for blacks. Even more ominously, some states provided that blacks without jobs would be arrested as vagrants. Their labor would then be sold at auction. Black children could be taken from their parents and "apprenticed" to whites, who would keep them as workers until adulthood. The Black Codes indicated that white southerners still thought they had a right to control black lives and labor; as one Freedmen's Bureau official commented, white southerners had a hard time understanding that abolition meant blacks were free just like they were.

None of the southern states took Johnson up on his suggestion to give the vote to blacks with property. Instead, through the Black Codes, the states reduced antebellum free blacks, often educated property owners, to the same status as illiterate former slaves. Moreover, southern whites enforced white supremacy with violence, attacking blacks who acted "uppity"—that is, like free men and women.

When they formed new governments, southerners indicated that military defeat had destroyed neither their belief in the right to secession nor their loyalty to the men who had led the secession movement. Some southern constitutional conventions refused to nullify secession, an action acknowledging its illegality. Instead, these states repealed secession. Other states refused to repudiate the Confederate debt, again signifying a belief that the Confederacy had been a legitimate government. Mississippi and Texas did not ratify the Thirteenth Amendment, which abolished slavery forever in the United States. When new governments were formed in the summer of 1865, they looked very much like the old Confederate state governments, with a lot of ex-Confederate soldiers added. Southern Unionists complained to their Republican supporters in the North that the rebels were back in power and were taking revenge on men who had been loyal to the Union.

When Congress reconvened in December 1865, the composition of the southern delegations enraged northern politicians. The southern states sent to Congress nine Confederate congressmen, seven Confederate state officials, four Confederate generals, four Confederate colonels, and the former vice president of the Confederacy. To expect northern politicians to accept as colleagues men who had only a few months previously been shooting at their sons and brothers was politically naive at best. Congress exercised its right to rule on the qualifications of its own members and refused to seat the southern delegations.

Johnson vs. Congress

The new Congress immediately formed a Joint Committee on Reconstruction. Led by moderate Republicans, the joint committee at first had no plans for radical Reconstruction of the South. Instead, Republican moderates wanted to protect the freedmen. The chair of the committee proposed to Congress an extension of the Freedmen's Bureau and a civil rights bill that would have protected blacks from infringements on their liberties such as those enacted in the Black Codes. At this point, moderate Republicans seem to have envisioned a status for blacks, male and female, equivalent to that of white women. In most northern states, laws protected white women's rights to own property and to be secure from attack, but women were not allowed to vote and could be denied access to educational facilities and to employment on the basis of sex. Moderate Republicans wanted to stop southerners from reenslaving blacks but did not yet support full equality for former slaves. They had every reason to think that President Johnson agreed with their position.

Instead, Johnson vetoed the Freedmen's Bureau extension and the civil rights bill. The president said that the bureau was providing blacks with economic support that had never been given to whites. Johnson suggested that welfare would destroy the characters of the former slaves and make them dependent on the federal government. In addition, Johnson charged that the bureau was too expensive and too intrusive into the affairs of the southern states. As for the civil rights bill, Johnson said that it was a "stride toward centralization, and the concentration of all legislative powers in the national Government." Besides, Johnson said, by protecting black rights the bill discriminated against whites.

With these two vetoes, Johnson lost the support of moderate Republicans and pushed the entire Republican Party closer to radicalism. Congress passed both bills over the president's veto and set out to remove Reconstruction policy from the hands of the man one historian referred to as the "last Jacksonian Democrat."

The Fourteenth Amendment

In June 1866, Congress passed the Fourteenth Amendment, the keystone of the joint committee's Reconstruction policy. By defining as citizens all those born in the United States, the amendment overturned the *Dred Scott* decision and gave citizenship to the former slaves. It also required that states respect the rights of all U.S. citizens, thus making racially specific legislation like the Black Codes illegal. The amendment dealt with the issue of black suffrage by saying that states that refused to let citizens vote could not count those citizens for apportionment purposes. This would mean that southern states who restricted suffrage would lose representations, while northern states would not, since the black population in most northern states was minuscule. The Fourteenth Amendment disqualified from voting men who, as members of prewar state or federal governments, had violated their oaths to support the Constitution by joining the Confederacy. However, this disfranchisement could be removed by action of Congress. Finally, the amendment guaranteed the national debt and repudiated the Confederate debt. Of the Confederate states, only Tennessee ratified this amendment, and it was readmitted to the Union in 1866.

The congressional elections in the fall of 1866 became a northern referendum on Reconstruction. The Republicans presented the Fourteenth Amendment as necessary to save the peace for which so many northern soldiers had given their lives. Without it, the former Confederates would regain control of the South and the lives of the freedmen would be endangered. The latter argument was strengthened in May 1866, when a white mob in Memphis, including many members of the city police force, attacked a black neighborhood and killed forty-six people. In July a white

HARPER'S WEEKLY.

JOURNAL OF CIVILIZATION

VOL. X.—No. 491.]   NEW YORK, SATURDAY, MAY 26, 1866.   [SINGLE COPIES TEN CENTS.
[$4.00 PER YEAR IN ADVANCE.

Entered according to Act of Congress, in the Year 1866, by Harper & Brothers, in the Clerk's Office of the District Court for the Southern District of New York.

THE MEMPHIS RIOTS.

THERE was in Memphis, on the first two days of May, an excitement unequaled since the close of the war. The origin of the disturbance between the whites and negroes of that city was highly discreditable to the colored soldiers, and the riotous proceedings which followed were a disgrace to civilization. For that riot the lower class of white citizens were as responsible as were the soldiers of the Third United States Colored Infantry for the original difficulty. This regiment, whose reputation has been a bad one, had been mustered out, since which they had frequented whisky-shops in the southern part of the city, and had been guilty of excesses and disorderly conduct. On the evening of May 1 some drunken members of the regiment were on South Street, talking noisily, when in an insolent manner they were ordered by two policemen to cease their noise and disperse. Words ensued, followed by blows, throwing of missiles, and firing of revolvers.

To understand what followed it must be remembered that the police force of Memphis is composed mostly of Irishmen, whose violent prejudice against negroes was so shamefully displayed in the New York riots of 1863. The [illegible] correspondent thus described the riot:

Word was sent to police head-quarters, and the whole force at once proceeded to the scene of the fray, being joined on the way thither by armed and excited citizens. Meanwhile the firing had brought other negroes to the spot, some armed with clubs and some with revolvers, so that by the time the police force came up the two parties were about equal in number. The negroes held the original

position, and, upon the approach of the police, showing no determination to abandon it, were fired upon by the police and citizens who accompanied them. This fire was returned, and for a while both parties busied themselves in discharging their revolvers as rapidly as possible. Meanwhile word was sent to General Stoneman, who promptly dispatched to the scene of action a company of Regular cavalry, when the negroes were quickly dispersed and driven in every direction.

During the evening the wildest and most exaggerated reports soon spread throughout the city. Every symptom[illegible] of the intelligence of the fight told a different story, and the highest excitement prevailed. Each rumor placed a wave appear upon the affair than the preceding one, and only served to develop the pent-up prejudices against the negro. Soon after dark this excitement and prejudice found vent. Large numbers of armed citizens repaired to the scene of the fight and commenced firing upon every negro who made himself visible. One negro upon South Street, a quiet, inoffensive laborer, was shot down almost in front of his own cabin, and after life was extinct his body was fired into, and beat in a most horrible manner. In all parts of the city, wherever they could be seen, negroes were fired upon by policemen as well as citizens. They were shot while driving hacks, and quietly walking in the streets about their business. The police seemed to make it their special business to shoot every negro they could see, no matter where he was, or what he was doing. The result was that if 9 o'clock the colored population were in doors trembling with wild alarm. How many negroes were killed during the night it is impossible to ascertain, as firing was constantly kept up during the earlier hours in all parts of the city. It is estimated that from 15 to 20 were killed, as far as I have been able to learn, not a white man was fired upon by a negro during the whole night.

After the fight of Tuesday evening the negro soldiers and most of the colored population residing in the vicinity of the fight fled to the fort for security. They were perfectly quiet—in fact, were terribly frightened for their own safety. At an early hour yesterday morning every thing

SCENES IN MEMPHIS, TENNESSEE, DURING THE RIOT—BURNING A FREEDMEN'S SCHOOL-HOUSE.

[SKETCHED BY A. R. W.]

Republicans in Congress were stirred to action in May 1866 by news of white attacks on blacks in Memphis. Shown above is the front page of *Harper's Weekly*, giving details of the Memphis riots. Library of Congress.

mob assault on an African-American political meeting in New Orleans resulted in the death of thirty-seven blacks and three white Unionists. Faced with southern defiance and violence, northern voters agreed with the Republicans. Although Johnson campaigned vigorously against Republican candidates for Congress, the party of Lincoln won a two-thirds majority in both houses of Congress.

This was the majority necessary to pass legislation over a presidential veto, or to impeach a president, as Johnson found out when he impeded Republican Reconstruction plans. Impeached by the House of Representatives, he was acquitted after a Senate trial in 1868 and retired at the end of his term to Tennessee, where he went back into politics and was reelected to the Senate.

In 1868 Ulysses S. Grant won the presidency for the Republicans; he was reelected in 1872. A soldier without much talent for politics, Grant followed the congressional Republicans' lead on Reconstruction policy.

Congressional Reconstruction

Now firmly in control, Republicans in Congress passed the Reconstruction Act of 1867, putting the South back under military occupation. In each of five military districts, officers were charged with supervising the Reconstruction process. The Reconstruction Act required that each of the Confederate states allow all adult males to vote for delegates to constitutional conventions, which were then required to draw up new constitutions giving adult males, regardless of race, the right to vote. The states also had to ratify the Fourteenth Amendment. Men disqualified from voting by the Fourteenth Amendment could not participate in these elections. Having complied with these requirements, southern states' representatives would be admitted to Congress. To supplement this plan, the Second Reconstruction Act, passed a few weeks later, required that the generals in command in the South register eligible voters and get the Reconstruction process under way.

By 1869 Republicans realized that even military occupation was not enough to ensure black suffrage. Therefore, Congress passed the Fifteenth Amendment, giving black men the right to vote, and added this new amendment to the list of items southern states would have to sign off on before readmission to the Union.

Reconstruction in the South

Congressional Reconstruction lingered long in southern memories, where it was generally termed "Radical Reconstruction." A popular historian, writing in the early twentieth century, insisted that between 1867 and 1877 southern whites had been "literally put to the torture" by white Yankees who incited normally docile blacks to rebellion and to lust after white women. Modern historians have been unable to find any evidence of torture, or indeed of any atrocities enacted upon white southerners at the orders of the federal government. By the standards of the twentieth century, the postwar punishment meted out to the South was mild indeed. Rebel leaders were allowed to go home. Their lands were not confiscated. By 1867 many high-ranking Confederate officers had become successful businessmen. Lee himself took a position as president of Washington College.

The federal government did single out Jefferson Davis for punishment, keeping him confined in prison for two years. In addition, the commandant of the horrific Confederate prisoner-of-war camp at Andersonville, Georgia, was hanged for war crimes, the sole such execution in the Civil War-Reconstruction period. Compared with what victorious nations usually do to defiant rebels, the South got off easy.

Why, then, the long memory of Reconstruction as a period of degradation, humiliation, and "torture"? Recent historians have suggested that the real issue of Reconstruction was race. With the support of the federal government, blacks who had been slaves two years previously registered, voted, and held public office. Conversely, whites who had been the region's traditional leaders were disfranchised. To the restrictions on voting contained in the Fourteenth Amendment and the Reconstruction Acts, Congress later added more legislation allowing local voting registers to determine whether a person's participation in the rebellion disqualified him from voting. As a result, about 10 to 15 percent of the white electorate lost the right to vote. These restrictions did not last long; all had been removed before 1877. Yet in five Deep South states, white disfranchisement created black voting majorities. When white southerners boycotted elections, as they did periodically throughout the Reconstruction period, blacks also gained political power. With as much as 30 percent of the white electorate staying home, black votes could swing elections.

For southerners committed to white supremacy, a system allowing freedmen to vote while disqualifying whites was unnatural; blacks holding political power instead of whites, unthinkable. In a culture where voting was an attribute of manhood, Reconstruction voting restrictions stripped masculinity from whites and bestowed it on blacks: for a brief time, the freedman was "the man."

Southern whites' legends describe the freedman politician of Reconstruction as an illiterate former slave right out of the cotton fields. Although some leaders did emerge from the agricultural labor force, most prominent black politicians during Reconstruction were literate, educated men. Many had been free before the war and owned businesses or plantations. Some had been runaway slaves. Many were the mulatto sons of plantation owners. Still others were natives of the North, come south to pick up on opportunities for black men not available in the northern states.

Former slaves learned about politics through "Union Leagues," political clubs formed to promote Republicanism in the South. There, teachers, preachers, and skilled craftsmen often took the lead in educating freedmen. Although southern whites scornfully asked how illiterate former slaves could possibly understand politics, observers noted that the freedmen clearly grasped their own political situation: they were poor and powerless and needed economic opportunity and political rights. For that matter, southern politicians had long expected illiterate whites to participate in politics, and no restrictions had ever prohibited them from voting.

Former Confederates also detested Reconstruction because it brought to power poor whites and men from the North. Many of the southern common folk had exhibited limited support for the Confederacy, and as noted earlier, the mountain districts of the South had been bastions of Unionism. At the end of the war, with their old political adversaries from the plantation districts disfranchised, men from the hill-country districts emerged as political leaders, joining the newly organized southern branch of the Republican Party. So did former southern Whigs. Unreconstructed Confederates called southern-born Republicans "scalawags," a term usually denoting poorly bred, runty cattle. For many members of the traditional southern elites, common folk, like blacks, were inferior beings incapable of political leadership.

Yet old rebels saved their most biting contempt for those northern-born newcomers to the South who went into politics: the carpetbaggers. In the 1860s, a carpetbag was the cheapest form of luggage. The term "carpetbagger" implied that the northern-born politician was a poor man who had come south to get rich, like a vulture battening upon the fallen South. In fact, many northerners had come to the South after the war to start businesses or to plant cotton; some worked as Freedmen's Bureau officials, while others were Union army veterans who simply liked the climate and the people of the South.

With the support of the federal government and the backing of federal troops, coalitions of blacks, southern whites, and northern newcomers formed local and state Republican Party units in 1867 and proceeded to follow Congress's plan for Reconstruction. By the winter of 1867–68, Republican-dominated state conventions began to draw up new state constitutions. These constitutions were more liberal than many in the North. Most mandated universal manhood suffrage, while many northern states still did not allow blacks to vote. In addition, the new southern state constitutions created the region's first real public school systems and other institutions of public welfare ranging from asylums for the orphaned, blind, and mentally handicapped to systems of poor relief. After fierce debates, some of the conventions wrote into their constitutions provisions disfranchising ex-Confederates, but when these voting restrictions proved unpopular, they were removed from the constitutions or quickly repealed. (Many black political leaders, committed to universal manhood suffrage, were less supportive of voting restrictions than white Unionists.) Ultimately, only Arkansas disfranchised large numbers of former Confederates, and even there voting restrictions were removed by 1872.

Almost overlooked in the controversies over schools, segregation, and voting restrictions was an issue that proved of great long-term significance: taxation. White southerners had a long tradition of opposing anything but the most minimal taxation to support the most minimal state governments. The new state constitutions proposed much more active state governments than had ever existed in the region before. This would require tax increases. One major source of prewar tax revenues, the tax on slaves, had disappeared with the institution. Therefore the new state constitutions included new state taxes on land. Many delegates to the conventions approved of higher land taxes for social and economic reasons as well: by hiking the land tax above the ability of planters to pay, they could force the sale of lands to freedmen.

Once written, the new state constitutions were then submitted to the voters for approval, with a majority of registered voters necessary for ratification. Southern Democrats, seeing an opportunity to thwart Reconstruction, urged white voters to boycott the elections, but Congress passed in March 1868 yet another Reconstruction Act saying that constitutions could be ratified by a majority of those voting. With as many as half of the South's eligible white voters staying home, Republicans carried the ratification votes throughout the region and then formed new state governments, which then ratified the Fourteenth Amendment. In June, the U.S. Congress voted to readmit seven former Confederate states to the Union; the remaining three, Texas, Virginia, and Mississippi, were readmitted in 1869.

Southern Democrats believed that their last hope of staving off "black rule" lay in the 1868 presidential election. They still found it hard to believe that white Yankees would vote for policies designed to enfranchise and empower blacks. The national Democratic Party leadership apparently agreed. The party platform denounced the Reconstruction acts as unconstitutional, and the party's vice presidential candidate accused the Republicans of having placed the South under the rule of "a semi-barbarous race" awaiting opportunities to "subject the white women to their unbridled lust." Calling for an immediate end to Reconstruction and the return of "white rule" to the South, Democrats throughout the nation joined to campaign for white supremacy.

In the South, whites formed terrorist groups and attacked Republican voters of both races. The most famous of these groups, the Ku Klux Klan, originated as a Confederate veterans' fraternal organization at the end of the war but was quickly transformed into a political terror group in 1868. The Klan and similar organizations throughout the South drew membership from all classes of southern society for their terrorist campaigns. During the months before the election of 1868, historians estimate that thousands of potential Republican voters, most of them black, died at the hands of terrorists throughout the region.

Reports of widespread disorder and violence in the South helped the Republicans carry the election of 1868. Ulysses S. Grant won the presidency, and the Republican Party kept its two-thirds majority in both the House and the Senate, thus ensuring that Reconstruction would continue.

Reconstruction State Governments

Between 1868 and 1870 Republican governments came to power in all the southern states. Long stigmatized as "carpetbagger governments" and lumped together in the public memory as uniformly corrupt and inefficient, the Republican governments actually varied widely from state to state. In Tennessee, which rejoined the Union early, in 1866, white Unionists dominated Reconstruction, while in Mississippi the Reconstruction governor was an idealistic northerner chiefly concerned about the rights of the freedpeople. In South Carolina, blacks formed the majority of the lower house of the legislature, while in other states whites, either northern newcomers or southerners, predominated. Some Reconstruction-era politicians used their power to enrich themselves with bribes, kickbacks, and insider information, while others, including prominent black leaders, were models of enlightened and honest public service. With so much diversity from state to state, it is hard to generalize about the famed "carpetbagger" governments. However, the governments did have certain things in common.

First, and most infuriating to the southern white elite, was the personnel of Reconstruction governments. Staffed by mountain people, poor whites, former Whigs, Union veterans, and blacks, the Reconstruction governments could never satisfy people who believed they had a hereditary right to regional leadership.

Second, Reconstruction governments greatly extended state services and required southerners to pay higher taxes, to the great disapproval of the farmers who made up most of the southern population. Small farmers, accustomed to paying little to no land tax, winced at the prospect of tax increases to pay for services they did not want, such as public schools and poor relief, and grumbled that the freedmen, who did want and need the services, paid no taxes because they owned no lands.

Third, Reconstruction governments attempted to bring the blessings of industrial capitalism to the South and failed disastrously. Convinced that railroads would open up the South for industrial development, most of the state governments encouraged railway construction by guaranteeing railroad bonds. When the railroads failed, as they often did, state governments were left with massive debts, the payment of which required still higher taxes.

Fourth, Reconstruction governments were corrupt, with personnel on the take at every level up to the top. Many Reconstruction political leaders had come into politics to make money; few had jobs or careers to fall back on if they lost elections. In the fast and loose atmosphere of post-Civil War politics, southern politicians who came into office with assets of a few thousand could leave with hundreds of thousands stashed away in banks. Although southern corruption paled before the mountains of boodle raked in by politicians in New York City, or in the national government itself, the fact of corruption played into the hands of people who did not believe that blacks or poor whites were fit to govern.

Fifth, and finally, all of the Reconstruction governments faced continual and violent opposition from unreconstructed rebels, determined to keep the South a white man's country. During the early 1870s white terrorist groups including the KKK attacked institutions of black advancement like schools and churches and terrorized black voters. Meanwhile, whites who supported the Republican Party found themselves ostracized by white society, while whites throughout the South complained of a rising crime rate.

The inability of Republican governments to keep the peace and protect property graphically illustrated how tenuous Republican control over the South really was. Reconstruction governments could not exist without the support of Union troops, still stationed in the South five years after Appomattox. Northern politicians, increasingly tired of Reconstruction, asked why the legitimate governments of the South could not defend themselves. In some cases, they could. In Arkansas and Tennessee, the governors sent in state militia units to put down the Klan in selected counties. However, in most of the South Republicans did not even organize resistance against the Klan, preferring to rely on the law and the protection of the federal government. Unlike the Klansmen, most of them Confederate veterans, blacks generally lacked military skills. Besides, black leaders believed that any attempt to organize militarily and fight white terrorism would create a white backlash. Taking the high ground, black leaders condemned white terrorists as the real "barbarians," and fought for their rights under the law.

In 1870 and 1871, the federal government passed a series of acts designed to attack the Ku Klux Klan by making interference with voting a felony. Empowered by Congress to use the U.S. Army to enforce the new "Ku Klux Klan Act," as it was popularly called, President Grant sent troops into counties known to be KKK strongholds and arrested thousands of suspected Klansmen. The resulting federal prosecutions helped drive the Klan underground but did not stop white southerners from resorting to terrorism in defense of white rule. Wearily, northern politicians, and President Grant himself, wondered how long the federal government would have to police southern elections.

Reconstructing Southern Society

White southerners who thought that the postwar South would be like the antebellum South, minus slavery, did not realize how impossible that dream was. The Civil War, emancipation, and Reconstruction brought rapid social changes for which most southern whites were unprepared. Accepting slavery as an organic part of their lives, white southerners did not know how deeply the institution was embedded in all southern institutions until, suddenly, it was gone. Filling in the vacuum required adjustments in every facet of southern life.

Land and Labor   When the war ended, freedmen throughout the South waited impatiently for the federal government to reward their loyalty by confiscating the rebels' land and giving to them each "forty acres and a mule." These hopes were most cruelly dashed. With rare exceptions, neither the federal government nor the Republican Reconstruction governments made any serious efforts to redistribute land. In fact, the federal government even evicted blacks from lands upon which they had been settled by the army during the war. As the head of the Freedmen's Bureau told black leaders, they had been given nothing but freedom. Freedmen wanted to be independent farmers like the white common folk around them, but without land that dream would remain unfulfilled.

The Freedmen's Bureau had its own plans for the former slaves: they were to become wage workers like the whites employed in northern factories. Imbued with the free labor ideology, bureau officials expected former slaves to save their wages and, through thrift and industry, rise in the world to become landowners and businessmen. Many of the bureau's policies, such as its sponsorship of schools, were calculated to speed the formation of a self-supporting black middle class. However, the bureau's plans ran aground against a basic fact of the postwar southern economy: southern planters had no cash with which to pay wages.

Planters wanted a labor system as close to slavery as possible. Insisting that blacks would not work without coercion, planters wanted to continue the system of gang labor typical of plantation agriculture before the war. Under that system, men and women worked in groups under an overseer's direction. Planters laughed at the idea of paying weekly wages, telling bureau officials that hands would immediately take their pay and leave, not to return until all the money was spent. Most of all, planters needed to be sure that their hands would not leave at critical moments in the agricultural year, such as planting and harvest. Moreover, planters wanted control over the freedmen's home life, preferring that their workers live in the old slave quarters under close white supervision.

In this conflict of goals and dreams, none of the parties could win. What eventually emerged out of the shambles of the postwar agricultural economy was a system no one really wanted: sharecropping. With bureau support, planters contracted to rent lands to tenants in exchange for a portion of the harvest. (The portion varied depending on whether the planter provided tools, draft horses or mules, seeds, and so on.) Because the worker would not be paid until after the harvest, the planter could be sure that he would stick around. On the other hand, freedmen extracted from planters an end to the gang labor system and a certain amount of privacy for their families. Freedmen demanded that planters give them a set acreage to farm on their own, without constant white supervision, and a cabin in which their families could live. Unable to get the land that made economic independence possible for white common folk, blacks approximated small farming as closely as possible through sharecropping. This system was not completely satisfactory to freedmen, planters, or the Bureau, but it seemed acceptable as a temporary expedient at a time of crisis. No one foresaw what would happen: the sharecropping system lasted until the middle of the twentieth century, to the great detriment of southern agriculture.

Domestic Relations: Work and Law   Southern jurists classified laws governing slavery under "domestic relations." With the removal of slavery, domestic relations for all southern families, black and white, went through a period of change, both legally and socially. For the first time, whites and blacks encountered each other as legal equals within the judicial system. Reconstruction governments wrote into their constitutions and their new legislation provisions significantly liberalizing family law.

Meanwhile, black families adjusted to gender role changes following upon emancipation.

Prior to the Civil War, southern family law followed the ancient English common law, by which women ceased to be individuals under law when married. As English legal scholars explained, by marriage man and wife became one person—and that person was the husband. Wives could not buy, sell, or make contracts without their husbands' consent. Through marriage, husbands acquired ownership of any property that wives brought to the marriage or earned by their own work. Although the northern states' original family law codes were similar, those laws had been modified to reflect the changing realities of middle-class family life in an industrial society. During Reconstruction, Republican legislatures reformed southern law to reflect the growing individualism of American society. In several states, married women were given the right to control their own property, a development conservatives denounced as part of "the mighty tide of progress which has already swept away the Constitution, and slavery, and State's rights." Conservatives protested that such laws destroyed the old domestic order under which only male heads of families had an individual relationship with the state. In addition, divorce laws were liberalized throughout the South, and judges became less likely to automatically award children, as a kind of property, to fathers.

The antebellum tendency toward patriarchy inherited from English law had been strengthened by slavery. Southern law codes and courts had argued that white male family heads needed to have almost all of the power within families, since they, as masters, were responsible for dependents, including their own wives, children, and slaves. Southern conservatives noted that antebellum southern society had hardly needed jails or prisons, since most "crimes" were domestic, occurring on plantations and dealt with informally by masters.

The Civil War destroyed this informal judicial system, and the more formal one as well. The result was a period of great confusion. Anecdotal evidence indicates that postwar economic and social conditions led to an increase in theft. With white refugees, freedpeople, and starving Confederate veterans floating through rural districts and crowding into towns, property owners guarded their food and money with guns. In the immediate postwar period, Union officers administered martial law in occupied territories, much to the relief of property owners, who found to their chagrin that they needed the Yankees' protection. After the war, the Freedmen's Bureau acted as a small-claims court to rule on conflicts between planters and workers, while the southern judicial system underwent its own reconstruction, with Republican judges replacing former Confederates on the bench, and blacks in the jury box, much to the disgust of many southern whites. Southern whites charged that the Reconstruction governments failed to protect their property, and both blacks and whites complained about racially biased courts, each charging the other side with failing to provide color-blind justice.

Antebellum southern laws had no provisions dealing with slave families, since under the law no such entities existed. For freedpeople, the right to form families and have the legitimacy of those families recognized by the state was one of the most cherished fruits of freedom. In 1866, a Freedmen's Bureau official gave a sermon on marriage to black Union troops stationed in Virginia and recorded the testimony offered by one of the soldiers, Corporal Murray: "*I praise God for this day!* . . . The Marriage Covenant is at the foundation of all our rights. In slavery we could not have *legalized* marriage: *now* we have it. Let us conduct ourselves worthy of such a blessing—and all the people will respect us—God will bless us, and we shall be established as a people." After emancipation, freed men and women hurried to legitimate long-standing relationships, often standing up before their children and grandchildren to say their marriage vows.

In freedom, black men insisted to their landlords that their wives and daughters would no longer take orders from white bosses as they had under slavery, and many withdrew their wives from field labor altogether. Whites disapproved when freedmen appropriated to themselves concepts typical of white society, such as the obligation of men to support women. Whites thought that a black woman carrying no more than the normal load of work for farm wives was not really working, and they mocked the pretensions of black "ladies." For their part, many freedpeople found middle-class gender roles impossible to sustain: survival required the work of the entire family, parents and children alike.

In a less striking fashion, Reconstruction saw the beginning of changes in gender roles for white southern families as well. The war had taken the lives of approximately one-quarter of the white men of military age in the South and had left many others physically disabled and mentally shattered. After the war, white women found themselves managing plantations and running businesses, jobs for which many of them had not been prepared, either educationally or emotionally. Their daughters and sons would grow up aware that patriarchy had its limitations. Contrary to myth, men did not always protect women from the harder side of life.

White women also became the chief mourners of the Confederacy. Unwilling or unable to let the memory of the men of the Lost Cause fade away, women throughout the South formed Ladies Memorial Associations in 1866 and created a new holiday: Confederate Memorial Day. Over the years, the Ladies Memorial Associations moved from decorating graveyards and putting up statues of Confederate soldiers to founding homes for the widows and orphans of fallen soldiers. Although memorializing the Lost Cause led white women into public activism, the ladies never ceased to uphold conservative concepts of white supremacy and the duty of white men to protect southern white womanhood.

The End of Reconstruction

The Rise of the Redeemers

Southern whites might have lost the Civil War, but they were determined not to lose the battle for home rule. Although Grant's reelection in 1872 seemed to signal that northern voters still supported Reconstruction, southern Democrats soon began a resurgence that toppled Republican governments throughout the South. When Democrats took power back from Republicans, they called it "Redemption," a word freighted with deep meaning drawn from law and religion: to pay all debts on a property is to "redeem" it; Christ's death "redeemed" the sins of the world. The southern Democrats called themselves Redeemers. By 1874 they had taken power in Virginia, Tennessee, North Carolina, Alabama, Georgia, Texas, and Arkansas.

The Redeemers began their return to power by winning the support of most white voters throughout the South. Never really reconciled to sharing power with blacks, white common folk also had reason to resent Republican governments' tax policies, which fell most heavily upon them. No one who valued good government could have approved of the level of corruption prevalent in many Republican-controlled legislatures and gov-

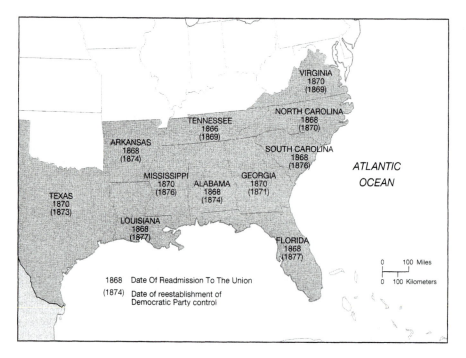

Reconstruction of the South, 1866–1877.

ernor's mansions. Finally, the Redeemers made cooperation with Republicans a distinct social liability. According to one well-known story, one southern man justified his decision to vote Democratic in the next election by explaining that he had five daughters, all single and all likely to remain that way as long as he supported the Republicans.

Republican disarray and factionalism also helped fuel Democratic resurgence. In several states, black Republicans charged that whites hogged all the patronage and offices, while in other states the party split, with some Republicans appealing for conservative Democratic votes and others drawing support mainly from blacks. In South Carolina, the only state where blacks held significant power during Reconstruction, black factionalism contributed to the Republican Party's difficulties. As educated black leaders became more prosperous, their interests more often coincided with those of conservative whites than with workers on the rice plantations.

Ultimately, however, the Redeemers took back power in the same way the Confederates had lost it: with guns. While encouraging white voters to support them, Democrats also discouraged blacks from voting, using the most forceful measures possible. Whites organized "rifle clubs" and other quasi-military groups to terrorize black voters. In Louisiana in 1874, "White Leagues" battled black militiamen in the very streets of New Orleans, took control of the city hall and arsenal, and were only put down by federal troops. In Mississippi in 1875, whites attacked black political meetings and rode through the countryside assassinating black political leaders, teachers, and ministers.

In previous years, such actions by unreconstructed southerners led to repeated federal intervention. However, by 1874 northern support for Reconstruction had waned. The entire nation slid into a major depression in 1873, and many voters worried more about their own economic prospects than about what many called the "Negro question." In the North, the children of the reform-minded people who had worked for abolition in the 1850s turned their attention to the problem of political corruption. Grant's own ability to govern, and his personal reputation, suffered when investigations revealed that several of his cabinet officers and his personal secretary were involved in schemes to defraud the taxpayers. Republican reformers found it difficult to defend Reconstruction governments noted for corruption.

Yet the North's retreat from Reconstruction represented more than just fatigue, distraction, or disapproval of corruption. Many northern politicians had supported abolition, citizenship for blacks, and suffrage for black men as ways of getting at the rebellious South. With the exception of true believers like Charles Sumner, who in 1875 pushed through Congress the last Reconstruction-Era civil rights bill, few northern politicians cared much about what happened to blacks in the South. Many northerners, as much convinced of white superiority as any southern Democrat, doubted whether blacks were, or ever could be, capable of governing themselves. The new popularity of Social Darwinism, which applied Charles Darwin's theory of evolution to economics and society, reinforced such prejudices.

To Social Darwinists, blacks were lower on the evolutionary scale than whites of British descent—but so were many other ethnic groups, such as the Irish immigrants who formed the majority of the working class in many northern cities. As labor strife rocked northern cities in the 1870s, upper-class Republicans found themselves thinking that perhaps the southern white elites were right: the working classes, whether white Irish immigrants in the North or blacks in the South, could not be trusted and needed supervision from their natural superiors. In addition, Social Darwinists, believing in the survival of the fittest in the socioeconomic world as in the jungle, thought that all people should be left alone to sink or swim on their own. Such attitudes reduced public support for continual federal intervention in the South to protect the freedpeople.

Reconstruction had failed, many northern leaders believed, and it was past time to withdraw support from a policy that simply did not work. Businessmen complained that investment in the South could never proceed until good governments and law and order replaced corruption, violence, and chaos. After almost a generation of political upheaval and war followed by more political upheaval, northerners wanted to forget the "southern question" and the "Negro question" and get on with their lives. As the *New York Herald* noted, "The plain truth is, the North has got tired of the Negro."

Therefore, when the governor of Mississippi, the carpetbagger Adelbert Ames, asked for troops to protect blacks and put down white violence, President Grant refused, saying "The whole public are tired out with these annual autumnal outbreaks in the South . . . [and] are ready to condemn any interference on the part of the Government." Grant's attorney general wrote to the governor instructing him to "Preserve the peace" in Mississippi with his own forces: "[L]et the country see that the citizens of Mississippi . . . have the courage to *fight* for their rights." Unwilling to send black militiamen into battle with whites for fear of provoking even more white violence, Ames negotiated a deal with Democrats that included disbanding the black militia. Without federal troops to back them up, the Republicans lost the 1875 elections in Mississippi.

The Compromise of 1877

In 1874 the Democratic Party made a surprising recovery from its years of unpopularity among northern voters, while the Republicans suffered public blame as the party that had presided over the Depression of 1873. Democrats won a majority of seats in the House of Representatives and made similar gains in many northern states. Hopeful of winning the presidency in 1876, the Democrats nominated Samuel Tilden of New York and issued a platform statement condemning "a corrupt centralism which, after inflicting upon ten States the rapacities of carpet-bag tyrannies, has honeycombed the offices of the Federal Government itself with incapacity, waste and fraud."

The Republicans nominated their own reform candidate, Rutherford B. Hayes of Ohio. Evoking the Civil War and capitalizing on white southern atrocities against blacks in Hamburg, South Carolina, the Republicans asked the northern public to rally once again, as Hayes wrote, against "the dread of a solid South, rebel rule, etc., etc." Though the Republicans expected their opponents to win most of the South, they had hopes of carrying the three remaining southern states under Republican governments—Louisiana, South Carolina, and Florida.

The election of 1876 produced one of the strangest outcomes in all of American political history: a kind of tie. With electoral and popular votes almost even, the winner of the election would be the man who was awarded the electoral votes of—Louisiana, South Carolina, and Florida, all of which had sent in two sets of returns, one certified by the Democrats and one by the Republicans. Which set one believed the "true" vote depended on one's politics, and in fact both sides cheated. Congress set up a commission to resolve the question, but the commission divided on party lines.

What followed has been the subject of considerable debate and conjecture among historians. We know that leading southern Democrats met in February 1877 with prominent Republicans from Ohio, Hayes's home state. We also know that after that meeting southern politicians in Congress withdrew their opposition to Hayes's election, and he was inaugurated in March. Apparently the southern leadership and Hayes's people cut a deal: the Republicans could have the presidency if Hayes would end Reconstruction. Although no documentation of such a bargain exists, historians have dubbed it the Compromise of 1877. Hayes removed all federal troops from the South, allowing Redeemers to take power in South Carolina and Louisiana; he made an ex-Confederate from Tennessee postmaster general, thus giving him control over highly coveted federal patronage jobs in the postal service; and he urged Congress to appropriate moneys for internal improvements in the South.

In 1877 the Republican Party gave up on Reconstruction, and with it, the party's long-term commitment to securing for blacks equal rights as American citizens. It would be eighty years before the federal government again dispatched troops to protect black rights in the South. The northern public acquiesced in this betrayal of black hopes. The leading journal of middle-class northern opinion, *The Nation*, welcomed the end of Reconstruction: "The negro will disappear from the field of national politics. Henceforth, the nation, as a nation, will have nothing more to do with him." Southern blacks understood their situation. As one Louisiana black leader said, "The whole South . . . had got into the hands of the very men that held us as slaves." Although Democratic leaders had promised to respect black rights, they clearly expected the freedmen to accept subordinate positions in southern society.

In 1861 southerners went to war to defend their way of life and by doing so destroyed it. Unable to salvage slavery out of the wreckage of the Civil War, white southerners mounted a successful resistance movement in defense of the other cornerstones of southern ideology, white supremacy and states' rights. Twelve years after Appomatox, the white South won the battle of Reconstruction. With the Old South dead, and Reconstruction over, southerners focused on a different kind of rebuilding: the economic transformation of the New South.

Suggestions for Further Reading and Viewing

PETER BARDAGLIO, *Reconstructing the Household: Families, Sex and the Law in the Nineteenth Century South* (1995)

W. E. B. DuBois, *Black Reconstruction in America, 1860–1880* (1935)

ERIC FONER, *A Short History of Reconstruction, 1863–1877* (1988)

JOHN HOPE FRANKLIN, *Reconstruction: After the Civil War* (1961)

THOMAS HOLT, *Black over White: Negro Political Leadership in South Carolina During Reconstruction* (1977)

J. MORGAN KOUSSER AND JAMES M. MCPHERSON, EDS., *Region, Race and Reconstruction* (1982)

LEON F. LITWACK, *Been in the Storm So Long: The Aftermath of Slavery* (1979)

ROBERT C. MORRIS, *Reading, 'Riting and Reconstruction* (1981)

MICHAEL PERMAN, *The Road to Redemption: Southern Politics, 1869–1879* (1984)

LESLIE A. SCHWALM, *A Hard Fight for We: Women's Transition from Slavery to Freedom in South Carolina* (1997)

KENNETH STAMPP, *The Era of Reconstruction, 1865–1877* (1965)

ALLEN W. TRELEASE, *White Terror: The Ku Klux Klan Conspiracy and Southern Reconstruction* (1979)

chapter

2

The New South, 1877–1900

In the 1880s southerners interested in boosting the region's economic development began to talk about a "New South." The Old South had been agricultural; the New South was to be industrial, urban, democratic— in short, much more like the North's idealized image of itself. New South promoters pushed for industrialization and urbanization, trumpeting each new factory or mine as a victory in the battle against the South's postwar economic defeat.

The South's economy and society did change radically in the two decades after the end of Reconstruction, but not always along the lines projected by the New South boosters. What, then, was "new" about the New South? Did the New South movement mark the final surrender of southern culture to the industrial North? Or was the New South as distinctively different from the rest of the nation as the Old South had been?

Boosting the New South

In 1886 a young newspaper editor from Atlanta prepared to make a banquet speech before the most Yankee of all venues: the New England Society of New York. Asked what he would say, Henry Grady replied, "The Lord only knows. I have thought of a thousand things to say, five hundred of which if I say they will murder me when I get back home, and the other five hundred of which will get me murdered at the banquet." The son of a merchant with no strong family ties to the prewar planter elite, Grady used his paper, the *Atlanta Constitution,* to boost his town, encouraging the development of industry, commerce, and urban growth—all things that antebellum southern white leaders had scorned as "Yankified," unnecessary, and unwanted in the agrarian South. Southern economic development depended on northern capital, so part of Grady's agenda in New York was to entice northern investors to Atlanta. On the other hand, any white southerner who appeared to be groveling before the victorious North risked losing the respect of the folks back home.

Grady's task could not have been made easier by the fact that one of his fellow speakers was General William T. Sherman, whose troops had burned Atlanta twenty-two years previously. Standing before the New England Society, Grady joked that General Sherman was regarded highly in Atlanta, "though some people think he is a kind of careless man about fire," and assured the group "that from the ashes he left us in 1864 we have raised a brave and beautiful city." Like Atlanta rising from the ashes, Grady said, a New South had been born: "We have fallen in love with work." Relieved of the burden of slavery, the New South might be "less splendid" than the Old, Grady said, but it was "stronger at the core: a hundred farms for every plantation, fifty homes for every palace; and a diversified industry that meets the complex needs of this complex age." Yet while boosting the New South, Grady was careful not to repudiate the old: "The South has nothing for which to apologize. She believes that the late struggle between the States was war and not rebellion, revolution and not conspiracy, and that her convictions were as honest as yours. . . . The South has nothing to take back."

With his combination of pride in the past and hope for the future, Grady best articulated the themes that New South promoters repeated constantly in the 1880s. Himself only a child during the Civil War, Grady was typical of a rising younger generation of white southerners who wanted to put the war behind them. Older men understood the impulse; as Alabama politician J. L. M. Curry wrote to his son in 1886, "of what avail is it to keep alive passion and cherish hatreds. . . . To go about shaking our fists and grinding our teeth at the conquerors, dragging [with] us a heavy weight, the dead, dead corpse of the Confederacy is stupid and daily suicidal. Let us live *in* the present and *for* the future. . . ." In the United States of 1880, industry, technology and urbanization represented "the future," while plantations seemed a vestige of a lost, doomed past.

Yet New South boosters could not, for political reasons, completely repudiate the Old South—and many did not want to do so. Many white New South promoters had fought with Lee and Jackson or had buried fathers who had done so; like Grady, they publicly expressed relief that the Old South had been swept away, but they would not condemn the men who had died believing the Confederacy to be just and right. Many had also grown up in churches where the fallen heroes of the war had been all but sanctified. One New South evangelist, J. William Jones, who had begun his career during the Confederate army revivals, went on after the war to urge young men to heed the example of Lee and to follow him, as Lee followed Christ. Jones began revival sermons with a prayer: "Oh, God! Our God, God of Israel . . . God of our fathers, God of Jefferson Davis, Robert Edward Lee, and Stonewall Jackson. . . ."

Many New South promoters also subscribed to the developing cult of the Lost Cause. During the 1880s white southerners began to rewrite history and edit memories to make up an Old South much prettier than the one that really existed. In this version of the Old South, white men were gallant, white women beautiful, and slaves loyal, docile, and contented with their lot; everyone lived on plantations; in 1861, all white men volunteered to go fight gallantly in defense of states' rights; the South lost the war only because of northern population and resource advantages. And so on. The Lost Cause myth seriously distorted the realities of slavery and war. Promulgated by the region's educated elite, it wrote common white and black folk out of the story and overstated southern support for the Confederacy. However, by ignoring race, class, and politics, Lost Cause propagandists created that extremely attractive cultural product, the "moonlight and magnolias" myth.

Preached in sermons, declaimed from lecture podiums, and eventually taught in schools, this bogus Lost Cause history captured the imaginations of younger generations of Americans, southern and northern alike. The late nineteenth century was a time of great social upheaval throughout the United States. Struggling with the changes brought by urbanization, immigration, and industrialization, many Americans found themselves looking back nostalgically to the antebellum South, when life was simpler—at least, according to novelists and popular historians. By the 1890s Americans had decided that the Civil War was romantic and the Old South, being doomed, most romantic of all.

In the South, businessmen joined with southern women's associations such as the Daughters of the Confederacy to contribute money for public memorials to the Lost Cause. In Richmond, "Monument Avenue" became a kind of Confederate theme park, with statues of Lee, Jackson, and Davis, but almost every small town in the Deep South had its statue of a Confederate soldier, often placed to face North in defiance. Some memorial associations, nostalgic for the old racial order, put up memorials to the loyal slaves.

By memorializing the Old South, New South promoters helped bury it. People rarely erect monuments to the living. While revering the memory of the past, New South promoters got on with the business of life in late-nineteenth-century America: making money.

The New South Economy

During the late 1870s the business pages of northern and European papers began to feature stories describing the South as one of the best fields of investment for enterprising capitalists. Drawn by the region's abundant assets, including previously unexploited iron and coal deposits and uncut timber, cheap labor, and low taxes, investors came south.

Exploitation of the South's natural resources required better transportation. The antebellum South had depended mostly on rivers to ship agricultural products from plantations to the coast. The region's lack of good railroads had been a factor in Confederate defeat. Although Reconstruction state governments had sunk millions in tax dollars into railroad bonds in the 1870s, the railroads had grown only about 25 percent by the end of the decade. In the 1880s railroad construction took off, grow-ing 135 percent. With an infusion of northern and European capital, rail-roads built an infrastructure linking the most remote southern villages with national and international markets. By the 1890s over three-fourths of all southerners lived in counties with rail connections.

Railroads transformed the southern way of life, replacing agri-cultural rhythms with machine time. In places where clocks had never been necessary, men began to set their watches by the daily passage of the 4:45 train. On southern farms, white boys dreamed of being engineers, while black boys aspired to one of the best-paying, most dignified jobs available for black men in the New South: railroad porter. Excited by the new, rapid transportation, southerners made up songs about trains and about mythic railroad heroes, such as the engineer Casey Jones and the steel-driver John Henry.

Yet railroad stories contained within them a note of caution. Casey Jones, the brave and handsome young white engineer, died trying to make up lost time: he pushed his engine so hard that his train jumped the track, and he was killed in the crash. John Henry, the black hero celebrated for his speed and strength, took up a challenge to compete with a steel-driv-ing machine and won, but the struggle broke his heart, and "he laid down his hammer and he died." In the New South, railroads represented moder-nity, power, and speed, a machine world with little respect for human needs.

Railroads and Governments

In the postbellum South, railroad management so intertwined with state government that at times it was hard to tell whether a state spon-sored a railroad, or whether the railroad sponsored the state: "The Louis-ville and Nashville is [as of 1889] now not only Birmingham, but Alabama," one Alabamian said. Anxious to obtain rail connections, antebellum state governments had backed bonds for railroad construction, a practice con-tinued and increased by Reconstruction governments, some of which had drained their state treasuries for railroads that never got built. Despite this bad example, southern state governments, particularly in Florida and Texas, continued to promote railroad construction during the New South period with grants of public lands.

The Redeemers who took power after the end of Reconstruction fulfilled their promises to lower taxes and cut back on state government but were often no more personally honest than the carpetbaggers they replaced. Though perhaps less likely to accept outright bribes, southern politicians of the New South period had serious difficulty understanding the concept of conflict of interest. Often owned and managed by northerners, railroads assured favorable treatment for their southern business by investing in politicians. From the state capital down to the smallest crossroads, politicians received small favors from railroads: "complimentary" tickets, special excursions to tourist centers, and so on. Railroads bought newspapers and used them to promote favorite politicians into positions of leadership. After long careers promoting the railroad's interests in state government, pet politicians retired to take up positions officially working for the railroad. While southern farmers fumed about high and often changing railroad shipping rates, politicians rarely favored railroad regulation.

Urbanization

Cities grew from railroad junctions. Atlanta, the virtual capital city of the New South, was a railway crossroads. Cities combining railroad and river connections, like Memphis, became regional centers of industry and commerce. Birmingham, a town of 3,000 in 1880, grew rapidly after the Louisville and Nashville Railroad ran up into the hills of northern Alabama to exploit coal and iron fields there. Essentially an L & N investment, Birmingham had 38,000 residents by 1900. Meanwhile, the relative importance of the older coastal cities within the regional economy began to decline, hastened by the unwillingness of many "old family" businesses to match the western newcomers' hustle.

In the new cities, "new men" without prestigious family backgrounds made fortunes from commerce and industry. Unlike antebellum elites, these new men made their money in town and often kept it there, building ornate brick and stone mansions in the latest styles. They might own plantations, but they rarely wanted to live in the country, and increasingly they looked down on the hayseeds, the "rednecks" from which many of them had come. In some southern states, antebellum planters watched aghast as the newly rich supplanted them in politics, as in wealth; in other states political clashes between agrarian and industrial interests became a feature of New South politics.

Blacks formed a high percentage of the population in most New South cities. During the Civil War, "contrabands" had flocked to Union camps in occupied southern towns. When the Union soldiers left, the freed men and women stayed, forming the nucleus of postwar urban communities. After the war, such communities grew rapidly. Industrial towns like Birmingham and Memphis offered work at better wages for black men, while black women could find jobs as domestics in white urban households. Living in town also afforded more security, since white terrorists usually attacked isolated black farmers, not black neighborhoods. Black parents often moved to cities so that their children could go to school. Overall, the cities drew the young, ambitious, and restless, a phenomenon typical of white immigrants to urban areas as well.

Although some southern cities industrialized during the late nineteenth century, many others grew as commercial centers. In cities and towns, southerners exchanged the raw products of the rural South for money and finished goods, often shipped from the North. Despite the bombast of New South promoters, the region's wealth still came from the countryside.

Forests, Mines, and Mills

In 1865 much of the South was still covered with uncut woods. Small farmers throughout the South hunted, trapped, fished, and foraged in the region's abundant forests and also pastured their hogs and cattle in the woods. Southern state laws required farmers to fence their crops but allowed livestock to roam free, enabling small farmers in the southeast to pasture cattle and hogs on the woodland "range" free of charge.

The Cattle Kingdom

American settlers moving onto the southwestern plains before the Civil War adapted quickly to a ranching economy pioneered in previous generations by Mexican and Spanish pioneers. Unconfined by fences, Texas longhorns roamed the plains, surviving on sparse water and tough, uncultivated vegetation. Ranchers rounded up these cattle once a year, branded their calves, and drove their steers to markets east. During the war, the cattle herds grew overly large. In the postwar period, cattlemen undertook "long drives" of huge herds to the nearest railhead—at first Sedalia, Missouri, and then (after 1867) Abilene, Kansas, then Wichita and Dodge City. Even these closer markets required a journey of hundreds of miles.

To move their cattle, ranchers needed cowboys. The American cowboy was essentially a hired hand, good with horses and skilled at his trade (roping, riding, and other aspects of bovine management). Although the mythological cowboy is an emblem of Anglo-Saxon American manhood, in fact cowboys were often Mexican or black. In any case, cowboys worked hard and long for low pay, particularly on the famous long drives, then spent most of their money on women and whiskey in Abilene, Wichita, or Dodge.

The cattle kingdom, so rich a source of American legend, looms large in the American literary and cinematic imagination. However, the heyday of the cowboy did not last for long. As railroads extended into the southwest, the drives became shorter and shorter. Cattlemen replaced the scrappy longhorns with more domesticated breeds that produced beef that was fatter and less stringy. Finally, ranchers began to enclose the open range with a new invention: barbed wire. By the turn of the century, the old days of the open range had already receded into romance.

After the Civil War, lands that had been open range rapidly became capitalist assets. Typically historians speak of the late nineteenth century as the Age of Iron, but it was also an age when building technologies required quantities of wood. Railroads ran on wooden ties. The new houses constructed in the suburbs then springing up around northern cities were built around wooden frames, had wooden floors, and—if families could afford it—lavish wooden ornamentation. Late Victorian furniture styles featured heavy, carved woods. To supply the needs of railroads, builders, and furniture makers, entrepreneurs turned to southern forests.

In the 1870s farmers in parts of the South began to cut their woods. Farmers cut logs, used mules to drag them to the nearest river, and tied them into mile-long rafts. When the river reached the appropriate flood stage, the raft crews cut loose and sailed their unwieldy crafts downriver to sawmills near railheads. At Nashville, a center of this kind of logging, log rafts sometimes stretched twenty-five miles above the city wharfs. However, full exploitation of the region's forests awaited the railroads. In the 1880s northern capitalists began to invest in southern lands. In Alabama, Arkansas, Florida, Louisiana, and Mississippi, big timber companies, mostly from the upper Midwest, bought approximately 5.5 million acres of public lands between 1881 and 1888. Other northern firms bought from smaller, locally owned lumber companies throughout the South. Sawmills became a prominent part of the southern landscape, springing up in the wake of railroads, and stacks of fresh-cut lumber lined the railroad tracks and piled up at depots, awaiting shipment to factories in urban centers.

Working in timber was dangerous. Accidents in the woods and mills maimed men and sometimes killed them. Yet for young men, life in sawmill towns was exciting as well as lucrative, and they flocked to sawmill work by the thousands. Farmers of both races uprooted their wives and children and moved to the woods, where workers' shacks or boxcars surrounded the company's offices and stores. As a Mississippi woman remembered, "In a few days it seemed the whole world had arrived, some with axes, saws, hammers, mule teams." While some people tried to bring civilization to the log woods, building schools and starting churches, others enjoyed the saloons and brothels that sprang up to serve the predominately young, male workers.

By the turn of the century the southern states supplied about 40 percent of the entire nation's timber. Timber companies clear-cut thousands of acres, destroying the natural habit and devastating the environment in parts of the South. When the trees were gone, the mill towns closed, and most workers drifted off to jobs elsewhere.

During the postwar period investors moved quickly to tap into southern coal and iron resources. Southerners had long known that coalfields lay under the Appalachian Mountains from Virginia and Kentucky down into Alabama. Farmers in the mountains often dug a little coal to supply themselves and their neighbors with heat during the winters, but without transportation by which to ship coal out, the industry remained localized. In the 1880s railroad companies, themselves major consumers of coal, began to build lines into the hills and to invest in coal lands. Other entrepreneurs, seeing opportunities in the hills, followed. In the 1890s southern coalfields supplied most of the coal used in midwestern industries.

Coal mining was statistically the most dangerous occupation in late-nineteenth-century America; some 2,000 miners died annually, with the southern mines contributing their share to that dismal total. Yet southern men of both races took jobs in mines because they paid well and offered a kind of independence. Miners furnished their own gear, worked at their own pace, and were paid by what they produced, not by the hour. Mining proved particularly attractive to black workers. At the turn of the century the coal companies could hardly keep up with demand; desperate for workers, they advertised and recruited in black neighborhoods in southern cities and offered black workers housing and wages similar to that afforded to whites. As long as the good times lasted, coal miners could, through hard work, make a good living—and pay back much of it to the company via rent on company-owned houses and purchases at the company store.

Nothing captured the difference between Old and New South more than the iron industry built in southeastern Tennessee and northern Alabama after the war. Like coal mining, iron production had been delayed because of lack of transportation. In the 1870s northern entrepreneurs began to build iron foundries, plants where raw ore was refined into usable forms. Chattanooga emerged as an early center of production before losing out to Birmingham by the end of the century. By the end of the 1880s Tennessee Coal, Iron, and Railroad Company was one of the largest producers of iron in the nation. To grow, TCI looked overseas, shipping to England, Europe, and Japan. In 1898 Birmingham was the third largest shipping point for pig iron in the world, and TCI was making plans to challenge Pittsburgh in steel production when United States Steel, a monopoly formed by investment banker J. P. Morgan, bought the company out in 1907. U.S. Steel gave priority to its Pittsburgh plants, requiring that southern steel prices be higher than that of steel produced in Pittsburgh, regardless of the actual cost of production. While Birmingham continued to thrive, the southern steel industry's growth slowed in the early twentieth century.

Tobacco

Pushed by innovative marketing and new technology, the Old South's oldest crop became one of the New South's most spectacular growth industries. The modern tobacco industry was born in the North Carolina Piedmont. Shortly after the war, Chapel Hill merchant Julian Carr began to promote a chewing tobacco manufactured in a nearby town. Spending spectacular amounts of money on advertising, Carr made "Bull Durham" an internationally known brand by the 1880s. However, Carr's success faded in comparison with that of the Duke family. Starting out as small-scale tobacco manufacturers in the postwar period, the Duke family fortunes soared when James "Buck" Buchanan Duke invested in a new machine to produce cigarettes. Duke marketed his new, machine-produced, cheap cigarettes aggressively and undersold his competitors. By the end of the century he had built a new business, the American Tobacco Company, which held a near-monopoly on the tobacco trade.

Although cotton mills had been built in the antebellum South, the postwar period saw a great expansion. In the 1880s town leaders in the Piedmont, the hill-country region west of the tidewater, promoted northern investment in mills. Some advocates of this "Cotton Mill Crusade" thought that the mills would instill "habits of industry" in the southern common folk; presumably being summoned to work at dawn by a mill whistle, putting in twelve hours of labor in the lint-clogged air of a mill, and being paid low wages would be good for the character of rural southern whites for whom mill jobs were reserved. Blacks were not allowed to work in textile mills, although they did hold jobs on loading docks and as janitors.

When the mills opened, they had no problem finding hands. Whole families moved to the mills, which employed fathers, mothers, and children as young as eight. The mills were a godsend for widows with daughters, offering such families one of the few options for economic survival off the farm. While middle-class reformers condemned southern child labor, scorning fathers who lived off the work of their children, the rural whites who flocked to the Piedmont mills were accustomed to putting young children to work in the fields. Mill owners built villages for their workers, complete with houses, schools, churches, and stores. For some rural whites, the mill villages appeared the height of urban living. Young people in particular enjoyed the social opportunities afforded by living in town. Later generations would question the hours, the pay, and the control that mill owners exerted over their workers and their villages, but for many rural whites in the 1880s, the mill villages were the best deal around.

Southern Labor

New South promoters lured northern investors to the region by promising them cheap, docile, Anglo-Saxon labor. This description was designed to contrast with the supposed characteristics of the northern labor force, composed increasingly of immigrants. When immigrant workers organized labor unions, campaigned for the eight-hour day, and struck for higher wages and better treatment, employers attributed this behavior in part to their ethnic origins. They alleged that the immigrants had been infected with dangerous socialistic ideas back home in Europe. Southern promoters promised that the region's workers would be different. As white men imbued with the national tendency toward individualism, southerners would be unlikely to form unions.

The logic of industrial life soon put paid to such notions. Employers treated workers as a collective unit, labor, which they tried to obtain at as low a cost as possible. Southern workers from farming backgrounds were used to acting independently, but anyone could see that an individual textile worker or miner was in no position to bargain with the boss. Like their northern counterparts, southern workers formed unions. In the 1880s some 50,000 southerners joined the Knights of Labor, the first big national labor union. The Knights' long-term goal was to build a union of all "producers," including farmers, housewives, and artisans, as well as factory workers. Noticeably liberal for their time, the Knights insisted on biracial unionism and also enrolled women, arguing that they should receive the same wages as men for the same work. Southerners participated in Knights of Labor strikes in numerous industries in the 1880s. Others joined unions in textiles, mining, and railroads. Many skilled or semiskilled workers belonged to craft unions, or "brotherhoods."

The Convict Lease System

In the late nineteenth century southern state governments rented out prisoners as labor to planters, railroad companies, and mines. This convict lease system had multiple advantages for the powers that ran southern states.

First, it kept taxes down. States did not have to build secure prisons, and they made money off convict labor.

Second, it acted as a deterrent to labor organization in the South. Companies threatened would-be union men with replacement by convict labor. Arthur Colyar, one of the founders of the Tennessee Coal, Iron, and Railroad Company, explained, "One of the chief reasons which induced the company to take up the system was the great chance it offered for overcoming strikes. . . . I don't mind saying that for many years the company found this an effective club to be held over the heads of free laborers." The TCI used convicts to develop its Birmingham lands.

Third, the convict lease system facilitated the use of prisons as a means of racial control. Black men and women, incarcerated for years for misdemeanors, could be employed as unfree labor on plantations belonging to those with state government connections, or put to work digging coal for New South industrialists. With justice, the convict lease system has been referred to as "state slavery."

Free laborers bitterly resented this competition from prisoners. In 1891–92 East Tennessee miners evicted the convicts from the coalfields, then fought the state militia sent to bring them back. Eventually the miners made the convict lease so expensive that the state abolished it, one of the few New South governments to do so. However, the Tennessee miners' victory was unusual. The convict lease system lasted into the early twentieth century, when most

states replaced it with a series of prison farms, also designed
to make convicts work for their keep.

State Power, Unions, and Race

Despite such examples, unions never took a strong hold in the
South, not because southern workers were ethnically opposed to them, but
because of factors in southern society. Manufacturers controlled much
more wealth and political power than did workers. When textile workers in
the Piedmont went on strike in the late 1890s, manufacturers united to shut
down the mills, locking out workers until the union was broken. In other
cases, industrialists called upon state government to send in the state militia to settle labor disputes. In 1894 the governor of Alabama used the state
militia to break strikes in the coalfields, and the governor of Louisiana did
the same in New Orleans. In both cases, the militia's presence protected
strikebreakers, known colloquially as "scabs." In many cases strikebreakers
were black. Shut out of many southern occupations by race, blacks comprised a reserve army of labor upon which southern manufacturers could
draw at need. Manufacturers and southern white workers alike understood
how the race card would be played: if white workers caused too much trouble, they would be replaced by blacks, who would work for even lower
wages.

White southern workers reacted to the race card in different
ways. In some cases, unions realized that admitting blacks to the brotherhood was essential; otherwise, employers would continue to undercut white
unions with black labor. However, the opposite reaction was more common. White workers saw blacks as threats to their jobs and mobilized to
drive them out of factories and mines. Occupations that had been integrated in the 1880s became much less so as years passed.

Agriculture: Southern Farmers
in the Wake of Defeat

New South promoters boosted industries and cities as the wave
of the future, but the roots of southern poverty lay back home on the farm.

While the northeastern United States made the transition to urban and industrial modes of life, the South remained stubbornly, persistently agrarian well into the middle of the twentieth century. As long as most southerners remained on the farm, conditions in southern agriculture determined the region's economic fate.

Before the Civil War, southern agriculture produced the nation's leading export, cotton, and put fortunes in the pockets of the planter elite. In the 1850s the "cotton nabobs" of the Natchez district in Mississippi were, per capita, the wealthiest men in the nation. Under the old southern system, a man's wealth was measured less in acreage than in slaves. All the wealth sunk into slaves disappeared with emancipation, leaving planters land-poor and freedmen simply poor, conditions that prevailed through the New South period.

However, the majority of southern farmers were neither planters nor former slaves. For white common folk, the farming families who comprised the majority of the southern population, the New South period brought with it new opportunities but also new problems. The political heirs of Jefferson and Jackson, white southern farmers believed that independence, that essential component of manhood, grew from land ownership. Postwar economic developments threatened the common white man's dream of achieving self-sufficiency on his own farm.

Sharecropping and Tenant Farming Sharecropping emerged as a temporary expedient in the Reconstruction period. Lacking land, former slaves contracted with landowners to work through the agricultural year and collect as pay a share of the crop once harvested. Neither landowners nor freedmen found the system completely to their liking. Landowners would have preferred to continue working their acres with gangs of laborers under the direct control of white supervisors, while freedmen would have preferred to have their own forty acres and mule. Sharecropping did give freedmen some measure of autonomy and the right to supervise their family's labor.

In the 1870s freedmen hoped that by sharecropping they could raise enough money to buy their own land. Like their white neighbors, southern blacks understood land ownership to be essential for political and social independence. For many, the first step was to make a transition from sharecropping to tenant farming. Unlike a cropper, a tenant furnished his own equipment and paid a cash rent for the land he used. By dint of hard work and good management, some black men began as day laborers, became sharecroppers, then tenants, then managed to buy farms of their own.

Pursuing economic opportunity, thousands of black farmers accepted the inducements offered by white labor agents, who recruited sharecroppers for Mississippi, Arkansas, Texas, and Louisiana. As a Greensboro, North Carolina, white man wrote in 1890, "The negro exodus now amounts to a stampede. . . . I judge that between 5 and 10,000 have passed in the last fortnight." While many black farmers moved every year in search of better opportunities, others found themselves unable to leave, tied to plantations by debts they had incurred to the landowner. Despite the disadvantages facing them, many black farm families struggled desperately to climb out of tenancy to landownership, and by 1900 approximately 25 percent of the South's black farmers had succeeded. As that statistic indicates, however, about 75 percent of the region's black farmers remained stranded in tenancy.

They were joined by increasing numbers of southern whites. By 1900 most black farmers were tenants, but most tenant farmers were white. Ten percent of the South's white farmers were cash tenants, while 26.5 percent were sharecroppers. There were 279,861 black sharecroppers and 491,655 white sharecroppers in the south central and southern Atlantic states (divisions used by the U.S. Census). The increased rate of tenancy among southern whites reflected a quiet, slow-growing crisis in southern agriculture. For black farmers, sharecropping was a definite improvement over slavery, but for most southern whites, it represented failure.

Yeoman Farmers and the Slide into Dependency   New South promoters, residing in southern cities and unfamiliar with agricultural conditions, liked to lecture southern farmers about making farming pay, or managing a farm like a business. Farmers sometimes countered by pointing out that farming was not a business but a way of life. Most farmers put out crops with family labor. A farmer's productivity often depended on the age and sex of his children, the health of his wife, and other factors not under human control. He could not lay off his workers if markets fell. Traditionally, southern farm families had raised crops and livestock to feed the family, and marketed surpluses of food crops. For generations, farmers understood that diverting acreage and labor from food crops to staples like tobacco or cotton was risky. If the staple crop failed to make a profit, the farming family would have neither food they had grown nor money with which to purchase food. Therefore, antebellum southern farmers entered the staple crop market cautiously, if at all.

After the Civil War, economic necessity drove many small farmers into the staple crop market. When farmers came home from the war, they often found their lands devastated by the passage of armies and the depredations of war. To rebuild would require capital that returning veterans did not have. Since the Civil War had reduced the world supply of cotton, small farmers turned to the cotton market for a quick profit. In the postwar period cotton production spread out of the Black Belt and into the hills of North Georgia, Alabama, and South Carolina; in the West, farmers planted cotton in areas of Texas and Arkansas considered marginal or unsuitable for plantations before the war.

To get started in cotton production, up-country farmers had to have equipment, supplies, seeds, and especially fertilizer. For all these items, they turned to merchants at country stores, who shipped in supplies and sold them to farmers on credit. To secure their own profits, merchants required that farmers sign contracts promising to pay the merchants first once the crop was marketed. These contracts, or "crop liens," were in effect mortgages on crops not yet planted. During the cotton-growing season, many merchants sold food on credit to farmers too busy tending cotton to plant gardens or tend livestock. The credit price was often at least a third higher than the cash price. At the end of the season, merchants often bought the crops on which they had liens, ginned the cotton, and shipped it to market via the new railroads. The potential for abuse in such a system is obvious. Unscrupulous merchants dealing with uneducated farmers could easily jack up the farmer's debt and take too high a cut from the final profit. Although blacks recited the little poem, "A jot is a jot, and a figger is a figger / It's all for the white man and none for the nigger," white farmers understood the principle as well. However, the disaster that came upon southern farmers was not caused by the merchant at the country store.

Hundreds of small farmers in the American South entered cotton production at just the wrong time. The British government began encouraging cotton production in its tropical colonies during the Civil War. By the 1870s, southern farmers were competing with farmers in India and Egypt. With cotton supplies increasing, the price paid for each bale of cotton fell. The more that southern farmers increased their productivity, the worse the situation became. As one farmer remembered, "The trouble about it was we started out making it at 20 cents, and then it went to 15, and then to 10 . . . and when we thought we had learned to make it at 8 it went to 6, and when we had learned how to make it at 6 it went to 4." In the mid-1870s cotton sold for 11.1 cents per pound; by the mid-1890s, for 5.8 cents per pound, a decline of 47.7 percent. As historian C. Vann Woodward noted, "The farmer got less for the 23,687,950 acres he planted in cotton in 1894 than for the 9,350,000 acres of 1873."

National fiscal policies added to southern farmers' woes. The currency question vexed politicians in the late nineteenth century; at one point James Garfield (later to be president) commented that only one congressman seemed to understand the currency issue, and he had gone mad. To avoid a similar effect on the reader, what follows is a very simplified explanation. The currency was deflated each year. Deflation is not a phenomenon very familiar to contemporary Americans, who are much more used to inflation, or the oversupply of currency. With inflation, prices go up, and the dollar is therefore worth less each year. Deflation means that not enough currency is in circulation. As a result, prices go down, and the dollar gains in value annually. This might sound like good news, but it was disastrous for farmers. A farmer who went into debt to put out a crop one year had to pay it back with money that was more valuable than that he borrowed. The currency situation compounded with falling cotton prices to lock farmers into debt. That is why southern farmers joined with midwestern farmers in asking for government action to inflate the currency.

One historian of the South has referred to the postwar cotton economy as a "vortex." The hopes of southern cotton farmers followed that vortex down. Each year cotton earned less per bale. To pay off their debts, farmers planted more the next year. Continuing overproduction led to lower and lower prices. According to basic economic theory, farmers should have realized that with supply exceeding demand, prices would continue to fall. Logically, they should have moved out of cotton production. However, the crop lien system prevented that. To clear their debts, farmers had to grow cotton, the only crop for which merchants or small-town bankers would advance money, since it was the only crop they could profitably sell. And so the downward spiral continued. By the 1880s, many farmers had lost their land and were tenants, often on acres they had previously owned.

The tenancy rate among white farmers also increased outside the cotton belt, largely because of the pressure of population on the land.

At a time when middle-class urban Americans were choosing to have fewer children, southern rural families continued to reproduce prolifically. On farms, as in textile mills, children were an economic asset, as farm families grew their own labor force. Traditionally, patriarchs had maintained their control over sons and sons-in-law by providing them land, either in an outright gift or at a minimal rent. As the decades passed, farms were divided again and again, until in parts of the South many farmers did not have enough acreage to survive in agriculture. Such farmers often made most of their money in off-farm occupations, like logging or mining, leaving wives and children to feed the family on the farm. White farmers whose fathers could not leave them even minimal amounts of land often became tenants, and like former slaves drifted from place to place in search of a better deal for their labor.

Tenancy rates varied from state to state but were high throughout the South by the end of the century. The fact that a farmer rents his land is not, in itself, a sign of economic hardship, since renting rather than owning land can be a wise economic choice. However, in the New South, few farmers chose to become tenants. Instead, white farmers were driven into tenancy by the combined pressures of the world market and the South's archaic credit system, while black farmers, coming out of slavery with no assets but their own labor, rarely managed to accumulate enough capital to buy land. Life on a New South farm was hard for families who owned their land. Tenants barely survived.

Southern Poverty

Historians have long contended that the postwar South's economy was essentially "colonial." That is, the South was to the rest of the nation as colonies are to imperial powers: a source of cheap resources and cheap labor and a market for finished products. Southern industries were extractive in that they took from the land nonrenewable resources, roughly processed them, and then shipped them north for finishing. Southern coal fueled manufacturing plants in the Middle West; southern iron was shipped north for processing into steel; southern timber was carved into fine furniture in the North and Midwest. All these processes added value to the product, thereby making it more profitable, but the profits went to the final manufacturer, not the southern laborers who extracted the raw materials.

Southern industries were also exploitive, paying the lowest wages in the nation. While some historians suggest that the southern racial system helped keep wages down, others point out that southern workers, often isolated in rural areas, lacking industrial skills and sometimes even basic literacy, were also a captive market for low-wage jobs. Southern industries would not approach national wage standards until the mid-twentieth century, when a combination of governmental policies and technological innovations better integrated the South into the national economy.

Labels and explanations aside, the fact remains that in the late nineteenth century the South was the nation's poorest region. In 1880 the southern per capita income was $376; that of the states outside the region, $1,086. In Mississippi, the per capita income was $286. By 1919, the southern per capita income was only 60 percent of the national average. The impact of southern poverty can be illustrated by looking at public health and education.

By the standards of modern medicine, the late nineteenth century was a particularly unhealthy time for everyone. Urban growth outpaced advances in sanitation and germ theory, and Americans throughout the nation died in epidemics of water-borne diseases now almost unheard of, such as typhoid and cholera. However, most Americans did not have dietary deficiency diseases, while many rural southerners did. With no land or labor to spare for food production, tenant families often subsisted on pork and corn bread, a diet lacking in essential vitamins. As a result, many southerners suffered from pellegra (a niacin deficiency disease that causes diarrhea, dementia, and butterfly-shaped blotches on the face) and rickets, a bone malformation caused by lack of vitamin D.

Being poor, southerners could not pay much in taxes, and many resented what little they did pay. Out of the meager tax revenues taken in by southern states, those states funded two school systems, one for whites and one for blacks. Typically southern schools ran for about three months a year. However, schools in country districts had even shorter sessions. While white children in urban areas could receive a good state-and-city funded education, and even attend high schools, white rural children usually completed no more than the five primary grades, if that. For black children, the situation was even worse. When country youth did attend schools, the quality of instruction they received was mediocre at best. As a result, the southern illiteracy rate was the nation's highest. In 1900, about 12 percent of southern whites could not read or sign their names. North Carolina led the South with a white illiteracy rate of 19.5 percent. No statistics exist to indicate the level of functional illiteracy, but a quick look at collections of letters from southern common folk of the period indicates that many had only the most minimal acquaintance with spelling, grammar and punctuation, and would have had difficulty reading newspapers or the region's favorite book, the King James Bible. On the other hand, only 50 percent of the black population was illiterate in 1900, a striking improvement from 1880, when three-quarters had been unable to read or write.

It was in this world, where white miners and loggers worked long hours in dangerous conditions for low wages, where white children toiled in textile mills, where white farmers were fighting a grim and losing battle against the world market economy, where white children grew up with twisted bones and neglected minds, that the postwar racial settlement evolved.

Jim Crow: The Height of White Supremacy

Antebellum whites, whether northern or southern, generally agreed that whites were superior to blacks and that it would be impossible for the races to live together as equals. However, northern racism and southern racism were different. Northern travelers in the antebellum South expressed shock at how closely, even intimately, the races interacted. Conversely, southern travelers in the antebellum North mocked northern pretensions to morality by noting that the Yankees cared about slaves in the abstract but would not tolerate African-Americans in their houses, places of work, or neighborhoods. Historians have noted that antebellum southern and northern attitudes about race fit into patterns labeled "paternalistic" versus "competitive." Under a paternalistic system in which whites were clearly dominant, such as the Old South, whites had little reason to act out dominance on a daily basis. Masters who can buy, sell, and punish slaves do not have to remind the slaves of their condition, and may in fact enjoy playing the benevolent patriarch to the people under their control. On the other hand, racism in the antebellum North was competitive or aversive: whites competed with blacks for jobs, refused to tolerate blacks in white neighborhoods, and expressed revulsion at physical contact with blacks.

With the end of slavery, the paternalistic racism typical of the antebellum South lost its social foundations, and in the late nineteenth century the New South moved closer to northern models of competitive or aversive racism. However, northern whites' competitive racism was directed at a very small minority, incapable of threatening white supremacy either by their numbers or by their votes. In contrast, southern whites' new competitive racism was directed at a much larger group of people. In some areas of the South blacks were the majority. Southern whites could not ignore blacks, who lived and worked in close proximity to them. Nor was it possible to push blacks out of the South, since the southern agricultural economy and many New South industries depended on black labor.

The change from paternalistic to competitive racism can be traced through the words of white southerners themselves. Before the war many white southerners spoke of blacks as a docile, childlike race in need of protection. The postwar cult of the Lost Cause included repeated reference to the good, loyal slaves who had protected white families from marauding Yankees. By the 1890s the tone had changed. White southerners charged that the first generation of blacks born or raised free were not like the "good old plantation negroes." Instead, whites said, they were immoral, shiftless, lazy and dangerous. Whites believed that the black women of the new generation were all sexually promiscuous, and they warned young white men that venereal disease was endemic in the black population. White women were warned from early childhood that all black men were potential rapists, eager to make themselves the equals of white men through possession of white women. Mourning the loss of supposedly obedient, subservient slaves, whites feared the appearance of the "bad nigger," a gun- or knife-carrying criminal who refused to bend to white authority. Living in a region containing most of the nation's black population, white southerners insisted that blacks be kept in their place lest white civilization be destroyed.

For white southerners, maintaining racial supremacy required a complex social, political, and economic effort. As this project unfolded, southerners labeled it "Jim Crow." No one is quite sure how the term originated, but it seems to have come from a minstrel show in which a white performer, his face blackened, did a "colored" dance routine: "Every time

I turn around / I jump Jim Crow." Perhaps the name derives from the system's ubiquity: every time they turned around, blacks in the New South had to jump to comply with the Jim Crow system. For blacks, the late nineteenth century was, as one historian said, the nadir of American race relations, during which black prospects for true political, social, and legal equality steadily diminished.

Disfranchisement

Black political power did not end immediately upon the withdrawal of federal troops in 1877. Voting rights for black men having been guaranteed in the Fifteenth Amendment, few southern whites cared to risk federal intervention by openly denying men the right to vote on account of race. Southern states continued to elect black men to state legislatures and to the U.S. Congress until the end of the century. Yet by the opening years of the twentieth century black men had been disfranchised—denied the right to vote—in southern states with large black populations, and various means had been devised to restrict black voting rights throughout the South.

The process of disfranchising black men began in the 1870s and continued through the end of the century. Some southern states greatly reduced the black vote by requiring all voters to register months in advance of voting. Others began to use printed ballots and other tactics designed to weed out the illiterate. Arkansas, Texas, Florida, and Tennessee initiated "poll taxes," fees that had to be paid well in advance of voting. None of these restrictions were overtly race-based, and in fact tended to disfranchise poor whites as well as blacks, an effect also appreciated by many southern politicians. In addition, southern whites continued to use violence to intimidate black voters.

The move to disfranchise black voters grew out of the complicated postwar southern political situation. Although the Democrats dominated the politics of most southern states, the Republican Party had two strongholds: black voters and mountain whites, who had transferred their Unionist allegiances to the party of Lincoln. The Republicans were strongest in the Upper South, and particularly in states like Tennessee and North Carolina, where they dominated the mountain sections and consistently sent representatives to the state and federal legislatures. By disfranchising black voters, southern Democrats removed the Republican threat to their control over state governments. Some Republicans also favored disfranchisement, believing that the presence of blacks in the Republican Party kept whites from leaving the Democrats to join the GOP.

However, it would be a mistake to see disfranchisement as simply Democrats against Republicans. Instead, disfranchisement served the ends of various factions of the Democratic Party in their struggles with other party factions. By the 1880s, some white Democrats had come to appreciate the usefulness of the black vote. In plantation districts, landlords often controlled the votes of their tenants and sharecroppers. As Wade Hampton, Redeemer governor of South Carolina, noted, the black voter "naturally allies himself with the more conservative of the whites." Political opponents from white districts charged that Black Belt politicians "voted" blacks as if they still owned them. If so, Black Belt politicians were guilty only of doing cheaply what other southern politicians did at greater expense. Politicians of all factions budgeted for entertainment, food, drink, and outright bribes for voters of both races. Buying votes was more efficient, as one North Carolina politician reported in 1880: "We don't propose to throw away money in barbecues and drinking, but to purchase directly the votes at the polls."

With all factions agreed that the corruption of southern politics had gone too far, the move to disfranchise blacks began as a cry for election reform. White politicians argued that if blacks were removed from the equation of southern elections, the system could be cleaned up. In 1890, Mississippi led the way. At the convention that rewrote the state's constitution to disfranchise blacks, one delegate explained his rationale:

> It is no secret that there has not been a full vote and a fair count in Mississippi since 1875—that we have been preserving the ascendency of the white people by revolutionary methods. In plain words, we have been stuffing ballot-boxes, committing perjury and here and there in the State carrying the elections by fraud and violence until the whole machinery for elections was about to rot down.

Mississippi's Democratic political leaders also worried that the state's Republicans, mostly black, would draw on federal support to contest fraud in state elections.

The Mississippi convention had to find a way to disfranchise blacks without actually mentioning race, since race-based voting restrictions had been prohibited by the Fifteenth Amendment. Black Belt leaders thought that it would be easy enough to cut blacks out of voting by enacting literacy and property requirements; if that reduced the number of white illiterate, propertyless voters, so much the better. Not so, said delegates from the hills: the rights of white men, regardless of class, had to be respected. Eventually the convention produced a set of voting restrictions designed to screen out almost all blacks while allowing whites to vote. To a combination of residency requirements, early registration, and poll taxes, the Mississippi convention added an innovation, the "understanding clause." The prospective voter had to read, or have read to him, a section of the state constitution, and indicate that he understood it. Through the understanding clause, white voting registrars could screen potential voters. White illiterates likely to vote the way the registrar wanted them to would pass the test, while blacks, no matter how educated, would not.

Other southern states soon followed Mississippi's example. Disfranchisement proceeded in two waves, the first in the 1890s and the second in the early twentieth century. The first wave was provoked by the rise of Populism (discussed below) and the second by southern progressivism, a reform movement covered in the following chapter. While the reasons white politicians gave for disfranchisement depended upon current politics, the impact on the black population did not. Despite the protests of black political leaders and of some whites, principally Black Belt politicians dependent on the African-American vote, between 1890 and 1910 southern states passed a variety of laws eliminating any potential for black political power.

The mechanisms used varied from state to state but generally included some form of the poll tax. In states with poll taxes only, blacks continued to vote, although in diminished numbers. Some poll tax states also enacted secret ballot laws, ostensibly intended to make elections more honest, but also designed to make voting difficult for the illiterate. Other states developed more elaborate schemes for disfranchisement. In Louisiana, men whose ancestors had voted before 1867 were exempted from literacy tests; this "grandfather clause" allowed illiterate whites to vote while disfranchising blacks. Virginia, Alabama, and Georgia had similar clauses applying to Civil War veterans and their descendants.

Delegates to disfranchisement conventions did not attempt to hide what they were doing. In statements before the conventions and to the press and public outside, white politicians made it clear that white supremacy was their goal. An Alabama delegate stated, "I believe as truly as I believe that I am standing here that God Almighty intended the negro to be the servant of the white man." Charged with discrimination, a Virginia delegate retorted, "Discrimination! Why that is precisely what we propose; that is exactly what this convention was elected for." As Senator James K. Vardaman of Mississippi said, "Shut the door of political equality, and you shut the door of social equality in the face of the black man; shut the door of social equality and you smother in his native savage breast the fury of his passion, which is but the blind craving of his soul to be the equal of the white man, and the partner of the white man."

In 1898 the Supreme Court upheld the validity of poll taxes and literacy tests, ruling in *Williams v. Mississippi* that such measures did not violate the Fifteenth Amendment. With this stamp of federal approval, all the states of the old Confederacy, and several border states as well, moved to limit black suffrage. In states with only poll taxes, black men continued to vote as long as it was in the interest of white political bosses for them to do so. In places like Memphis, political leaders like Edward "Boss" Crump "voted" black constituents in the old paternalistic manner well into the 1940s. In states with large black populations, like South Carolina and Mississippi, only a very few favored black men were allowed to vote. For black men, even attempting to vote became proverbially hazardous; blacks and whites alike understood the meaning of the saying, "sweating like a nigger going to the election." Black politicians disappeared from courthouses, state legislatures, and the U.S. Congress, where by 1898 George H. White of North Carolina was the last remaining black representative. His term finished, he retired to the North, stating, "I can no longer live in North Carolina and be a man."

Segregation

In the early twentieth century southerners began to use a new word to describe a new practice: "segregation," for legally enacted codes of racial separation. While masters and slaves had lived intimately together, the new racial order required that blacks and whites be separated in such a way as to demonstrate the dominance of whites.

The process of separating the races did not at first require legislation. When emancipation shattered the enforced togetherness of the plantation, blacks exercised their new freedom by forming separate institutions free of white supervision. Blacks pulled out of white churches to start their own. Black sharecroppers refused to live in quarters close to the "big house," preferring more isolated and private dwellings away from white scrutiny. When Reconstruction governments created new school systems, the schools were usually (but not always) for one race only, as were new hospitals, asylums, and so on. In general, black political leaders during Reconstruction acquiesced in racial separation as long as it was not imposed by law. Some hoped to use all-black institutions as centers of community and political strength.

Though whites and many blacks favored racial separatism in social venues, economic conditions made true segregation impossible. In rural areas, black and white men did the same kind of work, traded at the same country stores, hunted and fished the same woods and streams. In towns, black women worked in whites' houses, cooking, cleaning, and taking care of children. Many New South industries had biracial workforces. For white southerners, the presence of black people was a fact of life. Segregation evolved not out of a desire to remove blacks, but rather out of a felt need to control them. Ironically, the primary targets of segregation were not black servants or workers but the rising black middle class.

In the late nineteenth century some African-American men and women managed to accumulate capital, buy homes, and educate their children in the manner approved by the white middle class. According to the racial concepts shared by most white Americans, blacks were destined by nature to be unskilled workers, incapable of rising in the world. Whites who took for granted the presence of field hands and kitchen workers were affronted by gentlemen and ladies of color. Their very existence threatened the foundations of white supremacy. Moreover, money allowed the black middle class to go into places from which poverty barred poor people of either color, and to confront the white middle class as social equals.

In the 1880s, the new railway systems witnessed confrontations between blacks and whites over race and class. Trains typically had first-class, or "parlor," carriages, in which middle-class men and women traveled, and "smokers," cheaper carriages usually inhabited by men traveling alone. Smokers had reputations as places where men smoked, spat tobacco on the floor, cursed, drank and in general behaved badly. Therefore, middle-class people of both colors bought first-class tickets. However, whites protested when black men and women took seats in the parlor cars, contending that the proper place for blacks was in the smokers.

Whites' opposition to blacks in the parlor cars reflected concerns about gender issues that had been rendered more acute with the rise of an educated, well-spoken, well-dressed black middle class. The parlor cars were for ladies and gentlemen. If whites allowed black women to sit there, they had to acknowledge that black women deserved the protection and deference paid to ladies. This undercut the presumption of white supremacists that black women were morally inferior to white. White supremacists found middle-class black gentlemen even more threatening. As a Louisiana newspaper argued, train travel crowded whites and blacks together, "using the same conveniences, and to all intents and purposes in social intercourse." Therefore whites demanded that blacks be denied first-class seats.

In vain black passengers insisted that they were entitled to the seats they had purchased; conductors escorted blacks to the smokers, sometimes evicting them from their seats with the help of white passengers. If blacks refused to cooperate, whites put them off the train, often administering a beating in the process. Incensed, members of the black middle class sued railroad companies all over the South. During the 1880s, judges often ruled in favor of black plaintiffs, although less on racial than on contractual grounds: if the railroads sold first-class tickets to blacks, they had to provide first-class seats, although not necessarily in the same space allotted to whites. By the late 1880s state governments had begun to require railroad companies to provide separate cars for blacks, insisting (as in Texas) that the cars should be "equal in comfort."

In 1892 black activists in Louisiana decided to test that state's new railroad Jim Crow law in the courts. They chose as their designated lawbreaker Homer Adolph Plessy, a man of predominantly white ancestry whose one black great-grandparent made him a Negro under Louisiana law. Forewarned that Plessy was going to break the law by riding in the white car, officials of the East Louisiana Railroad had him arrested. Tried and convicted, Plessy appealed to the U.S. Supreme Court.

The Court's 1896 ruling in *Plessy v. Ferguson* gave federal approval to the final triumph of Jim Crow throughout the nation. Following the precedents set in lower courts, the Supreme Court approved of racially segregated facilities, requiring only that the separate accommodations be equal in quality. This "separate but equal" ruling upheld the railroad segregation laws already on the books in most southern states and encouraged cities and towns to enact municipal Jim Crow laws segregating blacks from whites in public transportation and other public facilities. *Plessy v. Ferguson* also validated the informal installation of Jim Crow already in effect in the South's educational systems.

After 1896, southern whites and blacks lived in a world where racial separation was enforced by law. This marked a significant turning point in U.S. race relations. With Jim Crow laws, racial separatism was no longer a private option but rather a social and legal mandate impervious to the good will of individuals. It no longer mattered much whether any one white man or woman was kind or cruel, tolerant, or prejudiced. Whites and blacks alike were caught up in a system that institutionalized racism to the advantage of whites while relegating blacks to "their place," a subservient one. In the new century, southern whites would come to think of Jim Crow as natural or traditional, as much a part of the southern way of life as hot weather. Jim Crow lasted until 1964.

Living in a Jim Crow World

In the late nineteenth century, travelers through the Deep South discovered that black men had created a new form of music. Waiting for trains at dusty Texas depots, walking down back streets in Memphis or New Orleans, whites heard blacks playing guitars in a new way, sliding notes, creating syncopated rhythms. To this music performers sang lyrics that reflected life in the Jim Crow South. There were songs about love, lust, gambling, drinking, and traveling. There were songs about "bad niggers" like Stagger Lee, who shot his friend Billy over a game of cards. But there were also songs about politics and economics. This new music, the blues, became one of the roots of rock and roll. As historian Leon Litwack has noted, it can also serve as a window into black life in the South at the turn of the last century.

Got one mind for white folks to see,
'Nother for what I know is me;
He don't know, he don't know my mind,
When he see me laughing
Just laughing to keep from crying.

Racial Etiquette

During the Jim Crow years white southerners elaborated an entire code of manners through which blacks were daily reminded of their place. On streets, whites expected blacks to give way on the sidewalk and to avoid eye contact. Good southern manners required that people be addressed by their proper titles, such as Mr. and Mrs., and that respect be paid to age and dignity. Whites applied these rules to whites only and habitually referred to blacks, no matter what their stature or age, by their first names, as if they were children. (Whites might refer to aged blacks they knew well as "Aunt" or "Uncle.") Black men, regardless of age, were boys, as in "Boy! Take my suitcase out to the depot." When blacks came to a white person's house, they went to the back door only. They rode in segregated Jim Crow cars on southern trains. In cities, blacks sat in the back of streetcars and were expected to give up seats if needed for whites. In stores, clerks waited on whites first, blacks last if at all.

Racial etiquette intertwined with gender. Whites drew the color line most clearly in places where white women might be near black men, and least clearly in places that were gender segregated. White and black men working together on some outdoor project might eat their lunches companionably together without violating Jim Crow etiquette. If they went to the white family's house for dinner, the black workers would be expected to eat in the kitchen or in the back yard. As white supremacists saw it, eating together was the first step toward "miscegenation" between black men and white women. In public places, white men could and did accost black women, who complained bitterly that not even the most ladylike and refined appearance protected them from sexual harassment. A black man who spoke familiarly to a white woman risked his life. More than one instance of lynching arose out of a white girl's terror-induced hysterics at being spoken to, or just looked at, by a black man.

From Lynching to Race Riot

Turn-of-the-century America was a violent place. In the West, the U.S. Army destroyed the last remnants of Indian independence during these years. (General Phil Sheridan, remembered for his conduct in the Shenandoah Valley, gave Americans a new catch phrase: "The only good Indian is a dead Indian.") In California, white workers guarded their jobs by attacking and killing imported Chinese labor. In the Northeast, management battled labor in a series of massive strikes. Concerned northern businessmen sponsored the transformation of the old state militias into National Guard units, staffed mostly by middle-class whites and designed to keep order and protect property.

The turn of the century also saw a great increase in lynching, the unauthorized execution without trial of a person accused of a crime. Lynch mobs hanged Mexicans in Texas and union organizers in Washington State. According to statistics compiled by the National Association for the Advancement of Colored People, 3,525 people lost their lives to lynch mobs in the period from 1889 to 1923, with the greatest burst of lynching occurring in the 1880s and 1890s. Although whites were lynched, the majority so killed, 2,795, were black. More lynchings, some 3,184, happened in the South than in any other region of the country (the South being defined in the NAACP stats as including Kentucky, Missouri, Oklahoma, and West Virginia, as well as the old Confederate states.) Other statistics compiled by African-American researchers indicate that from 1882 to 1930 Mississippi led the South in lynching, followed by Georgia and Texas.

Although all lynchings were different, historical records allow us to reconstruct the stereotypical lynching. Whites accused a black man of committing a crime, often rape of a white woman. The accused criminal was arrested and placed in the county jail. A white mob gathered and menaced the county sheriff and his deputies until they delivered the prisoner to the mob; sometimes law enforcement officials joined the lynchers themselves. The prisoner was then "lynched," a term that usually connoted hanging, but that also included preliminary torture, castration, and sometimes burning at the stake. White mobs committed these acts in full daylight, often cheered on by crowds of thousands, including white women and children. Photographs from twentieth-century lynchings show gleeful, laughing whites standing over the mangled bodies of their victims. Lynchers often took body parts as souvenirs and displayed them publicly.

Jesse Washington was 18 years old when he was lynched by a mob in Waco, Texas, on May 15, 1916. Note the crowd of white men watching as Washington's body burns. Library of Congress.

Whites said they lynched to protect white womanhood. They charged that the younger generation of black men, swept away by bestial urges, raped white women in order to destroy white chastity and to avenge themselves on white men. Although whites insisted that hundreds of white women's lives had been destroyed by interracial rape, historians have been unable to find any evidence for this supposed rape epidemic and have concluded that black southerners were correct when they stated that lynching was not about sex but about "keeping the nigger down." To this insight, historians have added another: lynchings occurred most often in situations where blacks and whites did not know each other personally. Thus lynching was relatively uncommon in the old plantation districts on the east coast, and most prevalent in places like the Mississippi Delta, not cleared and settled until the 1880s.

After her closest friend was lynched by a Memphis mob, young black journalist Ida B. Wells began to investigate lynching in the early 1890s. As she explained later, she had accepted the white version of lynching and had rather agreed that rapists deserved death. But her friend, Thomas Moss, had committed no crime against white womanhood. A store owner, he had been arrested and then lynched because he defended his store when attacked by whites. Wells and other Memphis blacks agreed that Moss's real crime was economic: he was just doing too well for a black man. In disgust, many left Memphis to join the Exoduster migration of blacks to the plains of Kansas and Oklahoma. Instead of leaving, Wells began to investigate lynchings. Using reports published in white southern newspapers, Wells concluded that lynchings could arise out of almost anything "from murder to a misdemeanor," but that they had the cumulative effect of terrorizing blacks and keeping them in their place. In an editorial in her Memphis paper, the *Free Speech*, Wells also suggested that white men called any kind of relationship between white women and black men rape, whether it was consensual or not.

For suggesting that some white women chose black men as lovers, Wells incurred the wrath of white Memphis. A local newspaper, assuming that the author of the editorial was male, suggested that "he" be tied to a stake in downtown Memphis and castrated. A white mob burned the *Free Speech* office. Traveling in the North at the time, Wells realized that she could never go home to Memphis again. Like many other black critics of the Jim Crow South, she settled in Chicago, where she published a series of well-documented studies on the lynching phenomenon.

Although lynchings occurred throughout the nation, the frequency and viciousness of lynchings in the South made the crime appear to be a southern, rural one. The race riot, on the other hand, was an urban phenomenon in both South and North. In nineteenth-century terms, a "race riot" meant a white attack on black neighborhoods. One of the first and most deadly had occurred in New York City during the Civil War. Infuriated by class-biased conscription laws, Irish immigrants in New York took out their wrath on blacks, burning black schools and orphanages and killing black men, women, and children, whose bodies they strung from lampposts. When blacks migrated out of the South, as they did in increasing numbers throughout the late nineteenth and early twentieth centuries, their presence in northern cities led to an outbreak of race riots there. In 1908, white rioters in Springfield, Illinois, Lincoln's home town, stormed black neighborhoods, stating that they meant to show blacks their place.

In the South, race riots grew out of a complicated stew of politics and sex, as illustrated by events in North Carolina at the century's turn. By 1898 North Carolina was one of the few states left in which blacks actually exerted real political power. With disfranchisement proposals up for public vote in November, white politicians used various methods to stir up antagonism against blacks. Black politicians fought back. One of the state's most prominent black leaders, Alexander Manly of Wilmington, was the son of a slave woman and an antebellum governor of North Carolina. In August 1898, Manly ran an editorial in his daily newspaper attacking the idea that black rape caused lynching and suggesting that white women chose to have sex with African-American men, particularly those of mixed ancestry. Accusing whites of hypocrisy, Manly concluded: "[Y]ou cry aloud for the virtue of your women while you seek to destroy the morality of ours. Don't think ever that your women will remain pure while you are debauching ours. You sow the seed—the harvest will come in due time." White proponents of disfranchisement reprinted Manly's words in the Wilmington newspaper every day until the election, which the disfranchisers won. After the election, whites burned Manly's office, killed twelve blacks who happened to be nearby, and by a combination of threats and violence drove Manly and other black leaders out of Wilmington. Approximately 1,500 prominent Wilmington blacks fled to the North. Whites confiscated their property for back taxes. The white leader of the riot was elected mayor.

A Separate World

Segregation laws that prohibited blacks from using the same public accommodations as whites led to the creation of alternative services within the black community. By the 1890s, black neighborhoods in southern cities had their own schools, colleges, churches, business districts, and entertainment facilities. Segregation enabled the rise of a small black middle class, composed of professionals and businessmen, who provided services to the community.

It was in this context that the best-known black leader of the late nineteenth century, Booker T. Washington, emerged. President of Alabama's Tuskegee Institute, a vocational training school for blacks, Washington gained support from white northern philanthropists for his message

A class in dressmaking, Hampton Institute, Hampton, Virginia, 1899. Library of Congress.

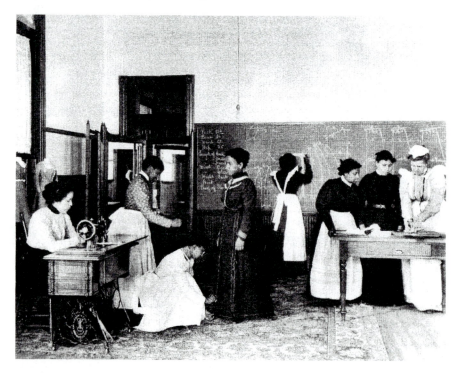

of "accommodation" to Jim Crow. Washington argued that blacks should give up striving for social equality and concentrate on self-improvement and the accumulation of money and property. In a famous speech given in 1895 at the Atlanta Exposition, Washington drew cheers from the white audience for saying, "The opportunity to earn a dollar in a factory just now is worth infinitely more than the opportunity to spend a dollar in an opera-house." Washington urged the leaders of the New South to employ blacks, and suggested, "In all things that are purely social we can be as separate as the fingers, yet one as the hand in all things essential to mutual progress." Although his message appealed greatly to whites, some of whom called him the greatest southerner since Robert E. Lee, it also appealed to many conservative blacks, who believed that agitating for votes and equal rights was both useless and dangerous.

In truth, Washington never gave up hope for equal rights or suffrage. Like other blacks, the Tuskegee president wore a mask, in his case one conciliatory to whites. By flattering whites Washington obtained money and political power. Northern industrialists contributed heavily to Tuskegee. Republican presidents consulted Washington on appointments to federal jobs in the South, and as the head of the "Tuskegee machine," he dispensed patronage to blacks throughout the region. Yet while Washington preached accommodation, he insisted that whites must respect black achievements. He liked to tell a story about two white men who passed on the street a wealthy black man. One of the whites said to the other, "My God! It's all I can do to keep from calling that nigger 'mister.'" Conservative blacks appreciated the message: the road to equality was lined with dollars.

The fate of more militant black leaders suggests the appeal of Washington's approach. During the 1890s Ida B. Wells, Alexander Manly, and a host of other defenders of equal rights were silenced by exile or death.

Fighting the Power: The rise of Populism

In the 1870s and 1880s farmers in the newly settled southwest formed organizations designed to work for better conditions in agriculture. The farmers' organizations culminated in the Farmers Alliance, founded in 1875 in Lampasas County, Texas, and the Agricultural Wheel, formed in Prairie County, Arkansas, in 1882. In 1888 the Alliance and Wheel united to form the National Farmers' Alliance and Cooperative Union of America, better known simply as the Alliance. Under the capable leadership of Dr. C. W. Macune, a rural physician, the Alliance drew members by promising to break the back of the crop lien system and deliver farmers from the middlemen who siphoned off their profits. As Macune explained it, farmers would unite to buy supplies and market crops cooperatively. The centerpiece of Macune's plan was the subtreasury system. Farmers would "deposit" crops in warehouses, where they would become collateral for loans made by the Alliance. The Alliance would hold the cotton crops thus deposited until cotton prices improved, as they usually did a few months after the prime harvest season. The Alliance also called for railroad regulation and currency inflation, both goals that could be achieved only through political action. Significantly, the Alliance declared itself nonpartisan but gave warning that Alliance votes would go to politicians who favored its goals regardless of party.

During the late 1880s the Alliance grew rapidly. By 1890 the organization had 852,000 members. Always strongest in Texas and Arkansas, the Alliance also built support in Alabama, Georgia, Florida, North Carolina, and Mississippi; it was weaker in Louisiana, Virginia and Tennessee. Alliance members were usually landowning farmers. Very few tenants joined, perhaps because landlords forbade them to. For that reason, the Alliance drew little support from the Black Belt.

The Alliance attracted politicians and reformers from agrarian districts throughout the South. Among them was Leonidis Polk, a successful North Carolina farmer who had served as that state's first commissioner of agriculture before resigning to found the *Progressive Farmer* in 1886. This paper became the voice of the Alliance throughout the South. In South Carolina, Ben Tillman, a prominent Democrat, became an Alliance supporter, as did Tom Watson in Georgia. In 1890 John P. Buchanan, president of the Tennessee Alliance, was elected governor of that state.

The southern political and social elite viewed the Alliance with dismay and fear. By the 1890s, the southern Democratic Party leadership was dominated by former Confederates, often called "Bourbons," not for their drink of choice but rather because, like the former royal house of France, they had learned nothing and forgotten nothing from the revolution that was the Civil War. Bourbon Democrats disapproved of the Alliance's stated intention to put the interest of farmers above party interests. Most threatening of all, some Alliancemen showed a willingness to accept political support from blacks and Republicans. Democratic newspapers poured scorn on the hayseeds, who retaliated by asking what the Democrats had done for them lately.

In 1892 members of the Alliance joined with a similar midwestern organization to form a new political organization, the People's Party, or Populists. The Populist Party adopted much of the southern Alliance's stance on economic issues but also emphasized a measure to inflate the currency by increasing the coinage of silver and included within its platform statements designed to appeal to industrial workers as well. At their convention in Omaha, Nebraska, the Populists nominated a balanced North/South ticket: the presidential candidate had been a Union general, and the vice president had fought for the Confederacy. With the creation of this new party, southern Alliancemen had to decide whether they were members of the older parties or Populists. Thousands of Democrats made the switch to populism in 1892.

By placing class issues ahead of race, the Populists threatened to upset the social contract that had defined southern life since colonial Virginia. Not racial liberals, the Populists supported segregation and white supremacy. However, Populist leaders like Tom Watson also assumed that as farmers, blacks and whites had the same economic interests. Watson appealed to black and white voters in 1892, saying, "You are kept apart that you may be separately fleeced of your earnings." When a black preacher campaigning for Watson received lynching threats, he went to Watson's plantation for shelter. Watson called for help, and 2,000 white farmers showed up with guns to protect the life of one black Populist. Populist organizations in Texas, Virginia, Georgia, and other states placed blacks in leadership positions. In other places, Populist leaders "fused" with Republicans, who promised to deliver black votes in exchange for Populist votes for selected GOP candidates.

The state elections in 1892 were among the most tense in southern history. Bourbon Democrats attacked Populists as traitors to their race and their Confederate heritage. When the Populist candidate for the presidency campaigned in Georgia, Democrats pelted him and his wife with eggs and rotten vegetables. They threatened Populist candidates with lynching. In several states mobs attacked Populist speakers, and in Texas Populists and Democrats fought duels. After the dust settled, observers concluded that the Democrats had stolen the election in many parts of the South. Much to the disgust of many Populists, Black Belt planters voted their black tenants for the Democrats, while in other places the victorious party resorted to simple fraud. In upper South states, such as Tennessee, Democrats won back wavering Populists by promising to support measures favored by the Alliance, such as inflating the currency.

Wounded but not dead, the Populist Party soldiered on until the presidential election of 1896. In the meantime, the nation slid into the worst depression in its history to that date. The Democratic Party splintered into factions favoring inflation through the increased coinage of silver ("Free Silver") versus those favoring the continuation of the federal policy basing the currency on gold. At the Democratic convention in 1896, the Free Silver forces won. They nominated for the presidency a young midwestern congressman, William Jennings Bryan, chiefly in response to a powerful speech he made extolling the virtues of agrarianism and silver. The platform on which Bryan ran called for Free Silver, but omitted mention of many reforms proposed by Populists. Nevertheless, the Populist Party decided in 1896 to second the Democrats by nominating Bryan as its candidate for the presidency. Despite protests from southern Populists, who warned that going back into the Democratic Party would be the end of the People's Party in the South, the farmers' party fused with the Democrats. Its only concession to independence was to nominate Watson for vice president. Having thus committed party suicide, the Populists went down with the Democrats to defeat in 1896. The GOP candidate, William McKinley, won by a landslide, elected primarily by the northern industrial states.

Populism was dead and with it hopes of a biracial political party. Angered that their enemies had used captive black votes against them in 1892, politicians representing small farmers were among the strongest supporters of the wave of disfranchisement that followed in populism's defeat. Observers noted the presence of Populists in the mobs that wrecked black Wilmington, North Carolina in 1898. The change in Tom Watson was emblematic. Watson, who had spoken so eloquently about the rights of farmers, regardless of color, eventually became one of the South's worst public bigots. Through his newspaper, Watson continued support for the common white folk but printed obscene diatribes against blacks, Catholics, and Jews.

A White Man's Nation

In 1898 the United States went to war with Spain, ostensibly over that country's oppressive government in its colony, Cuba. (Not coincidentally, the war also served the ends of American imperialists, who had their eyes on Spain's colonies in the Pacific.) Thousands of southerners of both races volunteered for military service in the Spanish-American War, among them some former Confederate officers. According to legend, one elderly officer became confused and urged his men forward in Cuba with cries of "There they are, men! Charge the Yankees!" Despite such lapses, most white Americans agreed that the Spanish-American War marked the final reintegration of the South into the Union.

The political climate in the North made that reunification easier. As noted earlier, white middle-class northerners began to reconsider their support for black rights as early as the 1870s. That support continued to deteriorate in the following decades, as more and more educated Americans came to subscribe to Social Darwinism. Believing that life was a struggle in which the fittest—individuals or races—survived and rose to the top, Social Darwinists surveyed the world around them and felt comfortable in asserting the superiority not just of whites but of Anglo-Saxons, whether British or American. The British presided over the world's largest empire, holding under their control peoples of color from Asia to Africa. Americans had similarly created an empire-sized republic, in the process decimating the American Indians. In the racial hierarchy constructed by Social Darwinists, Africans and those of African descent ranked far below even white immigrants who were not Anglo-Saxon, and even below Indians. Social Darwinists felt that evolution assured the survival of the fittest; if Indians did not survive, and if blacks struggled, that was nature's verdict on their viability as human specimens.

This racist consensus pervaded American society. White scientists produced research that validated the supposed superiority of whites over other races. History faculties taught younger generations of scholars that Reconstruction had been a tragic example of the inability of blacks to govern. Popular culture ratified these views, using song and story to depict blacks as comic buffoons. White immigrants quickly grasped the advantages their skin color brought them; African-Americans bitterly commented that the first word Europeans learned in English was "nigger." By 1900, the very concept that blacks could be equal to whites would have been as alien in New York or Chicago as in Little Rock or Atlanta.

White southerners had assured each other that by removing blacks from politics and public life, they could purify the southern politicial system and make it possible to reform southern society. They put those concepts to the test in the early years of the twentieth century, when the Progressive movement came South.

Suggestions for Further Reading and Viewing

EDWARD AYERS, *The Promise of the New South: Life After Reconstruction* (1992)

W. FITZHUGH BRUNDAGE, *Lynching in the New South: Georgia and Virginia, 1880–1930* (1993)

DAVID CARLTON, *Mill and Town in South Carolina, 1880–1920* (1982)

DON DOYLE, *New Men, New Cities, New South: Atlanta, Nashville, Charleston, Mobile, 1860–1910* (1990)

GAINES M. FOSTER, *Ghosts of the Confederacy: Defeat, the Lost Cause, and the Emergence of the New South, 1865–1913* (1987)

STEPHEN HAHN, *The Roots of Southern Populism* (1983)

J. MORGAN KOUSSER, *The Shaping of Southern Politics: Suffrage Restriction and the Establishment of the One-Party South, 1880–1910* (1974)

LEON LITWACK, *Trouble in Mind: Black Southerners in the Age of Jim Crow* (1998)

ROBERT C. MCMATH, JR., *Populist Vanguard: A History of the Southern Farmers' Alliance* (1975)

HOWARD RABINOWITZ, *The First New South* (1992)

ALLEN TULLIS, *Habits of Industry: White Culture and the Transformation of the Carolina Piedmont* (1989)

Ida B. Wells: A Passion for Justice (Video: The American Experience.)

CHARLES REAGAN WILSON, *Baptized in Blood: The Religion of the Lost Cause, 1865–1920* (1980)

C. VANN WOODWARD, *Origins of the New South, 1877–1913* (1951)

GAVIN WRIGHT, *Old South, New South: Revolutions in the Southern Economy since the Civil War* (1986)

chapter

3

Modern Times: The South 1900–1930

Symbolically reintegrated into the nation through combat during the Spanish-American War, white southerners began the twentieth century more optimistic and hopeful about their place in the nation than they had been in many years. Yet no one, North or South, would have contended that southern distinctiveness had disappeared. The differences between the South and the rest of the nation were still evident. Although the southern economy improved in the early years of the new century, the region was still the nation's poorest. The South's ethnic composition was also distinctive. During the early twentieth century millions of immigrants from southern and eastern Europe poured into the Northeast, dramatically changing that region's population and popular culture. In this age of mass immigration, the southern population remained as it had been for over a century: predominately British and African, with flavorings of French in Louisiana and Mexican in Texas. In addition to these statistically measurable ethnic differences, southerners would have cited cultural differences as well. Elaborate manners, a cultivation of leisure, a slower pace of business, a continued enjoyment of the outdoors, hunting and fishing, a devotion to evangelical Christianity—all these attributes contributed to a treasured "southern way of life," a cultural artifact in which many white southerners invested a good bit of emotion.

Northerners, too, had an investment in southern distinctiveness. While many were charmed by the South's old-fashioned ways, others found the region useful as a worst-case example of national problems. Interestingly enough, the ways in which the problems were defined changed over time, in ways corresponding to the social and political needs of the rest of the nation.

Did southern "problems" mirror those of the nation at large? Did the southern response to national events and movements of the early twentieth century demonstrate a distinctive southern spin? Was the region really integrated into the nation, or was the twentieth-century South even further out of the American mainstream?

Southern Progressivism, 1900–1930

At the turn of the century a diffuse impulse toward reform began to develop throughout the nation. Historians have labeled this movement "progressivism" and have traced its origins to the concern felt by a rising new generation of Americans over the failure of all levels of government to deal with conditions rising out of the nation's rapid industrialization and urbanization. Progressives thought that American government and society needed reform urgently but disagreed as to how to go about it, and they took their impulse toward reform into both of the major political parties, much to the disgruntlement of conservatives in both. Nonetheless, both parties sent progressives to the White House: Theodore Roosevelt for the GOP from 1901 to 1908 and Woodrow Wilson for the Democrats from 1912 to 1920.

A movement formed to address the problems of industry and cities might seem irrelevant to the South, still a mostly agrarian region. Yet despite a long-term regional aversion to strong government, southern progressives agreed with their counterparts elsewhere that the nation's changed economy required increased governmental activism. In the national government, southern politicians led the battle for progressive legislation and succeeded in obtaining passage of measures lowering the federal tariff, creating a graduated income tax, regulating corporations, and establishing a federally regulated national banking system—all goals accomplished under the leadership of President Woodrow Wilson, himself a southerner by birth. On the state level, progressives worked for better state services, including improved schools, public health facilities, highway systems, and above all, legislation prohibiting the manufacture and sale of alcohol.

The Religious Roots of Southern Progressivism

Although religion formed a component of progressivism throughout the nation, it was a driving force in southern progressivism. In the 1880s and 1890s religion provided the main challenge to the complacency of the New South. The region's most prominent evangelist, Sam Jones, organized segregated but biracial revivals at which he railed at the selfishness of the new rich, challenged the middle class to put their money to work in service of Christ, and thundered against the evils of alcohol: "[I]f there is a man on earth that ought to let whiskey alone it is the colored man. God bless you, you will need all the sobriety and manhood you can get, and whiskey cuts that grit from you every day you live." Reform movements sprang up in southern cities in the wake of Jones's preaching tours. Middle-class southerners founded charitable institutions ranging from day-care and educational centers for the children of working mothers to agencies for the relief of the destitute. In many cases, women were the organizers and fundraisers for these new philanthropic organizations.

Sam Jones's pet cause, Prohibition, linked the nineteenth-century religious revivals and twentieth-century progressivism. Southerners had come late to the temperance movement, which in the antebellum period had been associated with abolitionists and Republicans. However, after the Civil War southern evangelicals slowly came to agree with their northern brethren that not just drunkenness, but drinking in itself, was a sin. During the last two decades of the nineteenth century southern evangelicals preached a crusade of temperance to their own members. Having reformed themselves, evangelicals turned their concern to southern society. At their urging, laws prohibiting or greatly restricting the sale of alcohol were passed in most rural southern communities before 1900.

Prohibition proved unpopular in most of the South's cities, which remained "wet" by local option, and evangelicals' efforts to get southern states to enact mandatory statewide Prohibition in the 1880s and 1890s failed. (White evangelicals blamed the failure of Prohibition upon the black vote, especially as "voted" by urban political bosses, and became staunch supporters of disfranchisement.) The evangelicals did not give up. In 1900 the Southern Baptist Convention issued a resolution that summed up the position of many Baptists throughout the South: "[W]e favor prohibition for the nation and the state and total abstinence for the individual, and we do believe that no Christian citizen should ever cast a ballot for any man, measure or platform that is opposed to the annihilation of the liquor traffic."

Reform Movements and Conservative Opposition, 1900–1930

Most southern progressives began by supporting Prohibition and were led through that crusade to other progressive causes. Progressivism, unlike populism, expressed the interests of the new urban middle class. The movement drew upon a coalition of reform-minded clergymen, educators, philanthropists, women's groups, and (sometimes reluctant) politicians. Progressive southerners envisioned a region where the South's best graces—friendliness, hospitality, courtesy, and a commitment to Christian morality—could be combined with newer modern virtues, such as efficiency and good government. However, progressive reformers quickly discovered that advocating social reforms put them in conflict with one of the region's most deeply cherished values, the right of a white man to do as he pleased with his time, money, and dependents.

Prohibition Between 1907, when Georgia became the first southern state to enact Prohibition, and 1919, when the ratification of the Nineteenth Amendment brought Prohibition to the entire nation, "drys" and "wets" battled over liquor laws throughout the South. Support for Prohibition was strongest among rural southerners, among members of the new urban middle class, and among women.

For decades women reformers argued that drunkenness was the primary cause of spousal and child abuse, poverty, and violence. Protestant

This young textile worker was photographed in 1908 at the Mellville Manufacturing Company, Cherryville, North Carolina, by Lewis Hine, who became famous for a series of photographs of child laborers. Hine worked for the National Child Labor Committee, which used his photos in national campaigns for laws prohibiting child labor. Library of Congress.

women by the thousands joined the Women's Christian Temperance Union. In the South (as elsewhere in the nation) the WCTU and other Prohibitionist organizations introduced women to the arts of political pressure.

In some states, politics revolved around the Prohibition issue. In Tennessee, the feud between the pro- and anti-liquor factions led to a 1908 gun battle between prominent politicians on the downtown streets of Nashville, in which a former U.S. senator, a "dry," was killed. The ensuing public outcry pressured the state legislature to enact statewide Prohibition. Prohibition proved equally divisive, although not as bloody, in Texas, Alabama, and North Carolina. In other states Prohibition measures sailed through legislatures on a high tide of popular support. On the other hand, Louisiana, with its overwhelmingly Catholic population, never caught the evangelical Protestant enthusiasm for Prohibition and did not enact statewide anti-liquor laws.

Southern Prohibition had a mixed record. The passage of statewide laws drove the liquor trade off Main Street and out of grocery and drug stores. Southern towns and cities became quieter, more orderly places, where women and children could shop without being accosted by rowdy drunks. However, booze did not disappear. The fact that the middle class disapproved of drinking did not much impress either the white or the black urban working class, many of whom considered the right to a snort a matter of their personal liberty. Reflecting the wishes of their constituencies, urban mayors sometimes refused to enforce the new prohibition laws. This proved a boon to the illegal liquor trade. In the Appalachian South, moonshining (the illegal manufacture of liquor) became an attractive economic alternative for farmers. Although national prohibition ended in 1933, many southern communities retain to this day their laws against the sale of liquor.

Hurricane at Galveston

In Texas, one of the nation's worst-ever natural disasters led to an experiment with a new, progressive form of government.

In 1900 a devastating hurricane roared out of the Gulf of Mexico and all but destroyed Galveston. Present-day experts at the National Weather Service estimate that the 1900 storm was a category 4 hurricane, with winds up to 130–40 miles per hour and a fifteen-and-a-half foot storm surge. An estimated 6,000 people died during the storm, and 8,000 more were left homeless. After the storm, the parts of town closest to the beach looked as if they had been bombed. Rubble choked the streets, and the stench of death nauseated relief workers.

To cope with the emergency, Galveston re-created its form of city government. The governor of Texas appointed a mayor and four commissioners, each to be in charge of an aspect of city government. After the emergency ended, the city kept this experimental government but modified it to make it more democratic, allowing the election of mayor and commissioners. This was the first use of commission government in the United States.

Saving the Children: Child Labor, School Reform, and Public Health　Led to Prohibition by a desire to save the South's children from poverty and abuse, many southerners moved logically and easily to reforms designed to help the region's youth. Reformers campaigned to outlaw child labor, build better schools, and protect the health of the new generation. In each of these campaigns they received support, guidance, and funding from northern philanthropists.

In 1900 Alabama labor unions began to campaign for a law limiting child labor. To help them, the American Federation of Labor (AFL) sent an investigator, Irene M. Ashby, who reported that many Alabama textile mills employed children of eight or nine, who worked twelve-hour shifts for fifteen cents a day. Seeking local support, Ashby met with women's groups and church groups. In 1901 she made a convert of Edgar Gardner Murphy, an Episcopalian minister, who went on to lead the battle against child labor in Alabama and to work for educational reform throughout the South. In 1903 Murphy marshaled sufficient public support to obtain the passage in Alabama of the first significant child labor law in southern history. North and South Carolina soon followed.

After these early successes, the movement for child labor laws hit serious opposition and stalled. Understandably, mill owners opposed child labor laws, accusing Murphy and other reform advocates of conspiring to destroy the southern textile industry. The owners received support from an unexpected source: adult mill workers, who resented the reformers' intrusion into what they considered private, family matters. Moreover, mill workers found offensive reform propaganda that depicted life in the mills as degrading.

In 1904 northern progressives founded the National Child Labor Committee (NCLC) and named as its southern representative North Carolinian Alexander McKelway, a Presbyterian minister and journalist. McKelway investigated, wrote articles, lobbied, gave speeches, and helped coordinate state reform efforts throughout the region, with some success. By 1915 all of the southern states had enacted child labor laws of varying stringency. All southern states prohibited the employment of children under twelve, while some raised the age to fourteen or sixteen. Still, most southern child labor laws contained loopholes large enough for a ten-year-old to slip through. Encouraged by parents and mill owners, children continued to work, only slightly inconvenienced by the need to lie about their ages.

Discouraged, southern child labor advocates joined with their counterparts elsewhere to campaign for federal child labor laws. Their lobbying was influential in the passage of the Keating-Owen Child Labor Act in 1916. This act prohibited the interstate shipment of items manufactured by children under fourteen. North Carolina textile manufacturers challenged the law, and the Supreme Court declared it unconstitutional. No additional federal laws were passed until the 1930s. However, manufacturers knew that public opinion had turned against them. The number of child workers under fourteen gradually dwindled.

Good Schools   The southern campaign for better schools drew on the same constituents who opposed child labor and added to them a dedicated cadre of professional educators, whose efforts were funded by northern philanthropists. Some, like George Foster Peabody, a southern-born financier, began by funding reforms in African-American education. However, northern philanthropists soon realized that supporting schools for southern blacks while ignoring whites caused white resentment, thus endangering the very people the philanthropists were trying to help. Northern racial liberals came to believe that educating whites was the surest path toward racial justice in the region. Besides, as southern educationalists pointed out, white schools were almost as bad as black schools, and in almost as much need of help. No cause was needier than southern education, as University of Tennessee President Charles W. Dabney told a delegation of northern money men at an educational conference in Winston-Salem, North Carolina, in 1901. Inspired by Dabney and by North Carolina's "education governor," Charles Aycock, northern philanthropists provided funds for a southern educational reform campaign.

Robert Ogden, a New York businessman long associated with Virginia's Hampton Institute, and Peabody funded the Southern Education Board (SEB), designed to propagandize in favor of better schools. With Edgar Gardner Murphy as executive secretary, the SEB funded educational crusades throughout the South. Meanwhile, the Rockefeller family created its own organization, the General Education Board (GEB), to funnel money to education reform. The GEB and the SEB had interlocking directorates and cooperated on many pro-education campaigns. Thus the SEB helped pay for a pro-education propaganda office, the Bureau of Investigation and Information, run by University of Tennessee professor Philander P. Claxton in Knoxville, while the GEB funded the Summer School of the South, held annually at UT from 1902 to 1907. Approximately 11,000 teachers came to UT for the summer school's classes in educational reform and went home fired up and ready to work for reform in their home states.

With encouragement and advice from the SEB, local educators mounted campaign reforms in most of the southern states between 1903 and 1908. Reformers won their greatest victories in North Carolina, which drastically increased state and local funding for education, and in 1907 began to establish public high schools in each of the state's rural counties. Although other southern states failed to match North Carolina's achievements, most did begin spending more money for education. By the mid-1920s teachers were paid better, schools stayed in session longer, new buildings had replaced old cabins and shacks, compulsory education laws had been passed, and the illiteracy rate among white children had dropped by 50 percent. Yet despite the valiant efforts of educational reformers, post-reform southern school systems still failed to meet national norms.

Social realities undercut success in the progressive schools campaign. Although economic conditions improved in the early twentieth century, the South was still the nation's poorest region. A state like Mississippi could, and did, increase the revenues it spent on education by over 200 percent, without coming close to the funding level of wealthier northern states. To educate a population scattered through the countryside, counties had literally scores of small, one-room schools. Until new highway systems made consolidation possible in the 1920s, school reform in the rural South was all but impossible. Even then, the quality of facilities and instruction available in rural schools rarely compared favorably with those provided in towns and cities.

White supremacy also undercut school reform. States ran two school systems, one for whites and one for blacks, thus increasing the states' expenses. While segregated, the schools were by no means equal. In most southern states, white school authorities skimmed off most of the funding for white schools, leaving black schools underfunded, overcrowded, and badly supplied. (North Carolina's white superintendent of black teachers' colleges caused a statewide uproar in 1905 when he produced statistics indicating that blacks paid for white education, not the other way around.) The rate of illiteracy among southerners of both races aged ten and older dropped, but whites made more improvement than blacks. In 1920 white illiteracy rates ranged from a low of 2.9 in Florida to a high of 10.5 in Louisiana, while the illiteracy rate among blacks ran from 17.8 in Texas to 38.5 in Louisiana.

School reformers often complained that the southern population's attitudes toward education impeded progress. The attempt to build new public schools faced opposition from some members of the region's upper class and from many of the common folk. Upper-class southerners had traditionally sent their sons and daughters to privately funded academies and saw no reason why they should pay higher taxes to educate the children of the poor. Whites of all classes contended that educating blacks only spoiled good field hands and cooks. On the other hand, many white farmers complained that the new schools educated their sons away from the farm. Some southerners saw the new schools as a threat to their control over their children's lives and labor and questioned the legitimacy of state laws requiring school attendance.

In the long run, educational reform mattered most to white women. Throughout the nation women were more likely to finish high school than men, who often dropped out to take blue-collar jobs. High school educations allowed white women to take advantage of new economic opportunities in the 1920s.

Public Health   In the early twentieth century medical scientists successfully attacked many of the diseases that had plagued the South. Researchers discovered that mosquitoes carried malaria and yellow fever and began campaigns to eradicate them. The South suffered its last yellow fever epidemic in 1905; malaria, less deadly but still debilitating, disappeared by mid-century. Researchers led by Dr. Joseph Goldberger began investigating the causes of pellegra in 1914 and by 1915 determined that the disease was caused by dietary deficiencies. When a Mississippi flood caused a famine and an outbreak of pellegra in 1927, Goldberger advised the Red Cross to dose the sufferers with yeast. Convinced, the Red Cross began promoting better diets as a way of ending pellegra, and the condition became less common. Eradicating infestations of hookworm, an intestinal parasite, was the special mission of the Rockefeller Sanitary Commission. From 1909 to 1914, the commission took its traveling clinics to eleven southern states, tested over a million people, and treated almost half a million; they found infestations in almost 40 percent of the children they tested. The Rockefeller Commission's antiworm campaign aroused public interest in health reform. By 1913 all the southern states had created boards of health, charged with gathering statistics on disease and with educating the public.

In the long run, public health reforms depended upon changing people's habits. Many of the diseases endemic to the South were spread by poor sanitation. Farms, schools, and rural stores had no running water. People drew water from wells and shared dippers, thus spreading diseases. Farm families relieved themselves in barns or behind convenient bushes. Southern women and children went barefoot most of the year and picked up parasites from human and farm animal waste. Waste contaminated water supplies, leading to typhoid epidemics. The outhouse, now a comic symbol of rural backwardness, was a lifesaving innovation in the early twentieth century, demonstrated by public health agents at county fairs. The new schools bore the responsibility for teaching the rising generation better health habits. Simple things, like wearing shoes or using a privy, went a long way toward eradicating water-borne diseases in the South, and the populaton's health gradually improved.

Good Roads   The campaign to improve the South's highway system was perhaps the least controversial of all Progressive Era reforms, but it was critical to the region's modernization. As the southern urban middle class began to acquire automobiles, it quickly realized the need of state-funded interconnecting highways. Urban businessmen helped create road-boosting organizations such as the United States Good Roads Association, founded in 1913. To stir up support, road boosters created named highway associations, such as the organizations supporting the building of the Dixie Highway from Michigan to Florida. Senator John H. Bankhead of Alabama became a leading advocate of federal aid to highways and in 1916 was instrumental in obtaining the passage of the Federal Highways Act allotting federal matching grants to rural roads. Eager to get their share of federal funds, between 1906 and 1917 southern states created their first highway commissions and began work on state highway systems.

At first, many farmers opposed state highway programs, arguing that the new roads cost too much in taxes. Class resentment often motivated farmers' opposition to good roads. The first automobiles were lavish, expensive machines. Farmers considered them rich men's toys. But in 1914 Henry Ford began to mass produce the Model T, a car designed to be cheap, durable, and adaptable to rural conditions. As farmers bought cars, they changed their minds about the need for good roads.

The question remained: how were the new roads to be paid for? Anxious to get under way, most southern states decided to finance highways with road bonds, to be paid off with revenues from gasoline and other taxes. In the 1920s state governments poured money into highway building. Thousands of men got jobs in highway construction.

In addition to putting money in the pockets of southern working men, the new good roads helped break the isolation of the rural South. Country families who had gone to town once a year now drove in once a week to market produce and shop. Others opened up produce and crafts stands by the highways. The new roads made the southern tourist industry possible, spurring development of parks, roadside attractions, and beach and mountain property.

Road building supported southern prosperity in the 1920s, but at a cost. Financing roads with bonds, which are essentially loans, worked fine in times of prosperity, but when the national economy crashed in 1929, many southern states were left with debts they could not easily pay. In addition, road building offered opportunities for graft and corruption unmatched since the heyday of railroad construction.

Progressive Racists: Southern Politicians in the Progressive Era

Throughout the nation, progressives attempted to make the political system more responsive to the people. One method especially popular in the South was the state primary law, allowing voters to choose party nominees for all state offices. However, the institution of direct primaries also serves to illustrate the peculiar southern spin regional politicians put upon progressive reform. With the South solidly Democratic, primaries became the only election that mattered, since winning the Democratic nomination was tantamount to victory in almost all cases. Southern primaries also served as one more layer of disfranchisement. As private institutions, political parties declared their primary elections to be for whites only.

The example of the white primary should serve as a warning: southern progressives were not racial liberals. In fact, many southern politicians considered disfranchisement and segregation the cornerstone reforms that made all other progressive measures possible. Many of the southern politicians most supportive of school reforms, better roads, and prohibition rode to power on white supremacist tickets. North Carolina's Charles Aycock campaigned for disfranchisement in the 1890s before becoming the state's "education governor" in 1900. (Though a white supremacist, Aycock honestly believed in universal education and fought for funding of black schools.) In Georgia, Hoke Smith's successful campaign for the governorship in 1906 included calls for disfranchisement, which was enacted under his leadership in 1908, along with railroad regulation, Prohibition, tax reform, child labor laws, and educational reform measures.

In Mississippi, race and class combined to create a volatile political scene. The state's hill-country farmers had long resented the powerful planters, who controlled the votes of their black tenants. Disfranchisement in 1890 cut into planter political power, but the state's elite still controlled the Democratic Party's nominating conventions. In 1902 reformers pushed through a primary election law. Able to vote directly for their own political leadership for the first time in the state's history, Mississippi's common white folk overthrew planter power, a process referred to as the "revolt of the rednecks" by historians. In 1903 James K. Vardaman, a Greenwood newspaper editor, campaigned for governor on a platform that emphasized his disdain for the "special interests," including the planters, and for blacks.

To white plain folk, Vardaman was a gorgeous figure. Tall, handsome, with long flowing curly black hair, he dressed in white suits and hats and wore a red kerchief tied around his neck, thereby signifying his proud red-neck status. He made speeches denouncing blacks as animals and promised that every black man in the state would be lynched if necessary to preserve white supremacy. After being elected, he was the most progressive governor in the state's history to that date. His record was superseded by that of his protégé, Theodore G. Bilbo, who served as governor from 1915 to 1919. Bilbo was just as racist as his mentor and deficient in personal morals as well. Historian George Tindall pointed out that Bilbo's "political career began under the cloud of attempted bribery and progressed through accusations of fornication, adultery, graft, and slander." Yet with Bilbo as governor, Mississippi enacted tax reforms, educational reforms, Prohibition, reforms in county governments, aid to farmers, and many other progressive measures.

Southern conservatives called men like Vardaman and Bilbo "demagogues," men who rise to power by stirring up the masses. That label has also been applied to Jeff Davis of Arkansas and Cole Blease of South Carolina. Davis, the "Wild Ass of the Ozarks," rose to popularity by denouncing big business, but his terms as governor and senator produced little in the way of progressive reform. Cole Blease, elected governor in 1910, was an antiprogressive who won the support of South Carolina's factory class by crusading *against* compulsory education, child labor laws, and uppity reformers who thought they were better than the white mill workers. Vardaman, Bilbo, Davis, and Blease had little in common other than their racism, a trait they shared with more respectable progressives like Aycock and Hoke Smith, as well as with the conservatives who denounced their class-based politics. White supremacy was the lowest common denominator of southern politics. Although demagogues like Bilbo used rougher language than politicians from the region's upper-class elite, patrician politicians of the upper class were no more committed to racial justice than were the leaders of the redneck revolt.

Birth of a (White) Nation

In focusing their attention primarily on reforms designed to help whites, southern progressives did not differ from most of their colleagues in the North. In the northern cities where progressivism was born, reformers hoped through education to help immigrants assimilate and "Americanize." In effect, an Americanized immigrant became socially and culturally white. Liberal progressives believed that Italians and Slavs could learn to be Americans; more conservative progressives had their doubts. One sociologist of the period described Slavs as cavemen who could tolerate levels of dirt that would "kill a white man." If some progressives were not sure that blue-eyed blond Poles could become "white," where did that leave African-Americans?

In 1883 North Carolinian Thomas Dixon and Virginian Woodrow Wilson, both graduate students at Johns Hopkins, studied history with Herbert Baxter Adams. Influenced by Social Darwinism and by romantic notions of European racial origins, Adams taught his students that the spirit of democracy was essentially passed down to white Americans from their ancient Germanic ancestors. Not being of Germanic ancestry, blacks were incapable of self-government. Woodrow Wilson graduated from Johns Hopkins and went on to fame as a political scientist, governor of New Jersey, and president of the United States, in which office he presided over the racial segregation of Washington, D.C.

His young classmate Thomas Dixon went back to North Carolina, dabbled in law and politics, and in 1902 began writing novels. In 1902 he published *The Leopard's Spots: A Romance of the White Man's Burden, 1865–1900,* a historical novel that purported to describe the suffering inflicted upon whites by black rule during Reconstruction in the Carolinas. It was a runaway best-seller, but Dixon's next book did even better.

The Clansman: A Historical Romance of the Ku Klux Klan left a mark on American race relations still visible today. Continuing his Reconstruction saga, Dixon depicted black men as brutish sexual predators and glorified the southern white men who founded the KKK as heroes of the "Aryan race." The American public agreed, buying over one million copies of the book within the first few months of publication. When Dixon adapted his book for the stage, *The Clansman* played to sold-out audiences throughout the nation, despite the denunciations of newspaper critics, including southern editors who charged Dixon with stirring up racial animosity.

Sensing *The Clansman's* great dramatic potential, Hollywood director D. W. Griffith used it as the source of his first long movie spectacular, *Birth of a Nation,* the film with which American cinema history begins. The film opens with a statement by President Woodrow Wilson, who had viewed it at a special White House showing and testified to its historical veracity. Thus reassured, audiences in 1914 settled into their theater seats to cheer as the KKK first rescues innocent white women from rape by black soldiers, then uses violence to regain control of Carolina politics. Like all silent movies, *Birth of a Nation* is accompanied by written titles giving dialogue and explaining actions, but an immigrant just off the boat would have had no difficulty understanding the message.

Leo Frank

The 1913 murder of a young female factory worker in Atlanta set off a train of events leading to one of the nation's most famous lynchings. Mary Phagan, thirteen years old, pretty, and white, was an employee at the National Pencil Factory. She had gone to the factory during off-hours to pick up her wages and was killed there. To many Georgians, her fate symbolized the dangers now besetting young women, many of whom had to leave the shelter of their homes and work to help support their families.

After investigating several other possibilities, the Atlanta police arrested Phagan's employer and charged him with her murder. The evidence against him was not strong. However, Leo Frank was a northerner and a Jew. Prosecuting attorneys in the case used both circumstances against him, urging the jury to protect Christian womanhood by convicting him. Meanwhile, Frank's wife organized his defense, obtaining aid from prominent Jewish leaders in the North. To no avail: Frank was convicted and sentenced to death. However, Frank's wife and his friends did not give up the fight. They made his case a national cause, mobilizing support through the Anti-Defamation League.

In 1915, Georgia's governor commuted Frank's death sentence. The ensuing uproar drove him right out of the state. Two months later, a group of men from Cobb County, Phagan's home, kidnaped Frank from prison, took him to Cobb, and hanged him. This highly organized lynch mob included many of the leading citizens of Marietta, Georgia. They called themselves the "Knights of Mary Phagan."

Today, new evidence has convinced historians that Frank was innocent. Leo Frank remains one of the South's most famous lynch-law victims, and a martyr to anti-Semitism.

In 1915 an Alabama native who had made his living selling memberships to men's fraternal groups capitalized on the popularity of *Birth of a Nation*. Colonel William Joseph Simmons and a group of friends donned white robes and climbed up Stone Mountain, near Atlanta, to pledge themselves to the rebirth of the Ku Klux Klan. Simmons began to retail memberships in the new KKK from offices in Atlanta.

Progressivism in the Black Community

In 1906 Hoke Smith's campaign for the governorship of Georgia featured propaganda depicting black men as rapists, lustful beasts out to destroy white womanhood. In Atlanta, a local theater put on Dixon's *The Clansman*. After weeks of racist propaganda, in September an estimated 10,000 Atlanta whites rioted. After killing blacks in the city's business district, they rampaged through the city, attacking the homes of Atlanta's most successful middle-class blacks. Walter White, then the thirteen-year-old son of an African-American mail carrier, was riding through the town with his father when the riot began. Because the Whites were very light-skinned, they managed to make it home safely, but young Walter watched whites beat a black shoeshine man to death on Peachtree Street, and later that night joined his father in guarding their home from a white mob.

Young W. E. B. DuBois, a native of New England then teaching at Atlanta University, an all-black college, was out of town when the riots began. He rushed home to his wife and child. The professor bought a shotgun and "two dozen round of shells filled with buckshot. If a white mob had stepped on the campus where I lived I would without hesitation have sprayed their guts over the grass. They did not come." DuBois sat on his porch all night waiting.

By the time the carnage ceased, white Atlantans had killed twenty-five blacks. They piled bodies under the statue erected in honor of Henry Grady, spokesman of the New South.

Although many of the city's "best people" joined in the rioting, other whites were appalled. Some felt that as paternalists, whites had failed in their obligation to protect the "child-race." Others could not understand why white mobs would attack men like Dr. W. F. Penn, a physician who after the riot pointedly queried the town, "What are the requirements under which we may live and be protected?" In the wake of the riot, middle-class white Atlantans began to form interracial civil groups and prayer groups. The riot did not really represent Atlanta, they insisted; besides, all the rioters were white trash.

Blacks knew better. The Atlanta riot exposed the weaknesses of Booker T. Washington's Atlanta Compromise. Blacks who worked hard and got ahead were resented, not respected, by whites. For many blacks, the riot was a turning point. Already discontented with Washington's accommodationist strategy, DuBois and other blacks had formed the Niagara Movement in 1905 to fight for political and social equality. In the wake of the riot, DuBois became more militant. With his students at Atlanta, DuBois began publishing some of the earliest sociological studies of African-American life. In 1909 he left Atlanta for New York, where he became a cofounder of the National Association for the Advancement of Colored People.

Young Walter White grew up to be that organization's executive director. For all of his life, the blue-eyed, blond White remembered what the Atlanta riot had taught him about race: "I knew then who I was. I was a Negro, a human being with an invisible pigmentation which marked me a person to be hunted, hanged, abused, discriminated against, kept in poverty, in ignorance, in order that those whose skin was white would have readily at hand a proof of their superiority."

Headquartered in New York, the NAACP grew rapidly during the next ten years, spurred in part by black middle-class outrage over Griffith's *Birth of a Nation*. By 1919 the organization had 88,448 members, 42,588 of them southerners. For many middle-class southern blacks, paying NAACP dues was a duty owed to the race at large. The NAACP used its funds to investigate racial discrimination, publish reports, and challenge Jim Crow in the courts. It was a long, uphill battle, not to reach victory until the 1950s. Meanwhile, black migration out of the South increased every year, reaching a high point during the 1920s.

The South in World War I, 1917–1918

When war broke out in Europe in 1914, Americans debated whether or not the United States should enter the conflict. Antiwar sentiment was especially strong among farmers and among politicians representing agrarian interests, such as North Carolina Representative Claude Kitchin, Alabama Senator John Bankhead, Mississippi Senator James Vardaman, Martin Dies, Sr., of Texas, and old Populists like Tom Watson. However, as the war in Europe continued, the Wilson administration called for a buildup of U.S. military forces, and southern Democratic leaders joined him in advocating preparedness. When Wilson asked Congress to declare war on Germany in April, 1917, most southern politicians voted in favor of the declaration, leaving Vardaman and Kitchin among the last defiant holdouts.

Having given up on their opposition to U.S intervention in the war, southern agrarian politicians also fought a losing battle over the U.S. government's decision to use conscription to raise an army. Southerners still remembered Confederate conscription, and many opposed its use again. Agrarian politicians understood that conscript armies would draw on rural populations while exempting industrial workers. Despite such concerns, the U.S. government did enact conscription, requiring all military-aged men to register for service in June 1917. Populist Tom Watson sued in federal court on behalf of two conscripted men, contending that conscription violated the Thirteenth Amendment outlawing slavery. He lost the case, and the draft continued. When the federal government passed laws making criticism of the war or President Wilson illegal, the federal government shut down Watson's newspaper and other publications by southern antiwar dissenters.

The war brought prosperity to the South. Southern industries boomed, and new ones were created. The federal government built munitions plants in Alabama, Virginia, and Tennessee, and shipyards all around the coast from Hampton Roads to Pensacola and Mobile. Southern agriculture experienced its best returns since antebellum times. Most of the camps for World War I soldiers were located in southern states, since the mild climate allowed basic training year round. At training camps, Americans from all regions of the country learned to work together; the wartime experience did much to break down regional insularity.

World War I conscription drafted southerners of both races in disproportionate numbers, as a result of federal policies that encouraged draft boards to conscript the poor first. As the poorest men in the nation's poorest region, blacks were drafted in even higher proportions than whites. White supremacists argued that blacks could not make soldiers and that it was dangerous to give blacks arms and military training. Black leaders maintained that as Americans, black men had the same rights and duties of military service as whites. But after black soldiers in Houston expressed their anger over police harassment by shooting up the town, killing seventeen whites, southern political leaders insisted that blacks be trained in camps in the North. The U.S. Army was reluctant to use blacks as combat troops and placed most in construction or utility positions. In a violation of the usual American policy, some black regiments were placed under the command of the French army, which had no racial scruples about blacks in combat. Serving with the French, African-Americans won medals for their courage under fire. Meanwhile, white southerners participated in the 1918 campaigns in France, serving in the regular U.S. Army and in National Guard units.

Sgt. York

When Alvin C. York, a white farm laborer from Fentress County, Tennessee, registered for the draft in 1917, he indicated that he planned to ask for an exemption from service on the grounds "Don't want to fight." Although many southerners, black and white, had doubts about the moral correctness of warfare, conscription regulations in 1917 exempted only members of churches with a long tradition of pacifism, such as the Quakers, or with a creed that specifically prohibited participation in war. Holiness churches like the one York belonged to did not usually have such documented evidence of pacifism. So, like many other would-be southern conscientious objectors, he was sent off to army training.

In camp, York made his religious objections known to his officers. They convinced him of the essential righteousness of the American conflict with Germany, and he became an ardent soldier, distinguished by his marksmanship. In action in Germany in 1918, York's sharp eyes were put to good use. Alone, he attacked a German position, killed 20 Germans and captured 131. He received the Congressional Medal of Honor.

York's story seized the public imagination. A descendent of colonial Anglo-Saxon immigrants to America, York symbolized for many the traditional virtues of the rural nation then passing away. In the 1930s Hollywood put his story to another use. *Sergeant York*, a highly popular movie, used York's decision to go to war to urge U.S. intervention in the conflict then developing in Europe.

When blacks returned from service, whites determined to put them back in their place. Black folk legends tell of white attacks on African-American soldiers stepping off the train in full-dress uniforms and medals. After years of decline, lynching soared again, reaching a peak in 1919, the "Red Summer." Whites rioted in Longview, Texas, in Knoxville, Charleston, Chicago, Omaha, and Washington, D.C. Sporadic outbreaks continued into the early 1920s.

Postwar racial violence spurred the Great Migration of blacks out of the South. Although well aware that racial violence and prejudice existed in all parts of the country, blacks also knew that economic opportunities were better in the North, where the job market was less racially restricted. Drawn by opportunity and driven by violence, more than a million blacks left the South in the 1920s. Able to vote in the North, the new migrants constituted a sort of southern black community leadership in exile, exerting influence on northern politicians to intervene in southern race relations.

The South and the Jazz Age: 1920–1930

Sharing in national prosperity after World War I, the South embraced modern ways with enthusiasm. Newly paved highways helped break down rural isolation. Country folk came to town to shop in fancy new department stores, to gawk at the new skyscrapers, and to watch films—picture shows—in the palatial movie houses. Everyone who could afford one acquired a Victrola and records to play upon it; those without religious scruples against dancing learned the latest craze, the Charleston.

Yet modern times also included elements that disturbed conservative southerners. While respecting modern technology, religious conservatives deplored what they saw as the elevation of science above religion. Others hated the new national culture made accessible by movies, magazines, and (by the end of the decade) radio; they found it vulgar at best and sinful at worst. Social critics less motivated by religion still worried about the impact of modernism on southern communities and culture. Would cars destroy the face-to-face intimacy of small-town life? Would people desert the crossroads merchant for the new supermarkets in town? Did the fast pace of life in the 1920s mean the end of the slow, relaxed southern way of life?

Old Economic Problems, New Opportunities

American farmers experienced the best years ever from 1900 through 1919. Prices for U.S. agricultural products rose, reaching a high during the First World War. (Cotton prices fell abruptly in 1914, when the war began, but recovered rapidly.) However, when the war ended and European farmers returned from the trenches to the plow, increased production led to declining prices. In April of that year cotton sold for 41.75 cents a pound at New Orleans; by December, the price had sunk to 13.5 cents. For the rest of the decade, farm prices would rise and fall abruptly, but without reaching wartime highs again. During the 1920s farm prices in the South and in the nation as a whole continued to be depressed. While the nation experienced a decade of overall prosperity, the Depression began early for farmers.

On the other hand, southern industry bloomed. During the 1920s the southern textile industry grew rapidly, supplanting its old New England rival in number of workers and spindles. By 1933, 68 percent of the nation's textile workers lived in the South, most of them in the Piedmont hills from Virginia to North Georgia. Another Piedmont industry, tobacco, also experienced a period of rapid growth fueled by sales of cigarettes. Robert J. Reynolds's new brand, the Camel, led the field, pushed by new modern advertising techniques. In Atlanta, Robert Woodruff took the

The automobile facilitated the growth of the southern
tourist industry in the 1920s. Here, cars along
Daytona Beach. Library of Congress.

helm of the Coca-Cola Company in 1923 and used similar advertising to
make Coke first nationally, then internationally, popular. The southern
chemical industry got its start during World War I at federally funded munitions plants. Meanwhile, the region's list of extractive industries added
another, the extraction of aluminum from bauxite ore. In the second
decade of the century the Aluminum Company of America built company
towns at Alcoa, Tennessee, and Badin, North Carolina.

In 1901 Texas and Oklahoma got oil fever after a big strike at
Spindletop. The southwestern oil industry continued to grow throughout
the 1920s. In 1918 oil was discovered in Louisiana, and in 1921 in southwestern Arkansas. The southern oil fields quickly fell under the domina-
tion of corporate interests from outside the region. Companies funded by
northern investors, such as Rockefeller's Standard Oil and the Mellon family's Gulf Oil, controlled much of oil field development in the region by the

mid-1920s. Only a few companies, such as Phillips Petroleum, remained independent. Nevertheless, wildcat oil prospectors continued to search for the black gold; if they found it, they made fortunes peddling leases to the big oil companies.

During the 1920s Florida's sunny climate attracted the attention of real estate developers and tourist industry entrepreneurs. In 1925 the fabled Dixie Highway from the North to Miami finally opened, and the tourist trade took off. Lured by advertisements showing the good life in Florida, thousands of Americans invested in Florida real estate sight unseen. When they arrived in the Sunshine State, they all too often found that they had purchased several acres of undeveloped swamp. The Florida real estate boom began to deflate in 1925. Then in 1926 a major hurricane scoured the state from Miami to Fort Lauderdale and across to Pensacola, killing at least 415 people. Despite this unpleasant reminder that Florida's climate included storms as well as sunshine, the tourist industry had taken hold in the state.

In 1920 the Federal Bureau of the Census announced that the majority of Americans now resided in cities. This was not the case in the South, which continued to have a rural majority until the 1950s. Nonetheless, southern cities grew rapidly in the 1920s, more rapidly than in any other part of the nation. As the cities grew, southerners wondered: what would the region be like when it was finally cut off from its rural roots? Agrarian southerners shared with Thomas Jefferson a deep belief that cities were intrinsically evil places. In the hustle and bustle of the anonymous city, removed from the moral scrutiny of their neighbors, who knew what people might get up to? Yet, like Jefferson, who adored Paris, rural southerners were attracted to what they feared. This combination of attraction and aversion fueled social and political conflicts in the 1920s.

Modern Women

In many ways the young women of the 1920s typified all that southerners found exhilarating and disconcerting about modern times. Much more likely than their brothers to take advantage of the South's improved educational system, the new female high school graduates of the 1920s were no longer content with life on the farm. Equipped with high school business courses, thousands of young women fled the countryside for the cities, looking for jobs in banks, insurance offices, telephone companies, and other businesses. Whether black or white, the fashionable girl of the 1920s was a "flapper," with short bobbed hair, bright lipstick and skirts up to her knees. (Conservatives proposed laws requiring modest dress, but southern state legislatures refused to cooperate.)

The modern woman was no fragile belle. She could drive a car, live with roommates in an apartment, go out on unsupervised dates. She worried her parents and scandalized community fogies, who clung to old-fashioned gender roles with the same fervor that white supremacists devoted to traditional racial roles. Moreover, despite the determined resistance of generations of southern conservatives, she could vote. In 1920, southern women's rights activists won their long battle for women's suffrage and obtained the vote for women not only in the South but in the entire nation.

The Southern Suffrage Movement

Women's rights received relatively little support in the New South, for reasons related to the region's racial policies. White supremacists intended to keep the South a white *man's* country and justified lynching, disfranchisement, and segregation as necessary to protect white women. Equality for women threatened this hierarchical system only slightly less than equality for blacks would have. Dividing all roles by gender, southerners considered voting, like military service, an activity for males only. Therefore, the southern women's suffrage movement got off to a late and slow start, decades behind the national movement In the early twentieth century, elite proponents of women's suffrage found new support among women of the growing urban middle class. Through participation in women's clubs and activist groups like the WCTU, middle-class women became interested in suffrage as a way to work for civic and social improvement.

As the national crusade for women's suffrage heated up in the years before World War I, the leaders of the foremost women's suffrage organization, the National American Women's Suffrage Association (NAWSA), realized that without southern votes their cause was doomed. Yet despite growing support for women's suffrage among the educated middle class, most southern political leaders continued to oppose votes for women.

The suffrage movement had powerful enemies with deep pockets, including anti-Prohibitionists, railroad executives, and manufacturers who used child labor.

The small, but growing, southern suffrage movement was itself internally divided over how to obtain the vote. The NAWSA proposed a constitutional amendment to enfranchise women, as the Fifteenth Amendment had enfranchised black men. Many southern suffragists, loyal to the region's states'-rights heritage, insisted that the vote must come through state, not federal, action. When the majority of the southern suffragists sided with the NAWSA, a states'-rights minority denounced them. Some states'-rights suffragists even joined with anti-suffrage forces to campaign against a federal women's suffrage amendment.

During World War I most suffragists throughout the nation threw themselves enthusiastically into war work, hoping that by supporting the nation in time of crisis women could prove themselves worthy of full citizenship. Under the leadership of Carrie Chapman Catt, the NAWSA had organized suffrage workers down to the grassroots level. The NAWSA now mobilized these women for war work. Suffragists raised money for war-related causes, did volunteer work, organized local communities, and in general supported the war while continuing to work for women's suffrage. Meanwhile, a small radical faction of the suffrage movement, the Women's Party, picketed the White House, went to jail, staged hunger strikes, and kept the issue of suffrage alive before the public.

In 1918 President Wilson came out in support of the Nineteenth Amendment, giving women the right to vote. After a tough battle in Congress, the amendment passed both houses and made its way to the states for ratification. With thirty-six states necessary for passage, suffragists had to take their cause to the southern states. They considered their chances best in Arkansas and Texas, which by 1918 had given women the right to vote in primaries, and in Tennessee, where the state legislature gave women the right to vote in municipal elections in 1919.

As the southern suffrage movement gained momentum, an anti-suffrage movement arose to oppose it. In most southern states, conservative women, many of them from the old planter class, formed anti-suffrage organizations and countered suffragist propaganda with pamphlets of their own. Anti-suffragists played very heavily upon the Lost Cause theme, accusing the suffragists of selling out the South to northern interests. They reprinted sermons from conservative ministers attacking suffrage as "unscriptural and sinful" (in the words of a Methodist bishop). In addition to calling white suffragists ungodly, anti-suffrage leaders accused them of being racial liberals who would deliver the South to black rule.

White suffragists hastened to assure the public that they were not man-haters, unfeminine, ungodly, or race traitors. Rather to the dismay of their northern colleagues, southern suffragists played up their femininity, their happy family lives, their husbands and children. Women should vote, they cooed, because they were mothers; they would bring a woman's touch to politics. When attacked with Bible verses, they argued that enfranchised women would vote for Christian reforms like Prohibition. To the accusation that suffrage repudiated tradition, suffragists made a New South rejoinder: times had changed, and women's roles in society had changed with them.

On the race question, southern white suffragists were not united. Many of them assumed that the laws that kept black men from voting would work the same for black women. Other suffragists, often from the Black Belt, were rabid white supremacists who demanded votes for white women as a matter of race privilege. Georgia's Rebecca Latimer Felton, born in 1835, had experienced the Civil War and Reconstruction as a young wife and was convinced that blacks were not only inferior to whites but also dangerous. Speaking for women's suffrage in 1915, Felton declared, "Freedom belongs to the white woman as her inherent right." On the other hand, some white suffragists had no real objections to blacks of either sex voting. In their work for women's causes and reform in southern cities, many middle-class white suffragists had come to know women of the black middle class, and to respect them. However, in their public appearances suffragists took care to defuse the race issue whenever possible, and most kept the region's black suffragists at a safe, segregated distance.

With a presidential election coming up in 1920, suffragists throughout the nation pushed for quick ratification of the Nineteenth Amendment. National leaders of the Democrats and the Republicans joined in, hoping that their respective parties would receive credit for giving women the vote. Texas, Arkansas, and Kentucky ratified the amendment, but the other southern state legislatures adjourned without doing so. If women were to vote in 1920, one of the southern states would have to call a special legislative session to ratify the amendment. At the urging of President Wilson, North Carolina agreed to do so, but the legislature voted the amendment down. By the summer of 1920, the suffrage movement's last hope was in Tennessee, where Governor A. L. Roberts agreed to hold a special session.

Although the Tennessee senate approved ratification by a large majority, the speaker of the state house of representatives clearly intended to table the amendment, thus preventing a vote on ratification. However, the vote to table failed, and the amendment then passed by one vote. Much to the surprise of the suffragists, Harry Burn, a twenty-four-year-old Republican legislator from the mountains of East Tennessee, changed his mind at the last minute and voted for woman suffrage, thus enfranchising millions of American women. Burn later attributed his change of heart to three factors: his desire to free women from political slavery, his belief that his vote would allow the Republicans to claim credit for woman suffrage, and—most important—a letter he had received from his mother urging him to support votes for women.

Anti-suffragists had insisted that votes for women would destroy the American family; suffragists had promised that voting women would reform American politics. Both were wrong. When southern women voted in 1920, they usually took the same political positions as the men in their families.

Now that women could vote, they could also hold public office. In 1922 aged suffragist Rebecca Latimer Felton was appointed U.S. senator from Georgia, replacing a senator who had died in office. In Mississippi, where legislators had vowed to die fighting women's suffrage, suffragists Belle Kearney and Nellie Nugent Somerville were elected to the state legislature in the 1920s. Throughout the South, middle-class women became active in partisan politics and in the nonpartisan League of Women Voters.

Modern Times and Conservative Critics

For conservative southerners, the changes in gender roles symbolized by women's suffrage were but one more portent of social and moral decline. Yet, like anti-suffrage women, whose public role in opposing suffrage defied the very traditions they claimed to defend, southern conservatives found themselves unable to secede from their times. They used modern organizational methods and technologies to fight against modernism. Meanwhile, southern music traveled, via those same technologies, into the mainstream of American popular culture.

Country, Blues, and Jazz   The roots of much American popular music lie in the rural South of the late nineteenth and early twentieth centuries, where blacks and whites created a musical gumbo of styles and sounds. Although country was typically white people's music, played on fiddles and guitars and sung with a distinctive common folk twang, one of the stereotypical country instruments, the banjo, originated in Africa. Blues and jazz were supposed to be black and were certainly created by black musicians, but white country entertainers also sang the blues, and white southerners loved and played jazz. People of both races sang the same songs in church (although whites generally admitted that blacks sang them better) and both races enjoyed and copied tunes from traveling vaudeville and minstrel shows.

In the rural South, entertainers of both races worked days in the fields and played music at night for dances and parties. Rarely could any musician earn a living with his music. Moreover, religious folk of both races condemned secular music and dancing as sinful.

In the 1920s, two new technologies suddenly changed the southern music scene. The Victrola was to music what the Model T was to cars: a relatively inexpensive device affordable by the masses. As the Model T created a demand for roads, the Victrola created a demand for records. The second technology was radio. Radio transmission, originally of interest mostly to the military and to hobbyists, attracted the attention of entrepreneurs who grasped that this new medium could be used to make money by selling advertising. By the end of the 1920s, most southern cities had one or more radio stations, and small stations were beginning to proliferate in rural areas. To sell ads, station owners had to have air content that people wanted to listen to.

Radio and records created a new market for southern music. Country musicians who had previously worked in traveling vaudeville shows got jobs playing radio shows like the WLS Barn Dance, out of Chicago, and Nashville's WSM Grand Ole Opry. The growth of the blues market was even more spectacular. Black immigrants to the North wanted music that reminded them of home, while white sophisticates discovered blues and jazz. Black southern performers were among the highest-paid acts in 1920s nightclubs.

To market the new music, record company executives segregated the sounds by the color of the performers, selling country music as "hillbilly" and blues and jazz as "race records." On the southern musical home front, matters were never that simple. The first great country singer, Mississippian Jimmie Rodgers, sang the blues, and country bands thought nothing of tearing into W. C. Handy's classic *St. Louis Blues.* On the other hand, one of the Grand Ole Opry's featured performers in the 1920s was DeFord Bailey, who explained that he had grown up playing black hillbilly music. As always, southern performers continued to listen to the popular music coming out of New York's Tin Pan Alley, and the songwriters there returned the attention. By the 1930s, it was possible to hear a white country performer doing a song patterned after African-American blues written by a Jewish songwriter from New York.

That was just the sort of thing that most offended a less innocuous southern export of the 1920s, the Ku Klux Klan.

The Rise of the Invisible Empire   Founded to capitalize on the popularity of *Birth of a Nation,* the Atlanta-based KKK grew slowly until World War I, when the federal government's own propaganda encouraged xenophobia against Germans. After the war, government-sponsored hysteria targeted socialists and labor organizers as potential Bolsheviks out to replicate in the United States the 1917 Communist revolution in Russia. By 1920, many Americans had come to enjoy the pleasures of government-sanctioned ethnic and political hatred, and they missed the fervor of wartime.

In June of that year Colonel Simmons hired two publicity agents to sell the KKK, and memberships skyrocketed. Like the U.S. government during the war, the KKK sold "100% Americanism," but it wrapped it in the trappings of fraternal organizations. Klansmen wore robes, burned crosses, used an elaborate ritual language, and preached a message of hatred against the foreign, the strange, and the new.

Although the KKK promoted white supremacy, that was not its strongest selling point in a nation where most organizations from the federal government down to the local Rotary Club were already segregated. Instead, the KKK focused most on Catholics, Jews, immigrants, and people who violated small-town Protestant values. The Klan's slogan was "Native, white, Protestant supremacy," according to one of its leaders.

By the mid-1920s the KKK's membership had soared. It is hard to determine how many people joined the secret organization, but historians estimate that at its height the KKK enrolled about one-quarter of all native-born Protestant men in the United States. Unlike the original KKK, this new version attracted members throughout the nation. Primarily a middle-class organization, the Klan was particularly strong in Indiana, where it effectively controlled state government, and in Pennsylvania, where about a quarter-million people joined. In those states the KKK's appeal was primarily to anti-Semites and anti-Catholics. In the southern states, the KKK retailed similar religious bigotry but did not neglect to beat the drums for white supremacy as well. In parts of the South, the KKK briefly dominated state politics. Able to swing the votes of its secret membership, the Klan could make or break mayoral or gubernatorial candidates in some areas. To get ahead, some ambitious young politicians joined the KKK, while some older established political leaders, such as Alabama's Oscar Underwood and Texas's Jim Ferguson, defied it. In Louisiana, the governor had to call out the National Guard against the Klan.

Though the Klan made its greatest mark on the nation's memory by attacking blacks, immigrants, Jews, and Catholics, many KKK members insisted that they were primarily concerned with upholding traditional values. The KKK crusaded against the "filth" in movies. In many locales Klansmen threatened the owners of dance halls and "speak-easys," the illegal nightclubs of Prohibition-era America, and made bootleggers a special target. The hooded order shaved the heads of divorced women and terrorized abortionists.

In 1924 the federal government undercut the KKK's appeal by passing a stringent new immigration law that used quotas to restrict entry to the country. Under the new law, the kinds of people favored by the KKK—white and Protestant—had a better chance of coming to America than did peoples of color, Catholics, Jews, Italians, and Slavs, all groups targeted by the Klan. Historians suggest that Klan membership began to dwindle in the late 1920s in part because the KKK had obtained most of its stated goals. In the midwestern states, KKK membership declined when the Klan leader in Indiana went to jail for his involvement in the death of a young woman. By the end of the 1920s, the KKK's glory days were over. Despite persistent rumors of KKK actions, Klan-watchers today estimate that the organization has only a few thousand members.

The Klan's rapid rise and decline throughout the nation in the 1920s spotlighted the commonalities between regions. Crosses burned on hillsides in rural Pennsylvania to terrorize immigrant Catholic miners, and in Oregon the state legislature passed a law requiring Catholics to attend public rather than religious schools. (It was quickly overturned in court.)

The KKK led marches into northern immigrant neighborhoods, setting off riots. The Klan's popularity indicated that many of the values seen as "southern" were in fact shared by many people throughout the nation. So were the religious beliefs that led to the rise of Christian fundamentalism and with it, attempts to make illegal the teaching of evolution in public schools.

Fundamentalism and Darwinism   In the nineteenth century scientists in Europe, Britain, and the United States began to make discoveries that cast doubt on accepted Christian beliefs about the origins of the world. Geologists, biologists, and other researchers argued that the planet was millions of years old, and that life had not been created by God in a one-week burst, as Genesis stated, but had instead evolved over time, as hypothesized by British naturalist Charles Darwin.

Darwinism created an enormous crisis in the Christian world, one that has not completely abated to this day. To believe in evolution, Christians had to stop believing that the biblical account of creation was a literal description of actual events. By the end of the century, many Christians had made the transition to seeing Genesis's creation story as a metaphor describing humankind's relationship to God, an expression of religious rather than scientific truth. Other Christians refused to give up Genesis as fact and instead rejected evolution.

The controversies between Christian evolutionists and anti-evolutionists were only deepened by the activities of biblical scholars in the late nineteenth century. Using modern techniques of textual analysis, these scholars of the "higher criticism," as it was called, refuted traditional Christian and Jewish beliefs about the origins and nature of the Bible. According to these scholars, Genesis contained not one, but two, creation stories, which contradicted each other. Their research called into question Christians' traditional acceptance of the Bible as the inspired world of God and caused further upheavals in Christian churches and colleges.

Refusing to give up their traditional beliefs, conservative Christians fought back. In 1905 some California businessmen funded the publication of a pamphlet defending the "fundamentals" of the Christian faith, among them the accuracy of the Bible, the Virgin Birth of Christ, the Atonement of Christ's death, the Resurrection, and the Second Coming. Over time, Christians of various denominations who defended these beliefs became known as "fundamentalists."

In the South, as throughout the nation, fundamentalists worried first about the state of their churches, and second about society at large. In various locales fundamentalists worked to get ministers who accepted Darwinism or the higher criticism dismissed by their churches, but given the conservative nature of southern religion, ousted ministers were few and far between. More significantly, fundamentalists targeted professors at denominationally funded schools like Baylor in Texas and Wake Forest in North Carolina, succeeding in raising public uproar about what Christian colleges were teaching. When fundamentalists failed in their attempts to assure the purity of churches and schools, they usually withdrew to form their own congregations, denominations, and Bible colleges.

By the early 1920s, fundamentalists had widened their scope to attack Darwinism in the nation's public schools. Led by former presidential candidate William Jennings Bryan, fundamentalists argued that teaching evolution did more than destroy children's faith in the Bible. As fundamentalists saw it, Darwinism dissolved the very foundations of all systems of morality by reducing humans to animals. Southern anti-evolutionists made the same kinds of arguments as their colleagues around the nation, although they expressed them in the most extravagant southern rhetoric. Mississippi minister T. T. Martin's book *Hell and the High Schools,* published in 1923, called upon parents to be vigilant in defending their children from the "insidious, blighting curse" of Darwinism. Echoing William Jennings Bryan, Martin called for state laws to ensure that no teacher who believed in evolution could be hired in a tax-supported public school.

With Bryan spearheading the campaign, a number of southern states flirted with anti-evolution laws in the early 1920s. In North Carolina and Texas, governors ordered that all textbooks infected with Darwinism be removed from the schools. In Georgia, Representative Hal Kimberly spoke in favor of an anti-evolution bill: "Read the Bible. It teaches you how to act. Read the hymnbook. It contains the finest poetry ever written. Read the almanac. It shows you how to figure out what the weather will be. There isn't another book necessary for anyone to read." Despite Kimberly's advocacy, the Georgia measure failed to pass.

In 1925 fundamentalists rejoiced when the Tennessee state legislature passed a law forbidding the teaching of evolution in the public schools. The bill was written by John Washington Butler, a farmer, Primitive Baptist, and fan of William Jennings Bryan. The Butler Act swept through the legislature and was signed by Tennessee's governor, who considered it a legitimate symbolic gesture in favor of traditional social and religious values.

Quickly, the newly formed American Civil Liberties Union offered to pay the legal fees of any Tennessean who cared to challenge the law in court.

In Dayton, Tennessee, a small town in the hills northwest of Chattanooga, a group of town boosters took the ACLU up on its offer. Eager for publicity to put their town "on the map," they got a young substitute teacher, John Thomas Scopes, to agree to be cited for teaching evolution in the Rhea County High School. (The Butler Act made teaching evolution a misdemeanor punishable with a small fine; Scopes was never really in any danger of jail time.) Clarence Darrow, the best-known trial lawyer of his time, volunteered to defend Scopes, and William Jennings Bryan offered his services as prosecutor to the state of Tennessee. With nationally famous figures squared off to defend and attack Darwinism, the Dayton Monkey Trial opened in a blaze of media attention. In search of local color, journalists like Baltimore's H. L. Mencken described rural and small-town southerners as clowns too dumb to get modern science. Relatively few outsiders seemed to understand that for Dayton, the trial was a publicity stunt.

Darrow's strategy was to use expert witnesses to attack the portion of the Tennessee law prohibiting teaching evolution or any other theory contradictory to the Bible. He intended to ask his witnesses, who ranged from biologists to Hebrew scholars, what evolution said and what Genesis said. When the presiding judge refused to allow this approach, Darrow asked if he could question the prosecuting attorney, Bryan, about what the Bible said. Bryan happily agreed to discuss the Bible, and Darrow put him on the stand, where he proceeded to demolish the aged politician's pretensions to either scientific or biblical scholarship. This aspect of the trial attracted most public attention, but it was in fact just a spectacle without meaning. In the end, Scopes was convicted. Although Scopes's conviction was ultimately overturned by the state supreme court on a technicality, the court upheld the validity of the Butler Act, which remained on the books until 1967. Exhausted and ailing, Bryan died shortly after the trial. Complacently, many northern liberals believed that the anti-evolution cause died with him.

In reality, the Scopes trial amplified the impact of anti-Darwinism on public policy. Textbook publishers, understanding that many parents did not want their children to learn about evolution, censored their own books so that they would sell, thus extending the cultural imperatives of the South to the nation at large. Today school boards across the nation continue to clash over teaching evolution, with controversies perhaps more likely to erupt in California or Kansas than in Tennessee or Alabama, where schools tend to remain firmly under the influence of local culture, including local religious values.

I'll Take My Stand

In 1930, "Twelve Southerners," most of them faculty members at Vanderbilt University in Nashville, published a collection of essays entitled *I'll Take My Stand: The South and the Agrarian Tradition.* The Vanderbilt Agrarians had been irritated by media coverage of the Dayton trial that depicted rural white southerners as ignorant, backward, and all but subhuman. They also feared that the South was losing its distinctive rural culture and worried that southerners were selling out to the capitalist consumer economy. In a series of essays on religion, rural life, values, and race relations, the Agrarians defended southern tradition against the onslaught of modernity. Alas for the professors, rural southerners were quite willing to give up the mule and plow for the Ford flivver and a paying job in town. *I'll Take My Stand* had no perceivable impact on southern economics or society. However, the essays continue to be read for insight into the South during the 1920s, and also as critiques of the destructive effects of capitalism. The Agrarians were, in effect, opposing "globalization" and "consumerism" before the words had been invented.

Distinctive or Mainstream? During the 1920s the South solidified its reputation as the nation's most conservative region. As the historical record of southern progressivism indicates, that reputation was not completely deserved; conversely, the popularity of the KKK and fundamentalism throughout the nation raises questions about just how liberal the rest of the United States was anyway. Still, northern liberals appalled by conservatism in their region consoled themselves that things were much worse down South. By labeling the South a national cultural problem, northerners could project America's racism, sexism, and religious bigotry onto southerners—and away from themselves.

In 1929 cultural conflicts suddenly seemed less important. The stock market crash brought to an end a decade of relative prosperity and ushered in the worst economic downturn in American history, the Great Depression.

Suggestions for Further Reading and Viewing

GLENDA ELIZABETH GILMORE, *Gender and Jim Crow: Women and the Politics of White Supremacy in North Carolina, 1896–1920* (1996)

DEWEY W. GRANTHAM, *Southern Progressivism: The Reconciliation of Progress and Tradition* (1983)

ELNA C. GREEN, *Southern Women and the Woman Suffrage Question* (1997)

GRACE ELIZABETH HALE, *Making Whiteness: The Culture of Segregation in the South, 1890–1940* (1998)

JACK TEMPLE KIRBY, *Darkness at the Dawning* (1972)

EDWARD J. LARSON, *Summer for the Gods: The Scopes Trial and America's Continuing Debate over Science and Religion* (1997)

WILLIAM A. LINK, *The Paradox of Southern Progressivism, 1880–1930* (1992)

LEON LITWACK, *Trouble in Mind: Black Southerners in the Age of Jim Crow* (1998)

STEPHANIE J. SHAW, *What a Woman Ought to Be and to Do: Black Professional Women Workers During the Jim Crow Era* (1996)

ANASTATIA SIMS, *The Power of Femininity in the New South: Women's Organizations and Politics in North Carolina, 1880–1930* (1997)

GEORGE BROWN TINDALL, *The Emergence of the New South, 1913–1945* (1967)

MARJORIE SPRUILL WHEELER, *New Women of the New South: The Leaders of the Woman Suffrage Movement in the Southern States* (1993)

———, ED., *Votes for Women! The Woman Suffrage Movement in Tennessee, the South, and the Nation* (1995)

chapter

4

The South and the Nation, 1930–1946

During the 1930s, President Franklin Roosevelt referred to the South as the nation's number one economic problem. The poorest part of the country since the Civil War, the South was hit especially hard by the Great Depression. Yet the 1930s marked the beginning of the end of the southern way of life that had begun with Reconstruction, and World War II laid the foundation for the region's present economic boom.

How did the South capitalize on the nation's hard times? How did federal intervention transform the South? Did southern radicals repudiate the southern tradition, or build upon it? Are the historians correct who say that World War II was as important in southern history as the Civil War?

The Great Depression and the New Deal

In October 1929, stock prices on the New York Stock Exchange plummeted. Businesses began to try to reduce their inventories. Cutting production, they laid off workers. Banks and individuals who had lost money scrambled to cover themselves. Slowly, the impact of the crash rippled out of New York to the rest of the country. Banks closed, taking depositors' savings with them, and businesses went bankrupt, putting more and more people out of work.

Southern businessmen reassured the public and themselves that Wall Street's problems would have no impact on Peachtree, Canal, and Cotton Row. Yet as early as Thanksgiving, 1929, ominous stories of the suicides of prominent businessmen began to appear in southern newspapers. Bankers who had lost not only their own money but the money entrusted to them by the public sometimes felt that death was the only honorable recourse. In January, the owner of the New Orleans Pelicans baseball team shot himself after losing $300,000 in the crash. Each failed bank, each bankrupt business sent further shock waves through the region.

In November 1930, the South's premier investment firm, Caldwell and Company of Nashville, announced its bankruptcy. Caldwell and Company handled municipal bonds and owned subsidiary banks throughout the South. When the firm fell, it took with it 120 banks throughout the South. The mayor of Asheville, North Carolina, tried to save the local bank with the town's money. When that failed, he killed himself. Luke Lea, a politically powerful former U.S. senator from Tennessee, had used his political influence to get Tennessee state funds deposited in Caldwell and Company banks. When Caldwell crashed, the state lost $6.5 million. Although Tennessee's government avoided fiscal collapse, other governments throughout the South did not. Municipalities went bankrupt, and in 1932 Arkansas defaulted on the debts accumulated by road building. Investors there eventually recovered their principal but lost the interest they had hoped to earn.

By the end of 1930, the optimistic pronouncements of southern business boosters began to sound hollow; by 1932, they were a joke. People were beginning to use the word "Depression" to describe this worst-ever economic recession. Today, with the knowledge that the economic downturn lasted ten years, we call it the Great Depression. Still bitter in the memories of elderly Americans today, the Great Depression left a deep impact on the nation. For middle-class southerners, the Depression meant a curtailing of dreams: no college, no house, no car, delayed marriages, smaller families, sharing living quarters with relatives. For the southern common folk of both races, however, the Depression was catastrophic, pushing them over the edge from poverty into destitution.

As prices for the South's products—staple crops, textiles, and extracted raw materials—dropped, employers cut workers. Blacks were the first fired. Companies then dismissed married white women, then single white women, then single white men, then finally married white men. Some paternalistic mill owners, insisting that they would never fire their workers, instead cut the hours of labor for each so that all could get some small amount of pay. In Birmingham, Tennessee Coal and Iron took that course, but in 1933 it cut workers' pay by as much as 75 percent. Even in Houston, somewhat shielded from the crash by oil revenues, unemployment reached over 20 percent. As the South slid into the Depression, only the tobacco companies failed to feel the pain. As foreseen by tobacco executives, cigarettes proved to be "depression-proof," the last luxury to which people clung.

Pushed to the wall, white workers began to compete for jobs usually considered "colored." When white women took jobs as servants and white men as yard workers, blacks had nowhere to go. By 1933 the unemployment rate in many parts of the South had reached 30 percent, but in some black neighborhoods 75 percent of the workers were jobless.

The Depression hit southern agriculture hard. The price of cotton, already far below its WWI high, dropped even more, from 16.78 cents per pound in 1929 to 4.6 in 1932. Other southern commodities saw similar declines. The Depression accelerated the demise of small independent farmers in the Cotton South. Deeply in debt, many farmers were unable to even pay their taxes and had their farms sold out from under them by county governments. In 1932 one-fourth of the total area of Mississippi was up for sale. While landowners slid down to tenancy, sharecroppers could not make enough by growing cotton to pay their rent and feed their families. By the mid-1930s social workers reported cases of actual hunger among black and white sharecroppers, and many more cases of severe dietary deficiencies.

For southwesterners, a climatic disaster worsened the dire economic situation. For years residents of the Plains had overplowed their fields, creating a layer of loose topsoil. Then the rains stopped. By the early 1930s parts of Oklahoma, Texas, Arkansas and Kansas had been given a new name: the Dust Bowl. Prairie winds scoured the plains, sending choking clouds of dust high into the sky and piling dust up in drifts like snow. Old people and children died of respiratory failure. Unable to make a living in these conditions, thousands of "Okies" and "Arkies" trekked west, only to find California state troopers waiting for them at the border, where they were confined to labor camps.

As the economic situation worsened, southerners (like other Americans) drew upon old skills to cope. Black men boasted that their wives could find a way to feed a family on meats and vegetables that whites didn't even know how to cook. White common folk, laid off from city jobs, moved back to their parents' farms, put out big gardens, and taught their sons how to hunt squirrels and rabbits. Few expected help from state and local governments, which was just as well, for little help was forthcoming.

Though many southerners blamed the Republican in the White House, Herbert Hoover, for the Depression, most southern Democrats in public office insisted that their only responsibility was to enact frugal budgets and wait out the storm. The governor of Texas, Ross Sterling, believed that people who were hungry had brought their condition on themselves by poor management. In Houston, Mayor Walter Monteith proudly announced that his city provided no assistance for the unemployed. When a Presbyterian minister, William Jacobs, called upon the city's millionaires to give for the relief of the destitute, the pastor of the Second Baptist Church denounced him: "I do not believe a more dangerous doctrine has ever been preached in a pulpit in Houston." City leaders criticized Jacobs for feeding the poor and called on him to be more discreet. Other political leaders were more sympathetic but lacked both the funds and the administrative structure to help the jobless. Durham took care of its unemployed until it ran out of money, an experience replicated in other cities. By the spring of 1932 most cities and towns had exhausted their relief budgets. In Memphis, Boss Edward Crump's political machine provided apples for the poor to sell. In New Orleans, Mayor T. Semmes Walmsley supplied the jobless with oranges. (New Orleans, one of the biggest cities in the nation, had no programs for family relief.) In Birmingham, one of the hardest-hit southern cities, the city gave "food checks" to the unemployed.

Lacking established welfare bureaucracies, southern municipalities fell back on the vaunted private sector. Some individuals made valiant efforts to help their neighbors. In Atlanta, merchants created a work-for-food program, and theater owners sponsored a "Sunday Movies for Charity" drive, until pressure from local evangelical Christian leaders forced the city to shut them down. In Houston, movie theater owner Will Horowitz collected food at "Tin Can Matinees," distributing it to the poor. He also ran a private employment bureau, and in the winter of 1930–31 he opened up a soup kitchen, feeding about 900 people a day. In Jacksonville, Florida, Alfred I. DuPont (son of one of the nation's wealthiest families) created his own make-work project. He hired men to work in the city's parks for $1.25 a day. DuPont spent about $400 of his own money daily on this program until the federal government took it over in 1933. However, private charities, like municipal governments, could not cope with massive, nationwide unemployment. As the unemployed began to drift from place to place in search of jobs, many southern cities adopted even tougher policies. In 1934 Florida began to refuse admittance to transients; those turned back wound up in Atlanta, which did not want them. Memphis rounded up drifters and dumped them in Nashville.

In the early days of the Depression southern political leaders warned against turning for aid to the federal government. Still firmly committed to states' rights, southern white politicians understood that federal money would come with strings attached, in the form of federal supervision of programs within the states. Just the same, when the Hoover administration created a program to lend federal money to financial institutions, states, and municipal governments, southerners got in line with the rest of the nation for the handout. However, these funds proved inadequate to combat the ever-worsening Depression.

By 1932 President Hoover was the most hated man in the country. Democrats knew that their chances of winning the presidency were good. In a crowded field of presidential possibilities, many southern political leaders favored the governor of New York, Franklin Delano Roosevelt. Unlike many northern politicians, Roosevelt knew and liked the South. As a young man, Roosevelt had been stricken with polio, a viral disease that leaves its victims paralyzed. Unable to walk, he came to Warm Springs, Georgia, for physical therapy. There the pampered son of the northeastern upper class sweated and suffered with similarly afflicted common folk, many of them southerners. Although he never regained the use of his legs, Roosevelt bought a house near Warm Springs and spent time there annually. He joked that he was a "part-time" southerner. As affable and genteel as any scion of Virginia's First Families, Roosevelt appealed to southern politicians, who supported him for the Democratic nomination in 1932, and cheered when he won the presidential election in November.

Roosevelt openly acknowledged that he had no idea how to end the Depression, but he promised a "New Deal" for the American public. Roosevelt's New Deal began the economic transformation in the South.

Elected four times, the president became a hero to the southern common people and in doing so earned the bitter enmity of southern conservative Democrats.

Franklin D. Roosevelt spent many hours in physical therapy at Warm Springs, Georgia. Here he is shown shaking the hand of a child at Warm Springs during his 1932 election campaign. Although paralyzed from the waist down, FDR could stand with the aid of steel leg braces. Franklin D. Roosevelt Library, Hyde Park, New York.

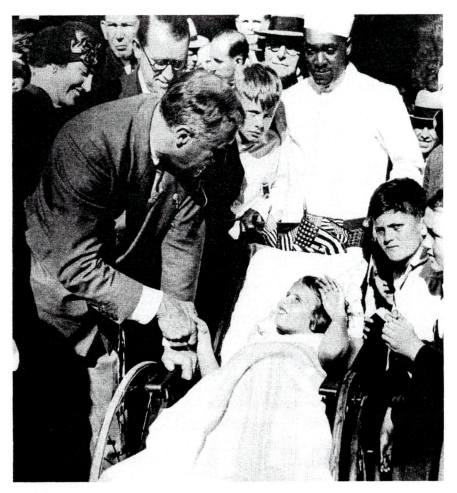

The New Deal in the South

Inaugurated in 1933, FDR pushed through Congress dozens of bills creating new programs to fight the Depression. The New Deal was national in scope and did not specifically target the South. However, in a time of widespread poverty, New Deal officials from FDR on down came to see that the South was a special case. Southerners were poorer, and had been poorer longer, than people in any other part of the country. Southern poverty was harder to attack, since it had structural origins in the very demography of the region itself. During FDR's second term in office, southern liberals obtained the president's support for a special *Report on Economic Conditions of the South,* issued to the public in 1938 and accompanied by a bombshell introduction by Roosevelt himself:

It is my conviction that the South presents right now the Nation's No. 1 economic problem—the Nation's problem, not merely the South's. For we have an economic unbalance in the Nation as a whole, due to this very condition of the South. . . .

It is an unbalance that can and must be righted, for the sake of the South and the Nation.

The report that followed FDR's introduction was blunt, detailing the South's demographic, ecological, economic, educational, and social problems. The average annual income in the South in 1937 was $314, while in the rest of the country it was $604. With the nation's highest birthrate and lowest incomes, the southern states had to "support nearly one-third of their population in school, while the industrial States support less than one-fourth." The southern illiteracy rate was the nation's highest at 8.8 percent. Only 16 percent of the children of the South went to high school, while 24 percent did in other regions. The report described the dismal condition of southern housing, even supplying statistics on the number of houses with indoor plumbing: 26 percent of southern urban households had no flush toilets, while in rural districts over 90 percent of the houses had no plumbing at all. The report focused especially on the southern population's lack of "purchasing power," explaining that southerners "need to buy, they want to buy, and they would buy—if they had the money." The report concluded that helping the South would help the nation: "Northern producers and distributers are losing profits and northern workers are losing work because the South cannot afford to buy their goods."

During the New Deal years, the nation discovered southern poverty. Funded by the federal government, writers, photographers, movie makers, and artists created portraits of the southern common folk designed to arouse public awareness of conditions within the "Nation's No. 1 economic problem." Many southerners writhed in embarrassment at having the region's deficiencies emblazoned in headlines throughout the country, pointing to a factor not mentioned at all by the 1938 report: the high proportion of African-Americans in the southern population. Fitzgerald Hall, head of the Southern States Industrial Council, suggested that the presence of so many poor blacks skewed the report's statistics to make the region look worse off than it was. He added "The question might be asked, Why does not the South do something about raising the standards for the Negroes? That problem is nationwide, for the relative economic position of the race is the same in every section of the country."

Other white southerners saw the New Deal as a chance to bring real systemic change to the South. These New Deal southern white liberals, many of them veterans of the progressive movement, took positions in the Roosevelt administration; it was at their urging that the 1938 report was prepared.

Meanwhile, New Deal programs created for the nation at large were implemented in the South, with mixed results. The New Deal created scores of new governmental agencies, all of which had some effect on the South. However, historians agree that the New Deal made its greatest impact in the region through work-relief projects, the Tennessee Valley Authority, and the Agricultural Adjustment Administration.

Work Relief and the Modernization of the South

In May 1933, the Roosevelt administration pushed through Congress legislation authorizing the expenditure of $500,000,000 in "relief," a term corresponding roughly to today's "welfare." The money was channeled to agencies or through state welfare departments. Under the Hoover administration, many conservative southern Democrats had insisted that relief was not a legitimate function of government. The newly destitute had fewer qualms. By the fall of 1933 more than one-eighth of the southern population was on the dole.

Although Franklin Roosevelt is remembered today as the father of the welfare state, he maintained a conservative attitude toward relief. FDR preferred programs that paid people for work done, no matter how trivial, to programs that simply gave people money. Among all the work-relief programs sponsored by the New Deal, none was more popular than the Civilian Conservation Corps, which enrolled unemployed young men and put them to work on conservation-related construction projects throughout the nation. The first CCC camp was in Virginia's George Washington National Forest; by 1941 there were over 100 camps throughout the South.

Of more lasting impact were the construction projects funded by two other New Deal agencies, the Public Works Administration (PWA) and the Works Progress Administration (WPA). The PWA, created in 1933, gave grants for construction to cities and states and ran some building proj-ects itself. The PWA built Virginia's Colonial, Blue Ridge, and Skyline parkways. In New Orleans, PWA workers dug sewer lines, restored the French Market, and built the Charity Hospital. In Memphis, the PWA funded the construction of Riverside Drive, a hospital, schools, and dorms at the UT medical facility. By the late 1930s, the PWA began constructing the nation's first public housing projects in Atlanta. Closely supervised by Interior Secretary Harold Ickes, the PWA built to last. Even today PWA-built highways, schools, libraries, and post offices serve southern towns and cities.

The WPA was intended from its creation in 1935 to put people to work, on useful projects if possible, with make-work if necessary. States and municipalities were required to kick in a share of the cost of WPA work relief, much to the dismay of southern governors and mayors, who insisted that they did not have the money. WPA administrator Harry Hopkins chided them: "[T]here is no state in the union that hasn't the power to take care of their unemployed." Despite the obstructive attitude of southern officials, the WPA put millions of southerners to work. Cotton Belt planters complained that the WPA made it hard for them to maintain control over their sharecroppers: "Ever since federal relief . . . you can't hire a nigger to do anything for you. High wages is ruinin' them."

Like the PWA, the WPA put men to work building new facilities for southern cities. WPA workers built Atlanta's sewer system, Tampa's airport, bridges in New Orleans, and so on. As historian David Goldfield has noted, the WPA paid for improvements in southern cities that northern cities had funded on their own. In effect, the federal government subsidized the modernization of southern cities, giving the South an advantage in the post-World War II period.

The New Deal's work relief programs rarely challenged the power of southern white politicians. Eager to win public support for the New Deal, the Roosevelt administration channeled much of the PWA and WPA funding through local political organizations, allowing them to share in the popularity derived from providing work in the middle of a depression. With Roosevelt in the White House, many southern politicians came to agree with Texas governor W. Lee "Pappy" O'Daniel, who in 1938 criticized the New Deal but added, "as long as he [Roosevelt] has the grab-bag open and as long as all the other states are grabbing, I'm gonna grab all I can for the State of Texas." Despite employers and landlords' complaints that the New Deal was ruining the South by paying workers too much money, New Deal wages for southern workers were linked to regional pay standards, which were lower than those paid in the North. Throughout the nation, New Deal projects observed traditional gender roles. The Roosevelt administration made work for men, who as heads of families were expected to support their women relatives. In the South, as elsewhere, relatively few New Deal jobs were available for women.

Most significantly, the work relief programs in the South followed regional racial norms. Whenever possible, southern WPA and PWA administrators hired whites before blacks. The CCC, administered by a Tennessean, ran segregated camps and in some southern states hardly provided CCC work for black youths at all. In Mississippi, a state with a black majority, over 90 percent of all "CCC boys" were white. The CCC had to threaten to withhold funds to get Georgia, Florida, Alabama, and Arkansas to enroll blacks. Whites throughout the region made it clear that they resented the use of federal money to support blacks. Make-work programs for blacks had to be carefully designed to avoid offending southern whites' sensibilities. One that succeeded was the WPA training program for black women: the Household Workers' Training Program.

The Tennessee Valley Authority: Groundwork for the Sunbelt

When present-day southerners move north, one of the many culture shocks greeting them is the cost of electricity. In most places in America, private power companies generate electricity and supply it to consumers at a cost sufficient to ensure their profit. In places where electricity is expensive, relatively few homes are "all-electric." By contrast, most houses built in the Southeast since World War II are lighted, heated, and cooled with cheap electricity supplied by an agency created by the New Deal, the Tennessee Valley Authority (TVA). By supplying cheap and reliable power, the TVA laid the foundations for the South's postwar prosperity.

That the South got the TVA was due to the persistence of a senator from Nebraska, George W. Norris. During World War I, the federal government had built a hydroelectric dam at Muscle Shoals, Alabama, using the power generated to produce explosives. Norris, a long-term advocate of public power, blocked postwar attempts to sell the dam to a private power company and repeatedly proposed to Congress that the dam be used as the starting point for a chain of similar hydroelectric projects along the Tennessee River. In the early 1930s, Norris's plan caught the attention of FDR, who in 1933 proposed the TVA to Congress. Encompassing seven states, the TVA was a massive building and renovation project that included flood control and conservation as well as the generation of electrical power.

Critics throughout the nation condemned TVA as socialistic, charging that the government was taking over functions that should be performed by private companies. Unmoved by charges of ideological impurity, most southeastern politicians supported the TVA, led by the formidable senior senator from Tennessee, Kenneth D. McKellar, who joined with Norris to push the enabling legislation through Congress. Although construction was slowed by lawsuits from private power companies, by the end of the 1930s TVA was well under way, constructing dams on the Tennessee River and its tributaries.

Most white southerners jettisoned their usual antipathy to governmental activism and welcomed TVA with open arms. TVA dams controlled flooding, supplied cheap electricity, eradicated malaria by destroying the habitat of mosquitoes, and sponsored soil conservation, libraries, and schools.

Although the agency's cheap power helped push regional industrial development, its most immediate impact may have been on the rural South. Private power companies had not extended services to the countryside. Federal legislation created the Rural Electrification Agency, which enabled rural southerners to form their own electrical membership cooperatives, obtain loans for construction, and tap into cheap TVA power. Throughout the rural South, farm families strung up lights and bought their first electrical appliances (usually something small, like irons). More prosperous farmers purchased radios, and they (and their neighbors) grew accustomed to hearing national news, soap operas, and musical programs. Gradually, the rural South became more integrated into national popular culture.

TVA's success did not come without ecological and social cost. The Tennessee, once one of the nation's wildest rivers, was tamed by dams and made navigable from Knoxville, Tennessee to Paducah, Kentucky, just short of the stream's entrance into the Ohio River. Although few people in the 1930s protested TVA's environmental impact, southerners whose homes were in the way of dam construction often resented it bitterly, even though TVA paid them current market prices or better for their land. Entire villages disappeared under the waters, displacing rural southerners to nearby towns and cities. Moreover, the TVA, like other New Deal agencies, followed southern racial laws and etiquette and discriminated against blacks in employment and housing.

The New Deal in Agriculture

The New Deal's programs in agriculture transformed southern agriculture. In the process, the New Deal helped destroy the sharecropping system that had marked southern agriculture since Reconstruction.

In 1933, farming specialists in the Agricultural Adjustment Administration promised government subsidies to farmers who volunteered to reduce their crops; lowering production would raise farm prices. In the South, producers of staple crops signed on to the AAA program with enthusiasm. The AAA made its most notable impact on cotton farming. In the spring of 1933, cotton farmers plowed under acreage that had already been planted. In 1934 Senator John H. Bankhead, Jr., of Alabama, introduced additional legislation designed to make controls over cotton production mandatory. Under the Bankhead Cotton Control Act, farmers who grew more than their government-allotted quotas would pay exorbitant taxes on their excess cotton. This Act effectively removed any incentive toward over-production. As cotton production fell, prices gradually rose. A similar program had the same impact upon tobacco production. By the end of the decade other crops had been added to the list of government-subsidized, controlled agricultural products. Although in 1935 the Supreme Court declared the AAA an unconstitutional extension of federal power over the states, the agency's crop limitation functions were continued under the Soil Conservation and Domestic Allotment Act, which created the Soil Conservation Service.

On the surface, the AAA and subsequent New Deal agricultural agencies were a great success. As the nation moved out of the Depression in the early 1940s, southern agriculture was more prosperous and less dependent on staple crops than it had been since before the Civil War. With government encouragement, scores of southern farmers got out of cotton production and experimented with new crops like soybeans. The mule, long a symbol of southern agriculture, gave way to new tractors paid for in part by government subsidy checks. By the end of the 1940s, parts of the agricultural South looked for all the world like farming districts in the lower Midwest.

Southern sharecroppers paid the price for the region's new prosperity. When cotton planters reduced their acreage, they no longer needed as many workers on the land. Although the AAA and subsequent New Deal programs contained provisions requiring planters to give part of the subsidies to their tenants, reports from the South indicated that in many places planters summarily dismissed sharecropping families. Throughout the region, a majority of sharecroppers were white. When dismissed by landlords, they had some small chance of finding work, particularly in government jobs. The situation on the other side of the color line was more difficult. Thrown out of work in the middle of a depression, black sharecropping families had little recourse and almost no chance of finding work. While some sharecroppers of both races joined agricultural unions and attempted to pressure the government for better treatment, many poor whites and blacks made their way to urban centers in the South and Midwest, where they wound up on relief rolls. Although liberals within the Department of Agriculture, which administered the AAA, fought hard to get the agency to intervene in favor of tenant farmers, their efforts failed. Programs created to help sharecroppers and small farmers proved ineffectual.

The AAA did not help small independent farmers much either. While the South's largest plantations received tens of thousands of dollars annually in government subsidies, small farmers' operations were not large enough to benefit much from government handouts. Farmers left the land in droves in the late 1930s, a process that only accelerated in the 1940s and early 1950s. Though regretting the suffering involved, Secretary of Agriculture Henry Wallace believed that the nation and the farmers would be better off in the long run: the South had more people on the land than agriculture could support. The solution was in "making more city employment."

Historian Roger Biles summed up the New Deal's impact on southern agriculture as follows: "Landowners prospered, and the landless suffered under the AAA." As sharecroppers had replaced slaves, tractors replaced sharecroppers, and plantations became agribusinesses.

Southern Politicians and the New Deal

The common folk of the solidly Democratic South loved FDR; they voted for him in 1932, 1936, 1940, and 1944, and would probably been in favor of a fifth term for the president had he not died in 1945. Roosevelt's relationship with southern white Democratic Party leaders was much more ambiguous. As Democrats, they supported the president, but as conservatives they often disagreed with New Deal liberalism. Because many southern states returned the same men over and over again to the Senate and to Congress, southern politicians had gained seniority in both bodies and headed key committees. The Speaker of the House of Representatives at the time FDR took office was Joseph W. Byrns of Tennessee; he was succeeded in that position by William Bankhead of Alabama and Sam Rayburn of Texas. To get legislation through Congress, FDR had to have the support of the southern delegations. For their part, most southerners in Congress understood that the people of their states needed federal help. In the early 1930s, therefore, the southern political leadership followed FDR's lead, balking only at measures that might upset traditional power relationships within the region.

The one great exception to this general rule was Huey Long of

Louisiana. But then, the Kingfish was an exception to almost all rules. For a brief moment in the 1930s, this amazing character bid fair to destroy the New Deal, not because it was too radical but because it was not radical enough.

The Kingfish

Even today Huey Long, nicknamed the "Louisiana Kingfish," stirs strong emotions. Born in Winn Parish, a place with a strong Populist heritage, Long was elected governor in 1928, and in 1930, U.S. senator. Long's rise to power in Louisiana awed his supporters and terrified his enemies. As governor, he employed corruption to gain control of key legislative leaders, turned the state police into his personal enforcement agency, and used the state's taxing power to punish his political enemies. Yet he was enormously popular among ordinary white voters because he actually supplied state services in a state where very few had ever been extended. His administration supplied free school books (a new thing in Louisiana) and built roads and bridges.

When Long came to Washington in 1932, his reputation as the near-dictator of Louisiana preceded him. He was instantly unpopular and did not win friends by his 1933 statement to his fellow senators: "Men, it will not be long until there will be a mob assembling here to hang Senators from the rafters of the Senate. I have to determine whether I will stay and be hung with you, or go out and lead the mob." Initially a strong supporter of Roosevelt and the New Deal, Long broke with FDR by 1933 and proposed his own solution to hard times: Share Our Wealth, a program that would confiscate the fortunes of American millionaires and redistribute wealth to guarantee all American families a middle-class income. By 1935 about 27,000 Share Our Wealth clubs had been organized throughout the nation, with a membership of over 4 million. Roosevelt's advisers believed the maverick senator was preparing for a run at the presidency in 1936.

Meanwhile, he consolidated his hold on Louisiana, pushing through the state legislature a bill giving the Long political machine control over state elections. Protesting that the bill disfranchised white Louisianans, Representative Mason Spencer called down vengence on the Kingfish: "I am not gifted with second sight, nor did I see a spot of blood on the moon last night, but I can see blood on the polished floor of this capitol, for if you ride this thing through you will travel with the white horse of death." The bill passed, making Long virtual dictator of Louisiana.

In September 1935, Long came home to Louisiana to attend a special legislative session in Baton Rouge. He was assassinated by a young Baton Rouge physician while walking through the corridors of the state capitol building. The Kingfish was only forty-two.

Even after Long's death, his political machine continued to wield power in Louisiana politics. While some of his top aides went to prison for corruption, his brother Earl was eventually elected governor, and his son Russell served as senator from 1948 to 1986. In the long term, however, the Kingfish's most significant legacy lay in his influence on national politics. In 1935, challenges from Long and other New Deal critics pushed the Roosevelt administration toward more radical attacks on the Depression. FDR pushed through Congress the legislation creating the WPA, which absorbed much of the nation's unemployed; Social Security; and a major tax increase for the rich. Roosevelt won reelection in 1936 by a landslide.

Southern Politics in the 1930s

Roosevelt's 1936 election win also inaugurated a new political phenomenon: the New Deal coalition. In the 1936 election the Democrats owed their victory to an unlikely combination of voters: white southerners, northern urban ethnics, organized labor—and blacks.

By 1936, the continuing migration of black southerners to northern cities had created a new source of black political power. Traditionally, blacks had voted Republican because of the Civil War and emancipation. Yet by 1936 blacks could legitimately ask what the GOP had done for them lately. Republicans took black voters for granted, rarely exerted any efforts in their behalf, and sometimes exhibited a lack of sensitivity on racial issues. By contrast, New Deal programs helped blacks, not because of their race but because of their poverty. Needing southern support in Congress, FDR was reluctant to support civil rights measures, such as a proposed federal anti-lynching bill. However, his wife, Eleanor, and high-ranking members of his cabinet publicly advocated racial equality and openly socialized as equals with black friends and political allies. In 1936 black political leaders in the North decided that enough was enough. After 1936, whenever and wherever blacks could vote, they tended to vote Democratic.

As blacks moved into the Democratic Party, southern whites grew restive. Southern white Democrats also owed their political loyalties to the memory of the Civil War. For many, the idea of voting for the party of Lincoln, Grant, and Sherman was unthinkable. On the other hand, sharing political power with blacks was unacceptable, too. On the state level in the South, the Democratic Party was still lily white, but at the national convention in 1936 southern whites watched aghast as integrated northern delegations took their seats, a black minister delivered the convocation, and a black congressman seconded Roosevelt's nomination. South Carolina Senator Ellison "Cotton Ed" Smith groused, "This mongrel meeting ain't no place for a white man."

The Democrats' new racial composition was not the only thing troubling southern white politicians. As early as FDR's first term, Virginia's senators Carter Class and Harry Byrd began to speak out against New Deal measures. Byrd feared the New Deal's centralizing tendencies, which he saw (with justice) as the beginning of the end for states' rights. Glass, whom FDR referred to affectionately as an "unreconstructed old rebel," denounced the New Deal as unconstitutional, uncivilized, and a disgrace to the nation.

Other southern political leaders went along with the first New Deal, but did not much like the programs passed in 1935, because those programs tampered with traditional power relationships on the grassroots level in the South. Relief programs threatened planters' control over their labor. Wage and hour laws threatened to destroy the South's traditional drawing card for attracting industry, cheaper labor. New Deal legislation encouraged workers to form unions. By offering farm credit, New Deal programs undercut the power of merchants and bankers. Whether intentionally or not, New Deal programs sabotaged the authority of the white small town elites who dominated southern society. The New Deal attempted to replace the southern paternalist "Big Daddy" of plantation, mill, or bank with a bigger daddy—the federal government. Though some southern white politicians remained wholehearted supporters of the New Deal, most of the region's entrenched political leadership had began to turn against FDR by 1936.

In 1937 FDR, worried that the Supreme Court would strike down the Social Security Act as it had previous New Deal legislation, set out to change the composition of the court. He proposed adding new members, whom he would of course appoint. When informed of the plan, Texas Congressman Hatton Sumners spoke for many of his fellow southerners: "Boys, here's where I cash in." Already concerned that the New Deal was centralizing too much power in Washington, southern congressmen and senators refused to support FDR's court-packing plan. As Senator Josiah Bailey of North Carolina explained, "Give the President control over Congress and the Court and you will have a one man government." In the court fight, FDR used all of his considerable political skills in vain. In coalition with Republicans, conservative southern Democrats blocked his court-packing legislation.

Attempting to purge his southern opponents, in 1938 FDR campaigned for liberal southern Democrats and against conservatives. With his help, Lyndon Johnson won reelection to Congress from Texas, and FDR-backed candidates also came in ahead in Arkansas, Kentucky, and Oklahoma. However, FDR's efforts to oust two of his most bitter enemies from the Senate, Walter George of Georgia and "Cotton Ed" Smith of South Carolina, backfired. Resentful of "carpetbagger" interventions in their internal political affairs, voters sent the conservative Democrats back for six more years. After the 1938 elections the rift between FDR and southern Democrats became permanent. Although the president could count on the South for support on foreign policy issues, southern Democrats joined with Republicans to block any further New Deal legislation.

By 1940 the Democratic Party itself had begun to show the strain of reconciling so many disparate factions. White southerners were Democrats mostly because their fathers had been so. As the national Democratic Party became more liberal on racial issues, however, white southern Democratic leaders felt less and less at home in it. On many issues, the ideological stances taken by southern Democrats were more compatible with the GOP's programs than with FDR's.

Which Side Are You On?
Southern Radicals and the New Deal

During the 1930s southern white liberals found within New Deal agencies a base from which they could work to change conditions in the South. Aubrey Williams of Alabama, a social worker who also published a

farmers' magazine, took a position with the WPA before becoming director of the National Youth Administration. Williams tried to make sure that
his agency treated blacks and whites as equals. To that end he appointed
Mary McLeod Bethune, a veteran black educator from Florida, to head a
special Division of Negro Affairs. Williams became so controversial in the
South that southern politicians blocked his appointment to higher administrative positions within the New Deal. The Reverend Will Alexander, a
white Methodist minister who headed the Farm Security Administration,
made sure that blacks got their just share of the limited relief funds within
his control. Clark Foreman, a white Georgian who worked with Alexander
at the FSA, was, like the older minister, a veteran of the Commission on Interracial Cooperation, a private Atlanta-based organization founded in the
post-World War I period. Foreman worked as a special adviser on racial matters for Interior Secretary Ickes and was instrumental in recruiting blacks
for positions in the New Deal. Hugo Black, senator from Alabama, had begun his political career by joining the KKK, back in the early 1920s when
the organization held sway over his state's politics, but in the 1930s he
emerged as one of the most liberal politicians in the region. In 1937, FDR
appointed him to the Supreme Court.

Most southern white liberals hoped to use the New Deal to attack the South's many economic problems. Although many of them ab-
horred the human damage done by Jim Crow, they opposed federal action
to end it, fearing that it would provoke southern whites to a bloody backlash. Instead, liberals pushed for better treatment for blacks within the Jim
Crow system; in effect, they wanted the nation and the South to live up to
the "equal" in "separate but equal." In 1938 a group of such liberals formed
the Southern Conference for Human Welfare, an organization designed to
work for racial justice. Mrs. Roosevelt attended the first meeting in Birmingham and sat in the "colored" section. When the city police, led by
Commissioner Eugene "Bull" Conner, came to force the president's wife to
comply with city segregation laws, Mrs. Roosevelt moved her chair into the
aisle between black and white and sat there defiantly for the rest of the
meeting. Although most members of the SCHW were not ready yet to advocate desegregation, Mrs. Roosevelt's actions won for them an undeserved
reputation as radicals on race issues.

Southern conservatives looking for radical enemies of the southern way of life mistook the nature of the genteel reformers gathered in
Birmingham in 1938. Southern radicals were more likely to be found in the

region's coal patches, textile mills, and cotton fields. During the 1930s southern labor, often libeled as docile, rose up and struck for better wages, shorter hours, and union recognition. In 1931 a miner's wife in Harlan County, Kentucky, wrote an anthem for the southern labor movement. To a haunting melody drawn from an old hymn, Florence Reece asked:

> Come all of you good workers,
> Good news to you I'll tell,
> Of how the good old union
> Has come in here to dwell
> Which side are you on? Which side are you on?

Organized Labor's Struggle in the South

Southern states had long lured northern investors by promising them native-born labor that would work long hours and never strike. Though unions did organize workers in the late nineteenth and early twentieth centuries, southern labor activism remained sporadic and small-scale until 1929, when white textile workers, mostly women, struck in towns all along the Piedmont. Divided between the United Textile Workers, the American Federation of Labor and the Communist-led National Textile Workers Union, labor faced unified opposition from textile mill owners, who adamantly refused to recognize the right to organize. The textile worker's strike and management's reaction to it presaged further labor tumult in the 1930s.

In 1933 a New Deal measure, the National Industrial Recovery Act, included a provision, Section 7a, stating that labor had a right to organize and bargain collectively. Encouraged, labor began an organizing drive, believing that the federal government would uphold the unions. In 1934 the nation's textile workers called a general strike. Two hundred thousand southern workers participated. Strikers and armed guards clashed at factory gates. Police in Honea Path, South Carolina, killed seven strikers, and in Atlanta teargassed workers. Governors in Alabama, North Carolina, South Carolina, and Georgia called out the National Guard to keep order; the federal government did not intervene. When it was all over, the workers lost: the final settlement gained them nothing of long-term significance. Down in northern Alabama, a strike by the biracial United Mine Workers also led to violence and ultimate defeat for the union.

In 1935 Congress passed the National Labor Relations Act at the instigation of Senator Robert Wagner of New York. The Wagner Act created a new agency, the National Labor Relations Board, charged with upholding the rights of workers to organize. With more support from the federal government for unionization than ever before in the nation's history, activist union leaders complained that the leadership of the American Federation of Labor was not moving fast enough to capitalize on new opportunities. In 1937 dissident AFL unions pulled out to form the Congress of Industrial Organization (CIO). Unlike the more conservative AFL, the CIO committed itself to organizing unskilled factory workers across racial lines. It began by attempting to organize workers in the midwestern centers of the nation's heavy industry and ultimately succeeded in forcing union contracts on the nation's major manufacturers.

However, the CIO did not neglect the South, understanding that as long as southern workers' wages remained low, industries would be tempted to flee the unionized North for the union-free South. When the CIO moved into factories in Birmingham, Memphis, Dallas, and elsewhere, local political leaders denounced the organization as a communistic threat to the southern way of life. In truth, the CIO did include some Communist-led unions, and Communists worked as organizers for mainstream unions like the UMW as well. Conservatives also criticized the CIO's biracial policy. Boss Crump of Memphis explained, "We aren't going to have any CIO nigger unions in Memphis."

City officials like Boss Crump made being a union organizer in the South one of the most dangerous jobs in the nation. In Memphis, thugs beat a United Auto Workers organizer so badly that he was hospitalized, then beat him again upon his release. No one was ever arrested. In Dallas, union members and organizers were assaulted repeatedly, and one was tarred and feathered. Local police did nothing. Nor did they intervene when mobs attacked women strikers marching through the business district and stripped the women of their clothing. In New Orleans and in Houston, the CIO failed in its drive to organize longshoremen; in both cases, management successfully played white and black workers off against each other. In the coalfields of Kentucky, Harlan County became a synonym for violent conflict between miners and local police acting as private armies for management. Throughout the South, workers and bosses' hired guns fought mini-wars.

Highlander

A group of white southern reformers opened up the
Highlander Folk School in rural Grundy County, Tennessee,
in 1932. Miles Horton, his wife Zilphia, and other members
of the Highlander staff wanted to help the South's rural
poor. During the 1930s, these ideological commitments led
the Highlander staff into union organizing. The folk school
became a center for worker education, much to the disgust
of regional conservatives, who accused the staff of being
communists. Despite repeated threats of violence, the
Highlander group worked for the CIO through the 1930s.
After World War II the school turned from union work to
civil rights organizing, offering workshops and meeting
places to such civil rights luminaries as Rosa Parks and
Martin Luther King, Jr., until the state and local authorities
finally drove them out of rural Grundy County in the early
1960s. Undaunted, Horton reopened Highlander in
Knoxville and continued the fight.

By 1940 it was clear that the CIO's organizing drive had failed.
Only about 10 percent of all southern workers belonged to unions, compared with just over 20 percent in the nation as a whole. In Birmingham,
the CIO came into the steel mills as a result of a contract between U.S. Steel
and the national union leadership; in Atlanta the UAW won a union contract from General Motors, again largely because of union pressure on corporate management in the North. The CIO tried again in the late 1940s,
but in the early fifties gave up, writing the South off as a perennial "open
shop."

In 1938 the Roosevelt administration took action to reduce the
wide gap between southern and northern wages, sponsoring the Fair Labor Standards Act (FLSA), which required that industries gradually raise
wages to forty cents an hour and reduce their workweek to forty hours. Although strong opposition by southern congressmen led to modifications

in the Act exempting agricultural workers, retail employees, and seasonal workers, the wage differential between workers in similar industries North and South began to decline. By 1939, southern workers earned 64.4 percent of what northern workers were paid; by 1946, 74.1 percent. While southern boosters still bragged about the availability of nonunion labor, they no longer claimed that southern workers came dirt cheap.

Reds in the Cotton

During the Depression many Americans flirted with leftist political parties. At a time when capitalism seemed on its last legs, socialism and even communism appeared attractive. The American left was itself fractured into many different factions. Socialists quarreled with each other and with the Communist Party. However, leftist parties of all ilks shared a belief that America's problems were based on the inequities of the nation's capitalist economic system. In addition, leftist parties were the only ones officially opposing Jim Crow. In the early 1930s leftists reached out to sharecroppers, arguably the nation's most oppressed group.

The Alabama Sharecroppers' Union (ASU) was organized by the Communist Party in 1932. A predominantly black union, the ASU achieved national attention after union members used guns to defend themselves from sheriff's deputies in Tallapoosa County, but it never had much success at collective bargaining.

The Southern Tenant Farmers Union was organized in 1934 in Tyronza, Arkansas, by two small-town socialists, H. L. Mitchell, former sharecropper and small businessman, and H. Clay East, a filling station operator. At the group's first meeting, an aged black sharecropper spoke in favor of an integrated union: "The same chain that holds my people holds your people too. If we're chained together on the outside we ought to stay chained together in the Union." The STFU decided that blacks and whites should work together and took as its anthem a union-friendly rewrite of the old spiritual "We Shall Not be Moved." Despite economic pressure and violence from planters, the STFU organized tenants and day laborers and struck for higher pay—a dollar a day. Although the strike failed, it got national attention, and the union spread into Oklahoma, Tennessee, Mississippi, Missouri, and as far east as North Carolina, receiving support from private philanthropists and church organizations. In 1937 the STFU affiliated with the CIO, but it pulled out in 1939 over the issue of Communist leadership in the CIO union with which the STFU had affiliated. Eventually the organization disintegrated, with members squabbling over race and which brand of leftist politics was better. By 1946 the STFU was effectively dead.

The Tuskegee Experiment

In 1932, the U.S. Public Health Service came to Tuskegee, Alabama, to study the incidence and medical progress of syphilis in the African-American population. Operating out of the prestigious Tuskegee Institute, founded by Booker T. Washington, the public health doctors collected data on about 400 men who had this dangerous venereal disease. All of the men were black and poor. The doctors were curious about the long-term effects of the disease. Therefore, the medical professionals involved in the study did not inform their subjects that they had syphilis, nor did they educate them as to how the disease was spread or offer them any treatment. Instead, they allowed the disease to take its course.

As horrifying as the early Tuskegee experiment was, it got worse. In 1946 penicillin became available. It would have cured the men in the Tuskegee experiment. But the doctors running the experiment did not administer penicillin to their patients, and they went out of their way to make sure that they did not get such treatment elsewhere. This went on for almost thirty more years, until 1972, when the experiment became public. By that time, more than 100 black men had died of tertiary (third-stage) syphilis.

The surviving test subjects and their families sued the federal government and received a $10 million settlement in 1974. However, the long-term effects of the experiment went far beyond rural Alabama. The news of what had been done at Tuskegee confirmed for many African-Americans their deepest suspicions of the white medical establishment.

When the AIDS epidemic began to spread in the 1980s, many African-Americans cited the Tuskegee experiment to justify their belief that AIDS had been created by the U.S. government to target peoples of color in Africa and the United States.

However, it had succeeded in dramatizing the plight of southern sharecroppers and helped influence the Roosevelt administration to create the Farm Security Administration to supply loans so that sharecroppers could buy land. Criticized by Black Belt politicians as nothing less than a modernized version of "forty acres and a mule," the FSA was chronically underfunded and made little impact on sharecropping in the South. Today, the agency is remembered mostly for its contribution to art. Photographers sent out by the agency to document rural poverty produced works that have become part of the nation's cultural heritage.

Ultimately, sharecroppers' unions and the FSA were too little, too late. In 1934, when the STFU was founded, few people envisioned an end to the sharecropping system that had been in place since Reconstruction. But the AAA had weakened tenancy, and World War II dealt it a knockout blow. Unable to get planters to pay them a dollar a day in 1934, sharecroppers and day laborers left the farms in droves in the early 1940s for war-related jobs paying that much an hour. As historian Pete Daniel noted, "The armed forces and defense work became the resettlement administration for rural southerners."

World War II and the South

The Second World War ended the Depression and brought more prosperity to the South than anyone then living could remember. From 1940 to 1945 the region's industrial plant doubled, as did its industrial workforce. In the coastal South, shipyards boomed. In Pascagoula, Mississippi, a Birmingham steel man took over an old shipyard and used it to produce the first-ever arc-welded ships, while in New Orleans Andrew Jackson Higgins became the champion small-craft producer. The population of Norfolk grew by 56 percent, and Mobile's by 61 percent; little Pascagoula grew from 4,000 to 30,000 in just a few years. Inland, southerners found jobs in munitions, petroleum, aluminum, chemicals, and aircraft plants. In Oak Ridge, Tennessee, the federal government built from the ground up an installation that employed over 100,000 workers on a secret project; not until 1945 did Oak Ridgers find out that they had manufactured the uranium isotopes for the first atomic bombs. In 1940, Oak Ridge did not exist; by 1945 it was the fifth largest city in Tennessee.

In addition, the federal government spent $4 billion on military installations in the region. As always, the South's mild climate made it the primary training ground for the nation's soldiers. Merchants in towns around army bases prospered, as did bootleggers and prostitutes. People in base towns complained about the low moral tone created by the presence of so many young men determined to have a good time before shipping out to war—and so many young women determined to help them. Folks joked about promiscuous "V-Girls," saying that they ought to be called "VD-girls," and indeed, venereal disease reached near-epidemic proportions among amateur "Khaki-Wackies," as women who pursued soldiers were also called.

Drawn by defense plant jobs, one-quarter of the rural South's population—about 4 million people—moved off the farms. Newspapers and magazines featured patronizing stories describing the culture shock experienced by ignorant country folk come to town. Between 1940 and 1941 the urban population grew by 35.9 percent—and that at a time when the region's civilian population was declining. With more jobs available than there were people to fill them, southerners job-hopped; worker turnover was high. For some southerners, opportunities outside the region looked even better. Thousands migrated to midwestern industrial centers like Detroit or Akron, Ohio, to help make tanks and tires for the war effort. Though some came home in 1945, others stayed "up north." Like other immigrants, they tended to cluster together in ethnic enclaves. Mississippians and Alabamians were taken aback to find that the natives up north referred to all such neighborhoods generically as "Little Appalachias." Black southerners left in droves for defense plant jobs in California, creating the first substantial African-American communities on the West Coast.

The War, Race, and Gender

In 1941 the main enemy of the United States was Nazi Germany, a regime based upon an ideology upholding the superiority of white (Aryan) males. Official U.S. propaganda condemned these ideas as the antithesis of the democracy for which American fought. Americans' actions belied their words. During the war, American citizens of Japanese ancestry were removed from their West Coast homes and held in concentration camps. In Los Angeles, whites attacked Mexican-Americans in the famous "Zoot Suit Riot." Lynching increased yet again, and race riots broke out in Mobile, Beaumont, New York City, Detroit, and elsewhere.

When American men went off to war, they served in segregated army units. The navy, unable to segregate ships, quietly integrated as needed, but generally placed blacks in service jobs. In 1940 all of the nation's officer training schools were desegregated except for those belonging to the air force. To train black pilots, the air force opened up a segregated flight school at Tuskegee, Alabama, the site of Booker T. Washington's famed institute.

Despite white opposition, blacks obtained defense plant jobs, an accomplishment due in part to action by the federal government and in part to the nationwide shortage of workers. In 1940 A. Phillip Randolph, president of the Brotherhood of Sleeping Car Porters (one of the nation's few successful black unions) threatened to expose American racial hypocrisy by staging a march on Washington in support of black access to defense plant jobs. To avert this public relations disaster, FDR issued Executive Order 8802, prohibiting racial discrimination in defense industries, and created the Fair Employment Practice Committee (FEPC), to which complaints of discrimination could be brought. The very existence of the FEPC angered white supremacists, but in practice the committee had little impact on defense plant hiring. Blacks got jobs because employers were in desperate need of workers.

The employment crunch also opened up jobs for southern women. Wartime propaganda urging American women to get into the workforce contrasted free American women with the women of Nazi Germany, who were depicted as baby-breeding machines. Although southern blacks had been quick to point out the discrepancy between American propaganda and American racial realities, southern women did not publicly make the same connections about gender; that would come a generation

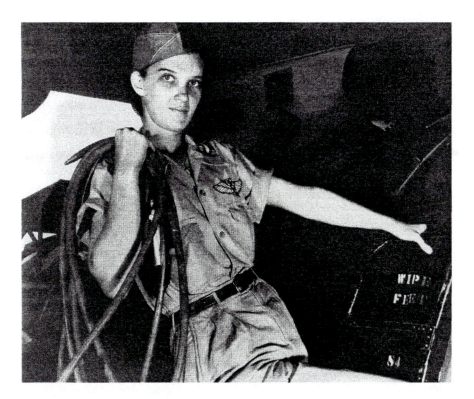

During the Second World War, many southern women found war work in defense plants and military bases. Lorena Craig, shown above, worked in a department store before taking a job at the Naval Air Base in Corpus Christi, Texas.

later. Nonetheless, they flocked to war employment, which paid better money than most had ever seen. Accustomed to doing heavy labor in house and field, many southern farm and mill women grasped eagerly at defense plant jobs, testifying that riveting and welding were a lot easier than chopping cotton. For some southern women, defense plant jobs provided a first taste of economic independence and pride. (The Pascagoula ship plant bragged when one of its workers was named the best female welder in the world.) Middle-class southern women with high school educations could find more traditionally feminine work as clerks in the enormous govern-mental bureaucracy that grew up around the war effort. In both cases, women were warned not to consider wartime opportunities permanent: when the war ended and the men came home, the jobs would belong to them.

Race and gender intersected in the rumors that swept through the white South during the war. Some were the usual—black insurrection, black soldiers after white women—but one was unique. White southerners spread the word that black maids were forming "Eleanor Clubs," civil rights organizations with the goal of putting "a white woman in every kitchen." Although no such clubs existed, maids and nurses did leave domestic work for better pay in defense plants, much to the chagrin of white housewives.

An American Dilemma

In 1938 the Carnegie Foundation, a philanthropic agency based in New York, hired Swedish sociologist Gunnar Myrdal to prepare a "com-prehensive study of the Negro in the United States, to be undertaken in a wholly objective and dispassionate way as a social phenomenon." Myrdal's study, published in 1944, was titled *An American Dilemma: The Negro Problem and Modern Democracy*. In the book's 1,483 pages, Myrdal discussed race re-lations north and south, touching on ideology, biology, sociology, eco-nomics, politics, the legal system, divisions within the black community, and more. He brought to the study insights into race in America that perhaps could have come only from a sympathetic outsider, and he generally main-tained the "dispassionate" tone requested by the Carnegie Foundation. The scientific tone of Myrdal's work enhanced its impact on the public.

Myrdal found that blacks were not treated as equals in any part of the nation, and he described with care the difference between the de facto segregation of northern cities and the legalized segregation of the South. He noted that few Americans, even in the South, felt comfortable admitting that white supremacy's primary function was to make life better for white people. Instead, most whites insisted that Jim Crow was necessary because blacks were innately, biologically inferior to whites. In measured prose, Myrdal concluded that there was no scientific basis for this con-tention. He zeroed in upon the tensions arising between America's public advocacy of democracy and the treatment meted out to black citizens. Writing in the early years of World War II, he warned Americans that the "treatment of the Negro is America's greatest and most conspicuous scandal. . . . For the colored peoples all over the world, whose rising influence is axiomatic, this scandal is salt in their wounds."

In his conclusion, Myrdal called upon the United States to live up to its own creed: "What America is constantly reaching for is democracy at home and abroad. . . . In this sense the Negro problem is not only America's failure but also America's incomparably great opportunity for the future. . . . America can demonstrate that justice, equality and cooperation are possible between white and colored people."

Southern white liberals were caught unprepared for Myrdal's report, which contradicted many of their most cherished illusions. White liberals had honestly believed that most blacks supported Jim Crow and that blacks would be content if treated equally in their separation. They believed that economics, not race, was the salient issue in the South. Myrdal's work indicated otherwise. When white liberals queried their friends in the black community, they were shocked to find that most wanted an end to segregation. Few southern white liberals were willing to go that far.

Lillian Smith

A writer who made her living running a summer camp for girls, "Miss Lil" was among the earliest white southern advocates of desegregation. In the early 1940s she published articles denouncing the cruelty caused by Jim Crow and exposing the old southern social contract by which rich whites played on poor whites' racial fears to maintain their own social and economic dominance. In 1944 Smith penned a best-selling novel, *Strange Fruit,* which created a national scandal by depicting a tragic interracial romance in a small southern town. Significantly, her book sold well in the South; moreover, unlike earlier white critics of the Jim Crow system, she was not ostracized or forced to leave the region. Smith went further in *Killers of the Dream,* her 1949 memoir of growing up in the South, where she described the ways in which white southern children were taught bigotry against their black playmates and friends. Characterizing the region as a "dark and tangled forest full of sins and boredom and fears," Smith said that guilt was the largest crop raised in Dixie. Outspoken and courageous, Smith called for an end to Jim Crow, and in the 1950s became a supporter of the black-led Civil Rights Movement.

Coming Home

Having spent up to four years in the service, some young men of both races came home after the war determined not to endure any longer certain aspects of traditional southern life. In 1946, an altercation between a black shopper and a white store clerk in Columbia, Tennessee, led the black community to fear that a race riot was about to break out. Black military veterans formed a defensive perimeter around their neighborhood and fought it out with white police and white mobs. Eventually, white police authorities arrested about 100 blacks, charging 28 of them with capital crimes. While the Columbia incident indicated a new militancy on the part of blacks, the denouement was even more striking: when brought to trial, 26 of the black men were acquitted by white juries.

Across the state in Athens, white ex-servicemen rebelled when a county political machine used a deputized force of thugs to keep their enemies from voting for the GI-sponsored reform ticket. When a deputy shot an aged black farmer who had tried to vote, the white GIs took weapons from the National Guard armory and marched on the courthouse, some 2,000 strong. They captured the deputies and the ballot boxes, counted the votes, and declared the reform ticket the winners.

Across the South, less dramatic GI political revolts brought younger politicians to positions as mayors and governors. Most of these men were not liberals on race or economics. Instead, they preferred to focus on building more efficient, less corrupt government and creating a favorable climate for investment. Whatever their private feelings about race, they knew that the old-style race-baiting hate rhetoric was bad for business.

It had also become politically risky. The NAACP brought suit against the white primary, and in *Smith v. Allwright* (1944) the Supreme Court found the primary unconstitutional. Although blacks remained disfranchised throughout most of the Deep South, *Smith* made it possible for them to vote in Democratic primaries—the only elections that really mattered—in parts of the South. Although statistics on the matter are hard to obtain, historians agree that black voting did increase in the late 1940s.

A New Day for Dixie

Historian Morton Sosna has suggested that World War II made a larger impact on the South than did the Civil War, and historians William Link and Marjorie Spruill Wheeler recently entitled a chapter in their reader on southern history "World War II: The War That Brought Old Dixie Down." What these historians are getting at is harder to quantify than statistics on jobs created and population movements. Historians have long contended that the war was a turning point for black southerners, who came back from fighting for democracy to demand some at home. The passage of time since 1945 has made it increasingly clear that the war was a turning point for white southerners as well. Perhaps Sosna is correct: for most southerners born since the war, the "southern way of life" that was built on stoic endurance of poverty is all but unimaginable.

In 1950 Mississippi novelist William Faulkner was awarded the Nobel Prize for literature for a body of work written mostly in the 1920s and 1930s. Faulkner's books had depicted the darkest, most tragic aspects of southern life; his characters were twisted by poverty, racism, and the incalculable burden of southern history. Despite his reputation as one of the nation's most pessimistic authors, Faulkner's Nobel acceptance speech was optimistic. He stated that he was unwilling to accept the demise of man. He expected man to endure, and more than endure, to prevail. Although few southerners had read Faulkner's notoriously difficult prose, the spirit he expressed was welcome in the postwar South.

Suggestions for Further Reading and Viewing

ROGER BILES, *The South and the New Deal* (1994)

DAN T. CARTER, *Scottsboro: A Tragedy of the American South* (1969)

DAVID L. CARLTON AND PETER A. COCLANIS, EDS., *Confronting Southern Pov-*

erty in the Great Depression: The Report on Economic Conditions of the South (1996)

JAMES C. COBB AND MICHAEL NAMORATO, EDS., *The New Deal and the South* (1984)

PAUL CONKIN, *The Southern Agrarians* (1988)

PETE DANIEL, *Breaking the Land: The Transformation of Cotton, Tobacco and Rice Cultures since 1880* (1985)

ANTHONY P. DUNBAR, *Against the Grain: Southern Radicals and Prophets, 1929–1959* (1981)

GILBERT FITE, *Cotton Fields No More: The Transformation of Southern Agriculture, 1865–1980* (1984)

DONALD H. GRUBBS, *Cry from the Cotton: The Southern Tenant Farmers' Union and the New Deal* (1971)

Huey Long (Video: Florentine Films)

GLEN JEANSONNE, *Messiah of the Masses: Huey P. Long and the Great Depression* (1993)

JAMES H. JONES, *Bad Blood: The Tuskegee Syphilis Experiment* (1981)

ROBIN D. G. KELLEY, *Hammer & Hoe: Alabama Communists During the Great Depression* (1990)

JACK TEMPLE KIRBY, *Rural Worlds Lost: the American South, 1920–1960* (1987)

NEIL R. MCMILLEN, *Remaking Dixie: The Impact of World War II on the American South* (1997)

GAIL WILLIAMS O'BRIEN, *The Color of the Law: Race, Violence and Justice in the Post-World War II South* (1999)

DOUGLAS L. SMITH, *The New Deal in the Urban South* (1988)

MORTON SOSNA, *In Search of the Silent South: Southern Liberals and the Race Issue* (1977)

PATRICIA SULLIVAN, *Days of Hope: Race and Democracy in the New Deal Era* (1996)

The Thirties (Video: Blackside Productions)

GEORGE BROWN TINDALL, *The Emergence of the New South, 1913–1945* (1967)

The Uprising of '34 (Video: First Run/Icarus Films)

T. HARRY WILLIAMS, *Huey Long* (1969)

"William Faulkner on the Web," http://www.mcsr.olemiss.edu/~egjbp/faulkner/faulkner/html

5

Free at Last: The South Since World War II

The South emerged from World War II with better economic prospects than the region had seen since before the Civil War. The region prospered in the 1950s and 1960s, benefiting especially from Cold War defense contracts. Like Americans elsewhere, Southerners moved to the suburbs, built ranch houses, bought televisions, and learned to dance to a new music, rock and roll.

During this time of prosperity, the nation's grandest drama played itself out in cities and small towns throughout the region. In the late nineteenth century, white southerners had enacted laws that denied blacks political power and enforced racial segregation. The Jim Crow system drew a color line through southern society, and blacks or whites who tried to cross it risked social and economic retribution at best, violence and death at worst. By the 1950s, Jim Crow had been the law of the land for almost three generations. Although black southern leaders had never given up the struggle for equal rights, most southern whites took Jim Crow for granted. In 1954 the United States Supreme Court declared school segregation unconstitutional, thus striking a blow at the roots of white supremacy. In reaction, many white southerners rallied to defend "the southern way of life," including states' rights and white supremacy, while black southern activists and their few southern white allies mobilized for a renewed attack on segregation and disfranchisement, forming the Civil Rights Movement.

By 1965 the legal foundations for Jim Crow had been destroyed. The Civil Rights Movement transformed the South in ways that few southerners, white or black, would have believed in 1950. The cost was great—civil rights workers paid for freedom with their time, prospects, peace of mind, relationships, faith, money, blood, and their very lives. Yet the cost could have been higher. Although most white southerners did not do anything to support the black freedom struggle, neither did most resort to violence to oppose the passage and implementation of federal legislation striking down segregation and disfranchisement. Despite threats by southern politicians and racist groups like the KKK, white southerners did not start a second Civil War in defense of Jim Crow. This leaves students of history with questions. How did the people in the Civil Rights Movement win their victories, and what kinds of victories did they win? How deep was the transformation wrought by the Civil Rights Movement, on the South and on the nation?

Dixie at Midcentury

During the postwar period most parts of the South completed the agrarian transition begun in the 1930s. By 1960 only 15 percent of the region's population lived on farms, while almost half lived in metropolitan areas. Previous generations of southern workers had moved into slum districts or crowded mill villages, but the post-World War II migration to town was different. Federal housing policies, which included loans secured by the Federal Housing Administration or the Veterans Administration, made it easy to buy single-family houses in the new housing developments that sprawled along the new highways (also federally financed) circling southern cities. In other parts of the country, people moved *out* from crowded cities to the suburbs. In the South, the suburbs often contained many people who had moved *in* from the farm. Though sophisticated urban folk might sneer at the suburbs' lack of social and cultural activities, simple one-story ranch houses and suburban amenities seemed wonderful to rural southerners.

The southern standard of living improved radically between 1940 and 1960. Georgia provides an example. In 1940 only 30 percent of the dwellings in that state were owned by their residents. Most houses did not have indoor plumbing. In 1960 a majority of Georgians owned their homes, 60 percent had indoor plumbing, 80 percent had televisions, and people were beginning to buy air conditioners. What happened in Georgia was typical of the region. Poverty remained connected to race, and black southerners did not prosper as much as whites in the post-war years. Nonetheless, never in the region's history had it been easier for ordinary people, white or black, to live comfortably. For their new prosperity, Southerners could thank the federal government, and the Cold War with the Soviet Union.

The Cold War and Southern Prosperity

In 1956 Mississippi novelist William Faulkner mourned the passing of the agrarian South. "Our economy is no longer agricultural," Faulkner said. "Our economy is the Federal Government." Faulkner explained that Mississippians no longer farmed cotton: "We farm now in Washington corridors and Congressional committee-rooms." Faulkner was right. During the postwar period Mississippi's prosperity depended on lobbying for defense contracts.

After World War II the United States and its wartime ally, the Soviet Union, began a period of hostility known as the Cold War, which lasted until 1989. Since the Soviets were communists, most Americans saw the Cold War as a battle between "communism" and "freedom." Hostility between the Soviet Union and the United States led both countries to create gigantic military establishments, armed with the most up-to-date weapons that either side could create. Although the United States and the Soviet Union never went to war against each other, the conflict between the superpowers occasionally led to real shooting wars, as in Korea and Vietnam, in which American troops fought communist forces supplied by the Soviets. The Cold War also led to competition in every aspect of international life, from sports to science, and to the creation of the space program, as the United States raced to beat the Russians to the first manned landing on the moon. The economic pressure caused by the Cold War helped destroy the Soviet Union, which disintegrated between 1989 and 1991. While it existed, the Cold War had a major impact on life in the South, in ways that we will explore throughout this chapter. But first of all, the Cold War fueled defense spending, which fueled Southern prosperity.

Because of the Cold War, the federal government did not cut military budgets as much after World War II as had been the case with prior wars. The southern economy benefitted. Southern agricultural interests sold the government the farm products necessary to maintain a large military. The continuing military buildup also helped the Southern economy because so many military bases had been located in the South. During the 1950s those bases stayed open, and even grew. However, the Cold War's impact on the southern economy was not just measured in dollars; the international conflict actually accelerated Southern modernization.

As the Cold War led the federal government to increase spending on defense projects, the South began to get not just military bases and tobacco contracts, but contracts for plants that used the newest technology of the period to build advanced weapons or space craft. By 1970, twenty-five percent of the nation's prime military contracts went to the South. In many states, defense-related industries became the largest employers. In Georgia, Lockheed (headquartered at Marietta) employed workers in 55 Georgia counties, and paid several hundred million dollars annually in wages and salaries. In South Carolina, Charleston's economy drew income from an Air Force base, a naval base, shipyard, submarine training station, and hospital, as well as plants operated by aircraft manufacturers and General Electric. When the space race began, Houston, Texas became the home of the National Aeronautic and Space Adminstration (NASA)'s Manned Spacecraft Center, now called the Johnson Space Center. Huntsville, Alabama, saw its population almost double between 1960 and 1970 after the federal government located the Marshall Space Flight Center there. NASA built Apollo rockets in New Orleans, tested equipment in Bay St. Louis, Mississippi, and launched its ships to the moon from Cape Canaveral, Florida.

New defense plants did more than supply jobs. They changed the region's population, its educational policies, and its relationship with the rest of the nation. First, the defense plants needed highly skilled labor—more skilled labor than the southern communities in which they were located could supply. For many decades southerners had left the region in search of good jobs. In the postwar period that trend began to reverse, and beginning in the 1960s more people moved into the South than moved out of it. This is not to say that migration into the region had an impact on every state or county, or that out-migration did not continue. Florida, Texas and Virginia received the majority of the newcomers, and rural areas of the South continued to lose population. In Florida, many new immigrants arrived from Cuba, as refugees from that island's communist government, while Mexicans continued to migrate into Texas. But in general, people who moved into the South from the North or West tended to be well educated, middle-class, and white—and those who moved out tended to be poorly educated, working people of both races.

Second, defense and space-program jobs offered an incentive for young southerners to stay in school, go to college, and specialize in high-tech fields. To encourage this, southern states formed the Southern Regional Education Board (SREB) in 1948 and began to work together to improve state universities' technological programs and to keep prospective scientists, engineers and other professionals in the region. While cooperating through the SREB, states competed with each other to offer the most hospitable southern welcome to high-tech industries.

Third, defense-based industries caused a multiplier effect. Houston makes a good example. In 1961 the federal government announced that the Manned Spacecraft Center would be located in Houston. A year later twenty-nine space-related companies had located in that city. These new industries created a demand for additional retail and service businesses. By 1965 Houston had become the greatest market, industrial, and population center in the Southwest.

Practical considerations led the federal government to locate space and military projects in the South. It was easier to build a new bomber plant in Georgia than to convert an aging tank factory in the Northeast to high-tech production. The space program chose Houston in part because it needed to be able to ship via the Gulf of Mexico. In addition, military contractors who located in the South could count on lower labor costs. Despite the CIO's organizing drives in the 1930s, the South remained the nation's least unionized region, with the country's lowest wages.

Southern states also won contracts because southern politicians went after them with great skill and gusto. One historian notes that Texas politicians (including Vice President Lyndon Johnson) thought of NASA as the Moses that would lead Houston and the South to the promised land of prosperity. Other southern pols looked for their own economic Moses in the Cold War military-industrial economy. In the 1950s and 1960s, southern congressmen and senators had attained seniority on many key congressional committees. They made alliances with the nation's defense establishment. Southern congressmen could be counted on to support defense budget increases, and members of the defense establishment made sure that the southerners' support was rewarded. L. Mendel Rivers, congressman from the South Carolina district that included Charleston, was so successful at obtaining defense-related installations for his district that he was teased about it by another southern congressman: "You put anything else down there in your district, Mendel, it's gonna sink." By some estimates, half the employment in Rivers's district was defense related.

NASA did not lead the South into the economic promised land. The region continued to have the lowest wages and highest poverty rates in the nation during the 1950s and 1960s. But an economy based in large part upon cooperation with the federal government went a long way to ending regional isolation from national trends, both economic and social, and made a defense of a distinctive Southern "way of life" increasingly anachronistic.

Black Soul, White Voices: Elvis Presley and the Birth of Rock and Roll

At midnight in Memphis in 1954, the truly cool kids tuned their radios to "Red, Hot and Blue," where a white disc jockey played black music. Still marketed as "race" music, rhythm and blues combined the deep emotion and dangerously sexual lyrics of blues with a dance beat. Rhythm and blues rolled out of clubs in every southern city and poured from radios throughout the South. But the market for this music was limited by the racism of the white American public. While white southern kids listened to R & B, and (like hip urban kids throughout the nation) sneaked into clubs to hear black musicians, the American musical mainstream in the early 1950s was dominated by white, middle-aged performers. There was no mainstream market for blues music—it was too black. Meanwhile, Nashville's country music had achieved national popularity in the 1940s, but its appeal was limited by class. To would-be sophisticates in the 1950s, country music, with its heartfelt lyrics about life's troubles, was at best quaint, at worst embarrassing: hillbilly music.

Sam Phillips ran Sun Records, a small recording studio in Memphis, turning out music for the race market. Phillips began telling friends in the early 1950s that if he could find a white singer who could sing like a black man, he could make a fortune. One day a truck driver whose family had moved to Memphis from Tupelo, Mississippi, wandered into the shop to make a record for his mother's birthday. Who actually discovered Elvis Presley has never been clear, but the young singer was invited back to make a real recording. During a break in the recording session, Elvis picked up a guitar and launched into a blues song. Phillips had found a white man who sang black. Phillips marketed Elvis as the "Hillbilly Cat." Presley's first record had blues on one side and bluegrass on the other. Rock and roll was born, a fusion of southern blues and country music.

During the 1950s Elvis rose to national stardom, delighting teenagers and horrifying parents. The young Elvis of the 1950s was energetic, strong-voiced and sensual, so sexy that television would show his performances only from the waist up. Phillips went on to produce Carl Perkins, Jerry Lee Lewis, and Johnny Cash, all of them known as "rock-a-billy" performers. Black performers sometimes resented the success of white musicians. Black rock-and-roller Chuck Berry accused whites of essentially stealing black music. Elvis and other performers copied black musical styles and tried to dress and sound black. Yet through white southerners, black southern music became mainstream American entertainment, and audiences who learned to listen to Elvis in the 1950s bought music by black performers in the 1960s.

Rock and roll infuriated white racists, who denounced it as jungle music. In truth, early rock and roll was musical "miscegenation," a marriage of musical styles created by poor whites and blacks in the South. There was no more southern music than that created at Sun Records in Memphis, and no music more subversive of the concept of racial separation. Elvis and the black performers he loved and copied performed the sound track for the 1950s. In 1954, Elvis gave his first concert in Memphis. The year is more memorable for a history-making Supreme Court decision: *Brown v. Board of Education,* in which the court struck down legal segregation in the nation's public schools.

Southern Politics, Race Relations, and the Cold War

Already disaffected by the New Deal, old-line southern Democrats became even more so during the administration of Harry Truman, who assumed the presidency in 1945 when FDR died. Elected in his own right in 1948, Truman was a Missourian, with a family heritage as Confederate as that of any senator from the Deep South. However, Truman presided over a national Democratic Party increasingly influenced by the prospect of winning black votes in key northern states. Running for reelection in 1948, Truman proposed to Congress a civil rights program that would have ended the poll tax, created a fair employment practices committee, made lynching a federal offense, and outlawed segregation in interstate buses, trains, and airplanes. Although the proposal never passed, it angered southern segregationists, as did Truman's decision that summer to desegregate the armed forces by executive order.

In protest, Deep South segregationists formed a States' Rights Democratic Party, better known by its media nickname, the Dixiecrats. At their convention in Birmingham, the Dixiecrats heard their keynote speaker, Alabama Governor Frank Dixon, denounce civil rights as a conspiracy to reduce white southerners "to the status of a mongrel, inferior race, mixed in blood." They nominated South Carolina Senator Strom Thurmond for the presidency. In November 1948, Thurmond won over a million votes. The Dixiecrats carried Alabama, Mississippi, and South Carolina and won a plurality in Louisiana.

However, Truman won reelection, in large part because of black voters' support for the Democratic ticket. In several key northern states, including Illinois, New York, Michigan and Pennsylvania, black votes swung the election to the Democrats. Whether they were racial liberals or not, Democratic Party operatives from key northern states had to be influenced by the electoral math.

In 1952 the Democratic national leadership retreated from civil rights, and the Democratic candidate, Adlai Stevenson, received support from most southern politicians. Some of the former Dixiecrats disagreed. They urged their constituents to vote for the GOP presidential candidate, former general Dwight D. Eisenhower, a move that presaged a party realignment still twenty years in the future.

During the 1950s Democratic defenders of the southern way of life found themselves becoming ever more politically isolated within the

Democratic Party. Nationally, the post-New Deal Democrats had become more conservative on economic issues, in part because the Cold War made it difficult if not dangerous for any politician to advocate class-based politics that might remind voters of communism, and in part because the nation was prosperous. Race replaced economics as the center of Cold War liberalism, as northern Democrats, influenced by increasing numbers of black voters in northern cities, spoke out against southern racial problems in terms drawn from Myrdal's *American Dilemma*. (Unlike Myrdal, most northern liberals preferred to assume that the nation's racial problems were confined to the South.) Therefore, southern Democrats in Congress found themselves more and more allied with northern Republicans, whose opposition to big government and social conservatism could accommodate support for segregation.

The Cold War itself had a deep, if somewhat confusing, impact on the politics of race. Since the Communist Party-USA was the only political party in the nation that had consistently supported racial equality and integration, southern segregationists accused anyone who did not support Jim Crow of being a Communist. (The reasoning went like this: Communists support integration; you support integration; you must be a Communist.) On the other hand, Americans perceived the Cold War as a struggle between the forces of good and evil, and the United States urged emerging nations in Asia and Africa to join in that struggle. It was hard to sell the United States as the "Land of the Free" to an African or an Asian when millions of U.S. citizens were denied the right to vote and the basic civilities of life because of the color of their skin. In 1950 the United States began a war with communist forces in Korea. That war was fought in part by black southern men who would not have been allowed to get a cup of coffee at a white-only lunch counter in their home states.

Brown v. Board of Education and Southern Resistance

In the postwar years progressive southern politicians and educators pinned their hopes for regional development on education. During the 1950s and 1960s southern states spent a greater percentage of their state budgets on education than did states outside the region. As southern universities began to receive federal grant money for science research, and as southern students increasingly drew tuition funds from federal subsidies for veterans' education, southern governments began to realize that their education systems now faced national scrutiny. The principle of the Supreme Court's 1896 decision in *Plessy v. Ferguson* was that segregated facilities were legal if the facilities provided were equal. This was a principle that had never been observed. Realizing that their own actions had placed segregation in peril, southern state governments began to increase funding for black schools in the early 1950s. Although black southerners welcomed better facilities and funding, state governments' reforms proved to be too little, too late.

In the 1940s, the National Association for the Advancement of Colored People (NAACP) funded a legal team that attacked school segregation by targeting lawsuits against inequities in graduate and professional education. Since southern medical and law schools were segregated, blacks who wanted a graduate education had to go out of state. The NAACP began to sue in such cases and to win. Southern states, hardly able to fund graduate and professional programs for white students, realized that they could not fund Jim Crow medical, law, and graduate schools. Some southern states tried ridiculous measures to give their black citizens a "separate but equal" education. In the late 1940s Oklahoma admitted a black student, George McLaurin, to the University of Oklahoma's graduate school of education but required him to attend classes by sitting in an anteroom separate from his white classmates, to eat at a separate table in the school cafeteria, to study separately in the library, and to use a segregated restroom. In Texas a black man, Herman Sweatt, sued to be admitted to the University of Texas law school; Texas authorities created a mini-law school just for him. The NAACP sued on behalf of McLaurin and Sweatt, and in 1950 the Supreme Court ruled that the students had been denied equal protection of the laws. After the decisions in the *McLaurin v. Oklahoma State Regents for Higher Education* (1950) and *Sweatt v. Painter* (1950) cases, many thoughtful southerners could see that segregation was doomed: the southern states' own failure to live up to the "equal" provision of *Plessy v. Ferguson's* "separate but equal" principle had left state governments without a legal defense.

During the early 1950s the NAACP legal team was headed by Thurgood Marshall, a Maryland native and Howard Law School graduate. Marshall, later to become the first African-American Supreme Court Justice, had made himself a reputation as a fearless NAACP lawyer during the 1930s and 1940s, filing suits on behalf of his organization in southern courts where no black man had ever dared to practice. In 1950, Marshall and other NAACP lawyers encouraged black parents to bring suit in federal courts, this time not to demand equal treatment within segregation, but to demand an end to segregation itself. Eventually five of these NAACP-sponsored suits made their way up through the appeals courts to the Supreme Court, where all were heard together under the heading of *Brown v. Board of Education of Topeka, Kansas.* In previous cases, the NAACP had sued to force southern states to live up to the principle of *Plessy v. Ferguson.* In these cases, the NAACP's lawyers charged that separate could never be equal: segregation itself denied black children the equal protection of the law. On May 17, 1954, the Supreme Court agreed. Chief Justice Earl Warren announced the unanimous opinion of the Court: "[S]eparate educational facilities are inherently unequal." Warren stated that segregating children "solely because of their race generates an inferiority as to their status in the community that may affect their hearts and minds in a way unlikely ever to be undone."

Brown v. Board of Education made segregation unconstitutional in public schools. Since southern states did not move quickly to desegregate their schools, the Supreme Court in 1955 issued another ruling ordering that public schools be desegregated "with all deliberate speed." While blacks in the South may have heard the word "speed," southern state governments, and the federal government itself, seem to have concentrated more on the word "deliberate," which might be used to describe the turtle-like pace of compliance with *Brown*.

Southern White Reaction and Federal Complacency

Southern state governments, with their long history of either ignoring or working around the Constitution, did not jump to comply with *Brown*. However, the region was not unified in defense of the so-called southern way of life. Deep South states with large black populations prepared for resistance even before the Supreme Court issued its verdict. In Georgia and South Carolina state legislators passed constitutional amendments that effectively allowed the states to close their public schools and provide tuition grants to private schools. Georgia Governor Herman Talmadge (son of Eugene) pledged in 1951, "As long I am governor, Negroes will not be admitted to white schools." However, many southern governors, particularly in the Upper South, were really more interested in promoting economic development than in risking prosperity by a die-hard defense of Jim Crow.

In Alabama and Louisiana, neopopulist governors continued to insist that class issues mattered more than race. Alabama Governor James "Big Jim" Folsom was 6 feet, 8 inches tall and weighed 260 pounds, liked to drink and chase women and had a reputation for corruption, but he was no great fan of the racial components of the southern way of life. He said, "As long as Negroes are held down by privation and lack of opportunity, the other poor people will be held down alongside them." While not an integrationist, Folsom was not a bigot either: "I could never get all excited about our colored brothers," he said. "I find them to be good citizens." Folsom's lack of interest in the politics of race found an echo in Louisiana, where Governor Earl Long, the younger brother of Huey Long, scorned race as a fake issue used by politicians to blind voters to their true interests. Long paid lip service to segregation in order to get elected but famously told a segregationist leader in Louisiana that when he got close with God, he would realize that "niggers is human beings!"

While the South's political leadership sorted out its response to *Brown,* the federal government did nothing to further implementation of the decision. From 1954, when the *Brown* decision was handed down, through 1955, when the Supreme Court urged implementation with deliberate speed, and on into the late 1950s, southerners were left to work out their adaptation to *Brown* without leadership from President Dwight Eisenhower. A war hero who had commanded American forces in Europe, Eisenhower was popular among white southerners, many of whom voted for him in 1952 and again in 1956, despite the fact that he was a Republican. Eisenhower privately disapproved of the *Brown* decision and expressed skepticism about the ability of a court decision to change the way the white South felt about race. Historians have condemned Eisenhower for his unwillingness to use his own power and enormous popularity to urge Americans to accept the concept of racial equality, and they have charged him with allowing southern conservatives to believe that the federal government lacked a firm commitment to enforcing *Brown.*

intend to make it difficult, if not impossible, for a Negro who advocates desegregation to find and hold a job, get credit, or renew a mortgage." The councils also targeted southern whites who indicated anything less than total support for Jim Crow and massive resistance. Former Georgia governor Herman Talmadge told a council meeting how to treat such men: "Don't let him eat at your table, don't let him trade at your filling station, and don't let him trade at your store." By 1956, the councils had become a powerful political force, capable of swaying elections and securing the defeat of liberals or moderates.

In Alabama, Big Jim Folsom fought the segregationists and lost. Folsom had other problems, including rumors of sloppy administration, public drunkenness, and corruption, but he helped complete the destruction of his political career when he invited New York Congressman Adam Clayton Powell of Harlem to have a drink with him in the Alabama governor's mansion. After sitting down for drinks and conversation with the black congressman, Folsom said, he couldn't run for dogcatcher. When Folsom tried to talk about legislation that would tax the rich, improve schools for the poor, and make it easier for labor unions to organize in Alabama, his working class supporters no longer wanted to hear it. As Folsom noted, the race issue had become the most important thing, and for some voters, the only thing.

In 1958 Folsom's chosen successor, Judge George C. Wallace, a defender of segregation, was defeated in the Democratic primary by an even stauncher segregationist. Embittered, Wallace made a vow never to be "out-niggered" again, a pledge he worked to live up to in his successful campaign for governor in 1962.

As southern states signified their willingness to defend Jim Crow, black southerners understood that *Brown* had not changed anything. Schools were still segregated and looked likely to remain so. Throughout the South, blacks who joined the NAACP, tried to organize politically, or protested segregation were still being terrorized, beaten, and killed. In 1955 a tragedy in Mississippi focused national attention on racial violence in the South. A black Chicago teenager, Emmett Till, was visiting family members in the Delta. Till was an outsider and may not have understood Southern racial mores. On a dare from other teenagers, he flirted with a female store clerk. For allegedly whistling at this white woman, Till was taken from his grandfather's home in the middle of the night and beaten to death. His killers, who made no real effort to hide their guilt, were tried for his murder but acquitted by an all-white jury. While most white Mississippians applauded the verdict, William Faulkner mourned: "[I]f we in America have reached that point in our desperate culture when we must murder children, no matter for what reason or what color, we don't deserve to survive, and probably won't." The murder of Emmett Till, like the *Brown* decision, was a turning point. For black Southern teenagers—and some whites—the murder was a shocking wake-up call. In later years, many civil rights workers would trace the origins of their commitment to racial justice to their dismay over the death of Emmett Till.

A Rising of the People

In December 1955, Mrs. Rosa Parks was riding the bus home from her job in downtown Montgomery, Alabama, when the driver demanded that she give up her seat to a white man. Mrs. Parks refused and was arrested. In protest, Montgomery activists organized a bus boycott that lasted almost a year, ending with a Supreme Court ruling declaring segregation on buses illegal. The Montgomery bus boycott attracted national attention to civil rights issues and introduced the American public to the Reverend Martin Luther King, Jr., the boycott movement's articulate spokesman.

Most Americans, including many historians, locate the beginnings of the postwar black freedom movement in the Montgomery boycott. But the story of the emergence of the Civil Rights movement does not begin in 1955. African-Americans' struggle for freedom and equal rights began in slavery days and continued during all the long years of Jim Crow. Aspects of the black freedom movement of the postwar period can be traced to Booker T. Washington's gospel of self-help and economic independence, as well as to W.E.B. DuBois's NAACP. In the 1920s, some black southerners had joined a black nationalist movement led by Jamaican Marcus Garvey. Since Reconstruction black men and women had used various means, from churches to unions to newspapers to community organizing, to fight as best they could for their freedom. The values and beliefs behind the Civil Rights Movement were nothing new.

However, the Movement of the 1950s and 1960s was operating

Mrs. Rosa Parks on a Montgomery bus in 1956, after the successful bus boycott. She is shown sitting in the *front* of the bus. Library of Congress.

in a new context. In the 1890s, blacks struggling for equal rights in the South had relatively few allies up North. But by 1950 many blacks had migrated out of the South to cities in the North and on the West Coast. Unlike most of their cousins down south, these African-Americans could vote. They put pressure on white politicians for action on civil rights.

The new context for the black freedom struggle also included television and the Cold War. Television made white terrorism against blacks national news, while the Cold War made the treatment of blacks in the South a point of international concern. How could the United States pose as leader of the free world while denying some of its citizens their constitutional rights?

The Civil Rights Movement extended far beyond Montgomery and Martin Luther King. It was a genuine popular uprising, in which sharecroppers, maids, schoolchildren, and church ladies enacted a revolution that destroyed Jim Crow. From 1955 through the 1960s, the South experienced years of upheaval. Blacks protested, boycotted, demanded better treatment and equal justice under the laws, and focused the attention of the nation and the world on southern race relations. Under pressure, the federal government intervened in the South with a force not seen since the 1870s.

Although two previous presidents had vacillated in their support for civil rights, in 1964 and 1965 President Lyndon Johnson, a southerner from Texas, pushed through Congress legislation that abolished every legal vestige of the Jim Crow system. The Civil Rights Movement led to changes so profound that historians of the South refer to the period as "Second Reconstruction."

These days many black Southerners over the age of forty, and some whites, like to remember themselves as having been "in the Movement." However, historians of the Civil Rights Movement note that in most places in the South most members of the black middle class failed to support the Movement until its success seemed assured. Many of them, including teachers, doctors, lawyers, and businessmen, had patronage ties that linked them to the white "power structure" (to use a Movement phrase) that dominated Southern towns. Some depended on whites for their jobs. Others had, by hard work and careful diplomacy, built up their incomes and established for themselves a place in society that they did not want to risk losing. Whites who supported civil rights faced similar economic pressures and also risked being cast out from their communities.

On the other hand, many black communities in the South had a small but tough and determined corps of activists. Some older people had worked for the CIO's biracial union-organizing drives in the 1930s or had participated in black unions like the Brotherhood of Sleeping Car Porters. Others were long-term members of the NAACP who chafed under that venerable institution's cautious and legalistic approach to fighting Jim

Crow. In Mississippi, many civil rights activists were landowning farmers. As Thomas Jefferson would have predicted, their economic independence made them more disposed to fight for political rights, and (like the landowning farmers of Jefferson's ideal agrarian republic) they had guns and knew how to use them to defend their homes. In parts of the rural South, women led the Movement; throughout the region, women acted as the Movement's foot soldiers, doing most of the drudge work of organization.

The Civil Rights Movement has a complex and tangled history. It was never united, and although Dr. King today is remembered as the heroic leader of the Movement, his leadership was often challenged and disputed at the time. The birth of the Movement in Montgomery illustrates some of the complexities. Rosa Parks herself was far from being a political novice or a naive woman who suddenly decided, all on her own, to resist segregation. An activist for most of her adult life, Mrs. Parks had attended a civil rights workshop at Tennessee's Highlander School just before she was arrested for refusing to give up her seat on the bus. As a long-term member of the NAACP, Mrs. Parks had worked with E. D. Nixon, a labor activist and NAACP leader who had been agitating for a bus boycott for some time. When she was arrested, Nixon immediately called for a boycott.

So did the Montgomery Women's Political Council, a black women's group. Under the leadership of Jo Ann Robinson, another long-term activist, the women's group mimeographed thousands of leaflets calling for a bus boycott and distributed them throughout the black community. With pastors of black churches, Nixon and the Women's Political Council helped form the Montgomery Improvement Association, the organization that implemented the boycott.

The association chose King as their spokesman in part because he was well educated and eloquent, but also because he was new in town and had not had time to become part of the local power structure. For whatever reason, the association chose well. For almost a year, King became the voice of the boycott, articulating the association's demands to the city, and explaining the Movement to the nation via the new medium of television.

The history of the bus boycott illustrates on a small scale the history of the Movement in general: white resistance to moderate black demands led to a hardening of positions on both sides, increased militancy from blacks, and federal intervention. At first the Montgomery Improvement Association asked only for modifications that would make segregation on the buses more humane. When Montgomery's white leadership refused to even negotiate, the association settled in for a long struggle. Blacks organized a carpool system to get people to work, and white women began driving their maids back and forth from work, much to the dismay of the city government. Whites fought back. In February 1956, a grand jury indicted Martin Luther King and eighty-eight other boycott leaders for conspiracy. White terrorists bombed King's home.

Facing intense white opposition, the association changed its tactics and goals, suing in federal court for an end to segregation on the buses. In November 1956, the Supreme Court ruled in favor of the association. The boycott ended, giving the fledgling Civil Rights Movement its first victory. The bus boycott made King a national figure, helped awaken Americans in general to civil rights issues, and encouraged blacks throughout the South to form their own "Improvement Associations" and to press for an end to Jim Crow.

In 1957 leaders of Southern civil rights groups, including King, formed the Southern Christian Leadership Conference (SCLC). As the name suggests, the group was led by ministers, mostly Baptists, from cities throughout the South. The formation of SCLC marked a transition in the history of the Civil Rights Movement. Prior to the 1950s, the NAACP had been the dominant civil rights group in the nation. The NAACP's strategy had been to attack Jim Crow through the courts. However, courtroom victories such as *Brown* had not been translated into actual change in the lives of black Southerners. The SCLC tapped into a different power source: the black churches. In most Southern towns, black churches, usually Baptist, stood as the community's only truly independent institution. Black ministers acted as community leaders. Based in the churches, the SCLC would turn from the NAACP's legal strategy to a strategy of "direct action." Under SCLC leadership, black Southerners and their white supporters would protest Jim Crow through boycotts and demonstrations. As SCLC leader, King called for militant, but nonviolent, resistance to Jim Crow: "We will meet your physical force with soul force," he said. King labeled Jim Crow a moral problem and proposed to combat institutionalized evil with Christian love.

The Religious Roots of Civil Rights Activism

Civil rights leaders and participants used the language of religion to talk about social reform. This was nothing new in American history:

reformers in the nineteenth century had often married religious rhetoric to secular purposes. But the Civil Rights Movement did more than talk religious talk. Under King's leadership, civil rights workers tried to "walk the walk" as well: to use tactics based on religious principles.

The Civil Rights Movement drew upon a long history of writing and thinking about the moral way to resist oppression. Back in the 1840s, the New England writer Henry David Thoreau refused to pay his state taxes to protest the Mexican War, which he saw as a land grab designed to acquire territory for the expansion of slavery. Briefly arrested for his protest, Thoreau wrote an essay, "Civil Disobedience." Thoreau asked, what is the citizen to do when the government (particularly a democratically elected government like that in the United States) takes actions that the citizen believes are morally wrong? His answer was civil disobedience: the citizen must refuse to obey the evil law and must be willing to take the consequent punishment—that is, to go to jail if necessary. Thoreau's essay became very influential among people who were pacifists for moral or religious reasons, because civil disobedience offered a way to resist oppression without resorting to violence. In the early twentieth century a young Hindu lawyer, Mohandas Gandhi, read Thoreau. Gandhi, a religious pacifist, developed techniques of civil disobedience, or passive resistance, that he used successfully in gaining India's independence from Britain in 1947. Gandhi's victory held out an example of the successful use of nonviolence to effect political change.

Some African-Americans looked to Gandhi for inspiration. In 1941 James Farmer, a young lawyer who was working for the Fellowship of Reconciliation, a pacifist organization in Chicago, joined with other students of Gandhi to form CORE, the Committee of Racial Equality, and planned use Gandhian tactics against segregation. Bayard Rustin, a New Yorker who became King's adviser, was first sent to meet King by the Fellowship of Reconciliation. Rustin, who had worked with the Gandhi movement in India, reinforced King's already strong belief in nonviolence as a tactic of protest.

By the end of the 1950s, some strategic individuals and organizations throughout the Movement were committed to nonviolence. Nonviolence meant that civil rights workers would deliberately break Southern segregation laws and take whatever abuse bystanders or police authorities gave back, including beatings and jail time. As King said, the goal was not to "defeat or humiliate the opponent, but to win his friendship and understanding."

Nonviolent resistance tapped into the deep Christian faith of many southern blacks. It also allowed civil rights workers to take the moral high ground while breaking the law. The Movement organized in churches and sent its people out into the streets fortified with hours of hymns, prayers, and sermons.

For many Movement people, resistance to Jim Crow became a religious duty, a calling to be pursued regardless of danger. As King told a supporter, "my obligation is to do the right thing as I am called upon to do it. The rest is in God's hands." The Reverend Fred L. Shuttlesworth, the combative leader of Birmingham's Alabama Christian Movement for Human Rights, survived his house's bombing in 1956. When warned by a Klan-affiliated policeman that he should leave town, he told the man, "I wasn't saved to run."

In Mississippi in 1963, female civil rights workers were arrested for attempting to integrate the Winona bus station. Local authorities ordered jail inmates to beat the women. Fannie Lou Hamer, a leader in the Mississippi movement, remembered hearing Annelle Ponder being beaten: "She kept screamin', and they kept beatin' on her, and finally she started prayin' for 'em, and she asked God to have mercy on them, because they didn't know what they was doin'. . . ." Guards beat Mrs. Hamer herself so severely that she suffered permanent damage to one kidney. The next day, Mrs. Hamer began leading her fellow inmates in gospel protest songs. When the jailer's wife gave her a welcome drink of cold water, Mrs. Hamer commented that she must be a Christian and suggested that when the woman went home she should get out her Bible and read Acts 17:26: "God hath made of one blood all nations of men for to dwell on the face of the earth." As Mrs. Hamer explained later, "It wouldn't solve any problem for me to hate whites just because they hate me. Oh, there's so much hate, only God has kept the Negro sane." When carried to trial, Mrs. Hamer asked her jailer, "Do you people ever think or wonder how you'll feel when the time comes you'll have to meet God?"

The religious tone of the Civil Rights Movement reflected the culture of the entire region regardless of race. Whites watched as civil rights workers knelt in prayer in public places and went to jail signing hymns—in many cases, the same hymns that echoed from white churches every Sunday morning.

Nonviolence also made great television. King and other Movement leaders understood that changing the South would require federal intervention. In most parts of the South, nonviolent protesters only had to appear on the streets to provoke a violent response from white mobs and local authorities. Movement organizers made sure that national network television filmed white teenagers beating up nonviolent blacks, or white policemen turning police dogs on demonstrators. Watching such scenes on television, Americans were first revolted, then angered, and began to pressure their federal representatives for action on civil rights. In essence, the Movement used televison to shame the South before the nation, and the nation before the United States' allies and enemies in the Cold War.

Nonviolence, however, was not an easy road to walk. Southern men of both races believed that defending honor sometimes required violence. Civil rights leaders asked participants to take abuse and not hit back. For some, that was just too hard to do. Many, perhaps most, Movement people felt no moral commitment to nonviolence. For them, it was a tactic that should be used if it worked and dropped if it didn't. While willing to use passive resistance in marches, they had no intention of allowing their families to be murdered in retaliation, and they stockpiled guns for home defense. Still others openly said that nonviolence was crazy—a point of view especially strong in Mississippi. Despite Movement workers' lectures on nonviolence, black farmers carried what they jokingly called "nonviolent Winchesters" to meetings. Hartman Turnbow, a Mississippi farmer, went so far as to argue with Martin Luther King himself about nonviolence: "He said that was it, said that's just his way, say he gon' finish up with nonviolent. I told him, 'Well you finish up in a cemetery you just keep following it.'"

The Struggle for School Desegregation

As the Movement organized, the nation's attention shifted to the dramas being played out in southern schools. In 1956 a black student was admitted to the University of Alabama by federal court order, but she was then driven from the campus by a white mob and expelled by the university when she charged that the school had "intentionally permitted" whites to create a dangerous atmosphere for her. In Texas that year, whites prevented the integration of schools at Mansfield and Texarkana; the governor had to send in Texas Rangers to maintain order, but the schools remained segregated. Although school desegregation began in a small way in Kentucky and Tennessee, many Deep South states refused to comply with

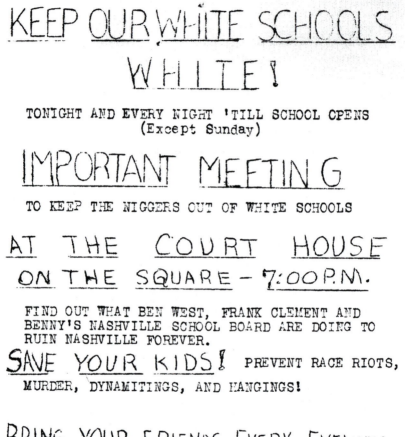

Copy of a handbill distributed in Nashville,
Tennessee, in 1957, illustrates opposition to school
integration. Library of Congress.

the Supreme Court's decision, and a clash between federal and state authority seemed imminent.

The clash finally happened in a place no one would have expected: Central High School in Little Rock, Arkansas. Arkansas Governor Orval Faubus, an industry-chasing prodevelopment moderate, had no deep commitment to segregation or states' rights. Little Rock, the capital of Arkansas, had no exceptional history of racial violence. When the Supreme Court issued the *Brown* decision, the school board of Little Rock announced that the city would comply with the ruling. By 1957, the school board had worked out a plan for desegregation. They planned to send nine black teenagers, specially chosen for academic achievement and good character, into Central High School. Meanwhile, the Citizens' Council had organized in Little Rock and began to hold rallies opposing segregation. In the summer of 1957, the council and the Little Rock school board both lobbied Governor Faubus for support. Faubus did not want to defy federal power. On the other hand, he did not want to lose white political support.

In the fall of 1957, Faubus made every effort to pass the buck. He contacted the Eisenhower administration, asking how the federal government would help if desegregation caused riots. Federal officials answered that the administration did not want to get involved. Faubus then obtained a state court injunction against the school board's desegregation plan, but a federal court overruled the state court. Fearing riots when schools opened, Faubus called out the National Guard and instructed them to prevent desegregation. When the black students showed up at Central High, the National Guard turned them back. Federal Court Judge Ronald Davies directed the administration to enforce desegregation and ordered Arkansas officials to stop interfering with the process. Faubus removed the National Guard, and desegregation proceeded.

Black students walked back into Central High through a mob of angry white people. As the mob grew in size and anger, the Little Rock authorities lost control of the situation and school officials feared that the students would be killed. One of the students, Melba Pattillo Beals, remembered later that "someone made a suggestion that if they allowed the mob to hang one kid, they could then get the rest out. And a gentleman . . . said, 'Uhn-uh, how are you going to choose? You're going to let them draw straws?' He said, 'I'll get them out.'" The state police took the students to the basement and loaded them into a car. The white driver was told not to stop. Beals remembered, "This guy revved up his engine and he came up out of the bowels of this building," and drove the black students out through the mob, scattering protesters right and left. Beals thanked him afterwards for the ride; she said later, "I should've said, 'Thank you for my life.'" Television cameras captured the spectacle of whites spitting and screaming obscenities at the teenagers.

The Little Rock crisis forced the Eisenhower administration to take a stand on integration. In the three years since *Brown*, Eisenhower had not so much as made a speech on civil rights. But the president could not allow a state to blatantly defy the national government. Eisenhower placed the National Guard under federal authority and sent in the 101st Airborne Division to enforce the desegregation of Little Rock Central High—the first federal military intervention in the South since 1877. With soldiers patrolling the halls, the black students finished out a year at Central High. But in 1958, Governor Faubus closed all the high schools in Little Rock in a last-ditch effort to prevent integration.

In 1958 federal courts ruled unconstitutional any kind of state support for segregated schools and determined that states could not close some schools to keep black students out while keeping others open. White Southerners faced a choice: either accept desegregation in the public schools or close the schools. Though many segregationists were willing to pay that price, others were not. Realizing that defying the federal government would not work, some white southerners began to signal that they would accept public schools that were not completely white, and some southern states began to move toward token school desegregation.

After Little Rock, grassroots "save the schools" organizations appeared in Arkansas, Virginia, Georgia, Florida, and North Carolina. Often started and staffed by white women, these organizations drew support from parent-teacher associations, state education associations, and business elites in cities throughout the region, most notably in Atlanta. Business leaders in "The City Too Busy to Hate" recognized the inevitability of desegregation and knew that open and violent opposition to it would ruin Atlanta's image and damage business prospects. As one banker put it, "If we behave like a banana republic, we shall get and deserve the economic rewards characteristic of a banana republic." Although Georgia's governor criticized the city for its willingness to surrender, Atlanta's business elite refused to go down with the segregationist ship.

In other places in the south, cities and counties began to desegregate their schools by admitting a token few African-American students.

Thus states could give the impression that they were complying with the law and avoid confrontations with federal authorities while still maintaining essentially separate black and white schools. By 1960 only Alabama, Georgia, Louisiana, Mississippi, and South Carolina still had school systems that were entirely segregated.

SNCC and the Kennedys

In 1960 a Democrat, John F. Kennedy, was elected president. During his election campaign, Kennedy had endeared himself to civil rights supporters by gestures of support for Martin Luther King, Jr., who was being held in jail after a protest. Kennedy had an undeserved reputation as a civil rights supporter. In fact, the new president was not especially well informed on Movement issues. Like Eisenhower, he thought of civil rights in terms of the issue's impact on the Cold War. Since treating blacks as second-class citizens made it hard for America to recruit peoples of color elsewhere for the struggle against communism, Kennedy supported civil rights. The president and his brother Robert, whom he made attorney general, simply did not understand the intensity of civil rights issues for people in the South. The Kennedys repeatedly took actions that indicated that their own political fortunes ranked higher in their priorities than civil rights, and they frequently urged Movement leaders to slow down or stop protests. Like Eisenhower, Kennedy intervened in the South only when he had to uphold federal power in the face of state defiance.

While school segregation proceeded slowly, and the SCLC struggled to define its role, southern black college students grew impatient. The Supreme Court had mandated school desegregation. No such court rulings required southern whites to desegregate public facilities or privately owned businesses, like restaurants or stores. Yet in terms of daily irritation, segregation in public accommodations was probably worse than segregated schools. Blacks could travel for miles on end through many parts of the South without finding a place to eat or even a public restroom to use.

In 1960, a group of black college students at North Carolina A & T in Greensboro decided to attack segregation by walking into Woolworth's, sitting at the lunch counter, and asking for service. The sit-in movement began in Greensboro and spread quickly to college towns throughout the state and into Virginia, South Carolina, and Florida. At sit-ins, college students took their place at lunch counters and were promptly arrested by local police and carted off to jail while the next wave of students took their places. The sit-in movement scored successes throughout the South, particularly in upper South cities like Nashville.

Most of the students had been in their early teens at the time of the Montgomery boycott five years previously, and they were not too impressed by Dr. King and his fellow pastors, who had accomplished little since then. In April 1960, Ella Baker, SCLC's executive director, invited student activists to a meeting. About 120 young people, most of them black southerners with a few southern whites included, attended. Although she worked for SCLC, Baker shared the students' skepticism about the organization. She urged the students to form their own group, the Student Nonviolent Coordinating Committee, SNCC (always pronounced "Snick").

The students who formed SNCC brought a new radicalism to the civil rights struggle. They disdained caution, organization, authority, and most people over thirty. (SNCC members referred to King as "De Lawd," mocking what they perceived as religious pomposity.) Going where the spirit moved them, SNCC members instigated or joined sit-ins and protests in towns throughout the South. In 1961 SNCC participated in CORE's freedom rides, an attempt to desegregate interstate buses in the Deep South. As vehicles involved in interstate commerce, Greyhound and Trailways buses fell under federal jurisdiction. By riding the buses, CORE and SNCC hoped to draw the Kennedy administration into enforcing civil rights in the South.

The freedom rides succeeded in dramatizing white resistance to integration. After white mobs in Alabama attacked the buses, burning one, the Kennedy administration pressured state authorities to protect the riders. But when the freedom riders' bus arrived in Montgomery on May 20, a white mob attacked the riders and also injured a Justice Department representative. On the following evening, King and other civil rights speakers came to a special meeting at First Baptist Church to honor the freedom riders. Despite the presence of federal marshals, a white mob surrounded the church and threatened to burn it with the crowd inside. Alabama Governor John Patterson sent in the National Guard, who protected the church until it could be evacuated the next morning.

Despite pleas from the Kennedy administration to stop the freedom rides, SCLC and SNCC joined CORE in continuing the campaign through Mississippi and Louisiana. In Mississippi, state troopers arrested and jailed freedom riders, most of whom refused bond and were sent to county jails or to the state's dreaded prison, Parchman, for the crime of sitting in the white sections of interstate buses.

The Kennedy administration wanted to channel the Movement away from direct action and toward political activities that might be useful to the Democratic Party. In June 1961, Attorney General Robert Kennedy told a meeting of civil rights leaders that they should turn their attention to voter registration in the Deep South and promised that the Justice Department and the FBI would protect such efforts. Private foundations provided funds to form the Voter Education Project, which financed attempts to educate and register black voters in the Deep South.

SNCC members moved to rural communities in Mississippi and Georgia and went to work. They quickly found out that Robert Kennedy's promise meant nothing: the federal government would not protect them. Indeed, many SNCC workers came to believe that the FBI was actively working against them. (FBI Director J. Edgar Hoover thought that the Civil Rights Movement was a communist plot, and southern FBI agents were certainly not friendly to Movement workers.)

From 1961 through 1964, SNCC workers and their local supporters were threatened, beaten, bombed out, and killed. SNCC people lost their idealism but found the strength to go on among the local people of the rural South. Faced with a situation in which some of the poorest elderly black women behaved with courage and dignity, while middle-class blacks wavered in their support for civil rights and the federal government reneged on its promises of protection, SNCC members became radicals. College students who had been aspiring members of the black middle classes put on overalls as a gesture of identification with sharecroppers and began to question the legitimacy of American society as a whole.

In November 1961, SNCC began a campaign for desegregation in Albany, Georgia, that produced the Movement's most famous defeat. As civil rights workers privately acknowledged, the Movement's success depended on the stupidity of its enemies. Nothing helped the Movement more than television pictures of Southern sheriffs flailing into nonviolent demonstrators or making speeches denouncing "niggers." Northern television audiences ate that up and gave more money so that the Movement could continue. In Albany, the movement ran aground on the rock of Laurie Prichett, the town's police chief. Chief Prichett did a very simple thing: he read King's book and studied up on Gandhian tactics. When the Movement came to Albany, he was ready. When SNCC led demonstrators into the streets, Prichett arrested them. He had already arranged to house prisoners in the jails of neighboring counties, so the Movement could not win by swamping the jails.

After a month of demonstrations and arrests, local leaders invited King and the SCLC to Albany, hoping that the Movement leader's charismatic presence would bring national media coverage to Albany. Prichett understood the media game as well and forbade his men to use violence against demonstrators, especially in front of television cameras. He simply enforced the law and treated King and other civil rights leaders with dignity. When demonstrators knelt in prayer, Prichett and his men took off their hats and bowed their heads, then arrested the demonstrators after the last "Amen."

After months of having nonviolence trumped by nonviolence, the Albany movement disintegrated. King and the SCLC left the town defeated but determined to go on. They planned their next assault on Jim Crow more carefully. To win, the Civil Rights Movement needed confrontations that made national news. In 1963, King and the SCLC took the Movement to Birmingham, Alabama, where such confrontations seemed inevitable.

Birmingham

National public opinion considered Alabama one of the most recalcitrant segregationist states. This reputation derived in part from the language used by Alabama's governor, George C. Wallace, and in part from the difficulties faced by the Civil Rights Movement in Alabama's largest city, Birmingham.

In 1962 George C. Wallace won the governorship of Alabama by pledging to oppose integration, a pledge he repeated in his January, 1963 inaugural address: "In the name of the greatest people that have ever trod this earth, I draw the line in the dust and toss the gauntlet before the feet of tyranny and I say segregation now! segregation tomorrow! segregation forever!"

As governor, Wallace came out swinging with public statements praising the Southern way of life and off-the-record comments suggesting that he would force the Kennedys to send in troops to integrate Alabama schools. By 1963, Wallace had built a national reputation as a die-hard segregationist and was gearing up to defy federal court orders to integrate the University of Alabama, as he had promised in his election campaign: "I shall refuse to abide by any such illegal federal court order even to the point of standing in the schoolhouse door." Wallace had close political ties to Birmingham segregationists and encouraged their resistance to SCLC and the Movement.

Fred Shuttlesworth and the Alabama Christian Movement for Human Rights had been fighting the battle of Birmingham since the late 1950s, despite opposition by conservative black leaders and a history of racially motivated bombings that had given the city the nickname "Bombingham." Birmingham's police force included many KKK members, and its Citizens' Council drew condemnation from other councils in the state for its blatant racism.

Birmingham was a steel town whose local bosses, referred to as the Big Mules, took their orders from corporate headquarters in Pittsburgh and New York. Most of the city's business leaders lived outside the city limits in incorporated suburbs "over the mountain." Thus, unlike most other cities, Birmingham lacked a civic elite whose fortunes would be damaged if the city authorities made fools of themselves on national television. In 1963, Birmingham also suffered from divided municipal leadership. As a result of a complicated and contested election, Birmingham effectively had two city governments, and no one was really minding the store, when King and the SCLC came to town. With the city's government in confusion, police commissioner Eugene "Bull" Conner took charge of the segregationist opposition.

Historians of the Movement have come to agree with Fred Shuttlesworth, who commented that "but for Birmingham" there would have been no civil rights legislation, no federal intervention—no "Second Reconstruction." The historical significance of Birmingham does not derive from the astute management of civil rights leaders there. Instead, Birmingham highlights the importance of the Civil Rights Movement's opposition. Bull Conner proved to be just the opponent the Movement needed.

The SCLC began demonstrations in Birmingham in April 1963, but quickly found that most local blacks did not want to be involved. When an Alabama court issued an injunction against the demonstrations, King and other leaders defied it and went to jail, where King wrote the classic "Letter from Birmingham City Jail," defending the Movement and nonviolent resistance. Movement leaders realized that unless something changed, the Movement would go down to an Albany-like defeat in Birmingham.

The SCLC decided to enlist high school and elementary school students as demonstrators. In a highly controversial decision, the Movement sent children into the streets, where they were arrested in droves. Police Commissioner Conner ordered fire hoses and police dogs turned on the children. The situation in Birmingham made newspaper headlines all over the world, to the nation's shame and the Kennedy administration's embarrassment. The administration brokered a settlement that allowed King and SCLC to declare victory in Birmingham.

The battle of Alabama was not over. In June, Governor Wallace signified resistance to integration and defiance to the federal government by standing in the door of the University of Alabama to keep black students from registering. (While television cameras focused on Wallace, the two students checked into their dorms and went about their business.) Segregationists continued to bomb in Birmingham, in September dynamiting the Sixteenth Street Baptist Church and killing four young girls at Sunday school. But with Birmingham, King and the SCLC seized the initiative and refocused national attention on civil rights.

In June 1963, President Kennedy spoke to the nation: "We are confronted with a moral issue. It is as old as the Scriptures and as clear as the American constitution." With a reference to events in Birmingham, he pointed out that black citizens' struggle for equality could no longer be ignored. He called upon Congress to pass a civil rights bill. That very night, a white assassin shot down Mississippi NAACP president Medgar Evers in his own front yard, a painful punctuation to Kennedy's call for national action on civil rights.

In the summer of 1963, King and all factions of the Civil Rights Movement joined to sponsor a march on Washington in support of civil rights legislation. A crowd filled the lawn before the Lincoln Memorial to cheer King's famous "I Have a Dream" speech: "I have a dream that one day this nation will rise up and live out the true meaning of its creed: 'We hold these truths to be self-evident, that all men are created equal.' I have a dream that one day on the red hills of Georgia, the sons of former slaves and the sons of former slave-owners will be able to sit together at the table of brotherhood." Although King concluded his speech, "Free at last! Free at last! Thank God almighty, we are free at last!" the Kennedy administration lacked the political clout necessary to get the civil rights bill passed. In

November, when the president was assassinated in Dallas, the bill had still not passed. Upon Kennedy's death, Vice President Lyndon Johnson assumed the presidency.

The Importance of Lyndon Johnson

Lyndon Johnson had Texas-size ambitions and appetites. As senator from Texas, Johnson became Senate Majority Leader in the 1950s. He built a reputation for ruthlessly effective political maneuvering. The "Johnson treatment" included smothering supporters with affection—and punishing opponents. In 1960, Johnson accepted the vice presidential nomination. He served for three years, becoming increasingly bored. Johnson had come into politics during the New Deal and admired Franklin Roosevelt. He wanted to make history. When he became president, he knew his hour had come.

Johnson moved immediately to muster congressional support for the civil rights bill. Congressional Democratic liberals and conservatives were both startled: as a politician from Texas, Johnson had no strong record of supporting civil rights legislation. When a Movement supporter asked him about his change of heart, Johnson quoted King: "Free at last, free at last, thank God Almighty, I'm free at last." In 1963, Johnson told his fellow Southern congressmen, including his old mentor Senator Richard Russell of Georgia, that he intended to have civil rights legislation, and that he would reward those who helped him and punish those who did not. Johnson broke southern resistance in Congress and put together bipartisan support for the 1964 Civil Rights Act, which he signed into law on July 2, 1964.

The Civil Rights Act of 1964 made Jim Crow laws illegal, mandated the desegregation of public accommodations, and authorized federal lawsuits to desegregate public facilities and schools. Under the act, any institution that took federal funding risked losing that funding if it discriminated against people on the basis of race, sex, or religion. The act also prohibited discriminatory hiring practices in firms with more than twenty-five employees and created the Equal Employment Opportunity Commission to enforce compliance.

While Johnson pushed the Civil Rights Act through Congress, the Movement turned its focus to voter registration drives, attracting national attention to Mississippi and Alabama. Television cameras failed to capture much of the pain of Movement days in Mississippi. SNCC workers struggled to register blacks to vote in rural counties far from media attention. White Mississippians retaliated vigorously against SNCC and the local people who supported it, using economic and legal pressure and some of the most vicious racially motivated violence in the South's history.

To coordinate Movement efforts, SNCC and other civil rights organizations in Mississippi formed COFO, the Council of Federated Organizations. In 1964 COFO decided to focus a national spotlight on Mississippi. The organization created the "Summer Project" to bring middle-class white northern college students to Mississippi to work in voter registration drives. With the help of northern liberals, COFO recruited hundreds of white volunteers, trained them, and tried to warn them that they were going into harm's way.

SNCC veterans and local Mississippians knew how dangerous the Summer Project was, but even they were stunned when three Movement workers (a local black man, a white SNCC veteran from New York, and a Summer Project volunteer from New York who had been in the state for one day) disappeared on June 21, 1964, on their way to investigate a church burning. The families of the northern civil rights workers aroused national attention. President Johnson ordered in U.S. troops to search for the men and sent the FBI to investigate the crime. In August their bodies were found buried under an earthen dam near Philadelphia, Mississippi. Using paid informants, the FBI found their killers, who were tried and convicted. Meanwhile, national opinion condemned Mississippi. "Freedom Summer," as it came to be known, rallied national support for a legislative attack on disfranchisement.

That summer and fall Lyndon Johnson campaigned for reelection, taking his support for civil rights into the Deep South. At a campaign dinner in New Orleans, Johnson spoke bluntly to an assembled crowd of southern politicians. Johnson described an old-style southern politician begging on his death bed to be allowed to give just one more "Democrat speech" about helping the common people. Johnson said that Southerners had not heard a real Democrat speech in years—all they had been allowed to hear was "nigger, nigger, nigger!"

Johnson's support for civil rights had limits. At his instruction, the Democratic National Convention refused to seat delegates from the Mississippi Freedom Democratic Party, which had been formed by COFO to challenge the segregationist Mississippi delegation's right to represent the state. Johnson preferred to deal with professional politicians, not with women like Fannie Lou Hamer or the other working people who formed the majority of the MFDP delegation. Instead, he supported the seating of the all-white official Mississippi delegation, with the admittance of two MFDP people as at-large delegates. His indifference to what SNCC saw as the justice of the MFDP's claims further radicalized SNCC members. However, Johnson went on to win reelection by a landslide.

The 1964 presidential election gave even stronger evidence of the southern political realignment that had been building since the late 1940s. Black voters turned out in droves to support Johnson and the national Democratic ticket. In states where blacks could vote, the southern Democratic Party became increasingly biracial. This displeased conservative southern whites, hundreds of thousands of whom began to consider affiliating with the overwhelmingly white Republican Party. The GOP leadership wooed southern support by opposing federal action on civil rights and labeling such action a violation of states' rights.

The Republican stand on civil rights helps explain why GOP presidential candidate Barry Goldwater carried five southern states: South Carolina, Georgia, Alabama, Mississippi, and Louisiana. Republican strategists, long accustomed to writing off the previously "solid" Democratic South, began making plans to capitalize on southern white voters' discontent with their old party.

Meanwhile, the Movement's focus shifted to voting rights. Although black political power could already be felt in the upper South states, many of the Deep South states still disfranchised black citizens. Movement people believed that federal intervention would be required to give blacks back the right to vote.

In 1965, SNCC and the SCLC opened a voter registration campaign in Selma, Alabama. Selma was picked in part because it had the kind of city authorities likely to supply the bloody drama required to get television coverage. Sure enough, Sheriff Jim Clark blocked the access of blacks to the voter registration office and formed an armed posse of local white men to keep order. In a town near Selma, a policeman killed a black protester who attempted to protect his mother from a police assault.

To protest, civil rights workers organized a march from Selma to Montgomery. Although Governor Wallace refused to give his permission, on March 7 demonstrators proceeded out of Selma. At the Edmund

Pettus bridge, Alabama state troopers blocked the road. Behind the troopers, Sheriff Clark's posse mounted up on horseback. Television cameras recorded the confrontation. The line of marchers, headed by SNCC's John Lewis and SCLC's Hosea Williams, stopped. Silence fell over the marchers. The state troopers' commander ordered the marchers to disperse. When they did not, the state troopers took out their clubs and attacked. Sheriff Clark's posse charged whooping into the crowd. Clark shouted, "Get those god-damned niggers! And get those goddamned white niggers!" The march ended in screams and blood. The television cameramen knew they had a winner. The film, quickly processed, made it to the networks by prime time. The ABC network interrupted a movie about the Nuremburg trials of Nazi war criminals to show Alabama troopers brutalizing civil rights marchers.

President Johnson told his attorney general to write "the god-damnedest toughest voting rights act that you can devise," and on March 15 went before Congress to call for passage of a voting rights act. Of the civil rights workers in the South, the President said, "Their cause must be our cause too. Because it is not just Negroes, but really it is all of us who must overcome the crippling legacy of bigotry and injustice. And we *shall* overcome." With Johnson's strong support, Congress passed the Voting Rights Act of 1965, which allowed federal intervention into voter registration in states that still had literacy tests or other disfranchising devices. The Voting Rights Act ended disfranchisement and made black political power a possibility in the Deep South.

Ten years after the Montgomery bus boycott had signaled the beginning of the Civil Rights Movement, all vestiges of the legal framework that had supported Jim Crow had been destroyed. The Civil Rights Movement had achieved a triumph hardly paralleled in American history. Ending legal segregation and disfranchisement did not end racism, which, as southerners pointed out, existed on both sides of the Mason-Dixon line. Nor did the Civil Rights Movement succeed in creating a color-blind America. But it did force the South to give up its system of legalized racial discrimination and become like the rest of the nation.

After 1965, the Movement dissolved into its component factions. Some black members of the Movement went on to conventional political careers, running for and winning public office in southern states. However, many of the young people in SNCC had been greatly disillusioned by mainstream politicians' willingness to betray the poor and powerless. Some dropped out of activism and tried to rebuild private lives that had been put on hold for years of activism. Others became advocates of Black Power, a movement for black pride, political power, nationalism, and separatism that grew in strength during the tumultuous late 1960s. The Black Power movement was not an exclusively southern phenomenon, but a national one, one more indication that racial issues once considered by northern whites to be peculiarly southern were now national in scope.

Radio Free Dixie

When military veteran Robert F. Williams returned to his hometown of Monroe, North Carolina, in 1955, he joined the local NAACP, only to see the middle-class membership dwindle as the organization faced white terrorism in the wake of *Brown v. Board of Education*. As chapter president, Williams enrolled working-class blacks and with their support made the Monroe NAACP one of the South's most active chapters. In one famous case, Williams mobilized support for two little black boys, aged eight and ten, who were sentenced to long terms in the state reformatory because one of them had kissed an eight-year-old white girl. Williams's efforts received international attention, and the two children were released after three months in jail.

By the late 1950s, Williams had become a nationally known advocate of black self-defense. He argued that since blacks could not count on justice from the police or the courts, they should defend themselves as needed when attacked. This put him on a collision course with the national leadership of the NAACP, which was publicly committed to nonviolence. In 1959 the national NAACP removed him from the presidency of the Monroe branch, even though Williams's stand was not that different from positions taken by other black leaders, including Martin Luther King.

Back in Monroe, Williams's situation became ever more precarious. Finally, in 1961, he was accused of kidnapping a white couple who had taken shelter in his home for fear of a black mob. Convinced he would not receive justice, Williams took his family and fled to Cuba. Under the sponsorship of Fidel Castro, Williams broadcast *Radio Free Dixie* from Havana from 1961 to 1964. He later moved on to China. Williams and his family finally returned to the United States in the late 1960s. By that time, Williams had lost enthusiasm for fighting for leadership of the black freedom movement. However, his ideas about self-reliance and self-defense, as printed in pamphlets and broadcast over Radio Free Dixie, had become influential among the younger generation of black activists. Historian Timothy Tyson considers Williams a major contributor to the rise of the Black Power movement.

During the late 1960s southerners, like other Americans, debated the virtues and defects of President Johnson's reform program, the Great Society, which provided a raft of social programs that attempted to make life better for the poor and aged. Johnson intended to declare a "War on Poverty." Poverty programs targeted areas of the Appalachian South as in special need of help and showered them with federal grants and social workers. Throughout the region, the poor of both races benefited from Johnson's programs, especially Medicare and Medicaid.

In the 1960s southern soldiers began to ship out for a Cold War conflict, the war in Vietnam. During the early years of the war in Vietnam, college students could obtain a draft deferment. Those who were too poor to go to college went to Vietnam. Since the South was still the nation's poorest region, the U.S. military drew its troops disproportionately from the southern states, and disproportionately from poor people, black and white.

After 1965 Dr. Martin Luther King became increasingly critical of America's involvement in the Vietnam War and increasingly vocal about his belief that poverty, not race alone, held African-Americans back. He seemed to be moving toward a critique of American society based on class, while he attempted without success to transfer the Movement to northern ghettos. In 1968, members of a predominantly black sanitation workers' union asked King to come to Memphis to support them in a strike. He died in Memphis, victim of an assassin's bullet.

The Transformation of Southern Politics

When the 1960s began, most white southerners still voted for the Democratic Party in most state and national elections. By the end of the decade, that had changed. For the first time since Reconstruction, the Republican Party became a contender in southern politics. Many white southern voters turned to the party of Lincoln because the GOP of the 1960s was much more conservative than Lyndon Johnson's Democratic Party. The national Republican leadership learned to capitalize on southern white discontent by watching the campaigns of an old-style southern Democrat, Alabama Governor George Wallace.

Wallace, Race, and Class

In 1963 George Wallace's inaugural address as governor of Alabama promised "Segregation now! Segregation tomorrow! Segregation forever!" In June of that year he stood symbolically in the door of the University of Alabama to block the admittance of black students. In 1964, Wallace challenged Lyndon Johnson for the Democratic presidential nomination. In Wisconsin, Indiana, and Maryland he got over 30 percent of the vote, much to the shock of northern politicians. Thinking of Wallace as a stereotypical southern segregationist, they could not fathom why northern voters would support him. In fact, the Alabama governor had received many telegrams and letters from northerners in support of his earlier white supremacist stands.

But Wallace's appeal was not just racist; it was also class-based. In 1964 and in 1968, when he ran for the presidency again as an independent candidate, Wallace upheld the values of the white working class. At a time when college deferments saved middle-class youths from service in Vietnam, Wallace praised the patriotism of the working class and called antiwar protesters "silver-spooned brats." He campaigned against the counterculture of sex, drugs, and rock-and-roll, and for "law and order," which many Americans took as a coded promise to crack down on black riots, antiwar demonstrations, and inner-city crime. He poured scorn on those he called "pointy-headed" intellectuals, on bureaucrats who tried to socially engineer solutions to the nation's problems, and on "limousine liberals" who supported school desegregation from the safety of all-white, affluent suburbs.

In 1968 Wallace drew tens of thousands of supporters to rallies throughout the nation—70,000 in Boston and 20,000 to a raucous gathering at New York's Madison Square Garden. Hunter Thompson, the counterculture journalist, described a Wallace speech as being like a political rock concert. Coatless, sleeves rolled up, sweating, Wallace worked a crowd like a revival preacher—or like Elvis. He was the farthest thing from cool or telegenic, a direct throwback to old-style southern stump speaking.

In 1968 the presidential race in the South was between Wallace and the GOP candidate, Richard Nixon. The Democratic candidate, Hubert Humphrey, carried only Texas. Nixon won Florida, Kentucky, North Carolina, Oklahoma, South Carolina, Tennessee, and Virginia, with Wallace coming in second. The Alabama governor carried his home state, Mississippi, and pluralities in Arkansas, Georgia and Louisiana. He ran in 1972, but his campaign was cut short by an assassination attempt that left him in a wheelchair, paralyzed from the waist down. Although Wallace made a stab at the presidential race once more in 1976, his thunder had already been stolen by the Republicans.

Southern Republicans

The national Republican Party learned a lot from George Wallace. Republicans, traditionally the party of big business and the country club set, realized that the Democrats were losing control over the old New Deal coalition. With Richard Nixon at the helm, the GOP began to reach out to disaffected southern whites and working-class northern ethnics. Richard Nixon promised law and order and swept the South for reelection in 1972. But if southern segregationists thought that Nixon would try to roll back the civil rights gains of the 1960s, they were wrong. As president, Nixon presided over a federal desegregation suit against Georgia for maintaining separate school systems, and he encouraged federal affirmative action programs for minorities and women.

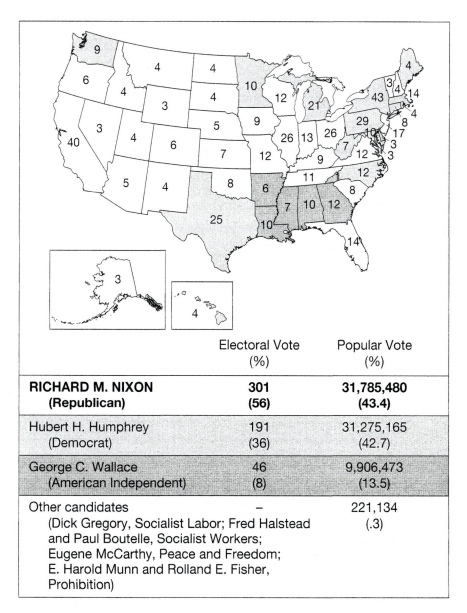

	Electoral Vote (%)	Popular Vote (%)
RICHARD M. NIXON (Republican)	**301 (56)**	**31,785,480 (43.4)**
Hubert H. Humphrey (Democrat)	191 (36)	31,275,165 (42.7)
George C. Wallace (American Independent)	46 (8)	9,906,473 (13.5)
Other candidates (Dick Gregory, Socialist Labor; Fred Halstead and Paul Boutelle, Socialist Workers; Eugene McCarthy, Peace and Freedom; E. Harold Munn and Rolland E. Fisher, Prohibition)	–	221,134 (.3)

Election of 1968

Traditional Southern Republicans

When hundreds of thousands of white southerners shifted their allegiance to the Republican Party in the late 1960s and early 1970s, they joined southerners whose families had maintained a loyalty to the GOP since the Civil War.

White southerners who were Unionists during the war usually joined the Republicans after it. In 1960, southern states had counties that had consistently voted Republican since the 1870s. Among these isolated outposts of Republicanism, the largest was probably East Tennessee.

Another source of traditional Republicanism remained in the conservative black communities of the South. Although most African-Americans shifted party membership to the Democrats in the 1930s, not all did so. Some black southerners stayed loyal to the GOP. Black southern Republicans remain rather rare, but they do still exist. They share with white southern Republicans a profound conservatism, particularly on religious and gender issues. In addition, many find social programs such as affirmative action insulting. The ideological heirs of Booker T. Washington, they prefer self-reliance to alliances with white liberals.

After a brief hiatus in 1976, when Georgia Governor Jimmy Carter capitalized on the nation's distrust for Republicans after the Watergate scandal to become president, Ronald Reagan won the South back for the GOP in 1980. The Republicans garnered support from the region's growing white middle class, who supported the GOP's economic programs and its conservative social agenda. As a Republican official told political scientist Alexander Lamis in 1981, "All you have to do to keep the South is for Reagan to run in place on the issues . . . fiscal conservatism, balancing the budget, cut taxes, you know, the whole cluster."

Republicans courted southern white voters, and conservatives throughout the nation, with rhetoric that promised cutbacks in social programs at home, a stronger military presence abroad, and action in favor of a conservative agenda that included constitutional amendments repealing abortion rights and reinstating school prayer. This appealed to many different types of voters. A candidate like Reagan could unite small-town businessmen, cold warriors determined to continue the struggle against the decaying Soviet Union, religious conservatives, and people who favored scrapping affirmative action and welfare on racial grounds.

It should be pointed out, however, that people who voted Republican for racial reasons were found on both sides of the Mason-Dixon line. Northern working-class whites who had liked Wallace became "Reagan Democrats" during the 1980s, for many of the same reasons as southern whites. Moreover, when elected, Reagan devoted most of his time to his economic and military agenda and spent very little political capital on causes dear to southern white conservatives. Although he did not enforce civil rights legislation with enthusiasm, affirmative action was still intact when he left office, as were abortion rights and the Supreme Court ban on school prayer.

Since 1980, the GOP has dominated presidential elections in the South, and the South has increasingly dominated the GOP. Southern senators and representatives hold high positions in the Republican congressional leadership. However, the southern Democratic Party is by no means dead.

Southern Democrats

As segregationists and conservative white men fled the Democratic Party, blacks and white women replaced them. Today, the Democratic Party in the South is one of the most racially integrated political groups in the nation. As Democrats, black politicians serve in public offices in all southern states (although still in smaller proportions than their percentage in the population.) Since the 1960s, black southern Democrats have built power bases in southern cities, and blacks have served, and continue to serve, as mayors in Atlanta, Charlotte, Birmingham, and elsewhere. Virginians elected Doug Wilder governor in 1989, becoming the first state in the nation to place a black man in the governor's mansion.

To win presidential elections in the post-Reagan era, the national Democratic Party turned to candidates from the South. This was profoundly irritating to northeastern liberals, who found southern Democrats too conservative. But after Massachusetts governor Michael Dukakis went down to a humiliating defeat in 1988, losing badly to Republican George Bush, the Democratic Party rallied behind a governor from Arkansas in 1992.

The South in National Politics

Bill Clinton held the presidency for two terms. His chief opponents in the House and Senate were southern Republicans. When Congress impeached the president, he was prosecuted by a House management team dominated by white southern Republicans and defended by (among others) black southern Democrats, including veterans of the Civil Rights Movement. By the late 1990s, national politics had taken on a distinctly regional accent.

In the 2000 presidential election, a Democrat from Tennessee, Albert Gore Jr., faced a Republican from Texas, George W. Bush. In many ways both men were products of the changing demography and politics of the post-World War II South. Gore's father, a pro-civil rights Democrat and long-term Tennessee senator, saw his political career destroyed in the early 1970s by the new-style southern Republican Party. George W. Bush's father, a rich upper-class New Englander, had been part of the postwar migration of well-to-do, educated white northerners into the South.

The idea that both national parties would field southern white men as presidential candidates would have profoundly shocked politicians in 1880 or, for that matter, 1950. But in 1992 a book by political scientists Earl and Merle Black, *The Vital South*, argued that winning the South had become essential for presidential candidates. According to the Blacks, the South's "unmatched size and potential unity make [it] . . . the grand regional prize of presidential elections." This was especially true for the Republican Party. The Blacks believe that if the GOP can carry the South, then they can ignore most of the rest of the nation, concentrating all their efforts on a few key non-southern states, California being the most important. After decades of being written off in national politics, the southern states were suddenly cast in the role of kingmakers.

The growth of southern political power reflects the region's continuing population growth. If the southern states continue to gain population, the region may be the key to the nation's politics for years to come.

White Resistance, White Accommodation

In 1963 Glenn Evans was a Birmingham police captain assigned to arrest children demonstrating for civil rights. As he and his fellow policemen loaded the students into school buses to transport them to jail, his coworker said to him, "Evans, ten or fifteen years from now, we will look back on this and we will say, 'How stupid can you be?'"

While civil rights workers and segregationists fought for the region's soul, most white southerners quietly made their peace with integration. The civil rights drama obscured deep divisions in the white population about the morality and practicality of continued support for Jim Crow. Pollsters working in the South after the *Brown* decision had discovered that about 20 percent of Southern whites accepted the decision, while about 20 percent were die-hard segregationists. The remaining 60 percent supported segregation but without the deep conviction expressed by groups like the Citizens' Councils and the Klan. By the late 1950s, polls showed that a majority of southern whites thought integration was inevitable.

Few white southerners openly supported the Movement. Those who did were often motivated by religion or conscience. Some white southern men and women marched with the Movement, or gave legal aid, or turned their homes into safe houses for activists on the road. There were white ministers whose support for the Movement cost them their pulpits. There were white journalists whose reports and editorials earned them community ostracism and crosses burned on their front lawns, and white businessmen whose support for civil rights cost them in money and community standing. However, if most southern whites over forty were asked by their grandchildren today what they did for civil rights, they could only reply, "Nothing."

But when the Civil Rights Movement came to a crunch, when the federal government made integration the law of the land, most white southerners did refuse to follow the die-hard segregationists into open defiance. To keep segregation, white southerners would have had to give up public schools and federal contracts and accustom themselves to the condemnation of national and world opinion. That was a price too high. Instead of fighting for segregation to the last ditch, southern whites minded their own private lives—and joined the Republican Party.

Deseg Academies, North and South

In some southern communities, segregationist whites accommodated to the end of Jim Crow by pulling their children out of public schools entirely and placing them in newly created private schools. Called "deseg academies," these schools sometimes had an official Christian orientation, but they were not open to Christians of color.

This flight from the public schools was most common in areas with large to majority black populations. In areas where blacks were a small to tiny minority, whites did not usually withdraw from integrated public schools.

Throughout the nation, most school segregation grew from residential patterns. The postwar suburbs circling northern and western cities were as resolutely segregated as those around Houston or Birmingham. To break up school segregation based on residential patterns, courts in the 1970s turned to busing, sending black students to schools in white areas and whites to schools in black areas. This proved overwhelmingly unpopular with white parents in every region of the country. White suburban and urban parents fled busing and the public school, placing their children in private schools instead. Unlike southern deseg academies, these schools were not always racially segregated, but their cost usually made them inaccessible to poor people of any race. The great exception to this statement is found in Catholic parochial schools, favorites of urban parents of all races and religions who want a good, safe education for their children.

Today, poll takers find that white southerners' attitudes about race are no longer strikingly different from those of Americans elsewhere. This may not be completely good news. African-Americans have been pointing out for years that racism is an American, not just a southern, phenomenon. As the South became more like parts of the North, southerners may have switched to northern ways of thinking about race. The region's adoption of northern housing patterns may be significant. In the pre-war South, poor and rich, black and white lived in close proximity, particularly in rural areas and small towns. The postwar suburbs, south and north, separated people by race and class in a new way. Living in homogenous enclaves, shopping in up-scale local malls, southern suburbanites and their northern counterparts can avoid people different from them, whether that difference is measured by race or class. Rather than contesting public space, suburbanites throughout the nation have withdrawn from it.

Elvis Presley spent most of the early 1960s making movies in Hollywood as the musical revolution he had helped start passed him by. When he made a comeback in the late 1960s, one of the songs he chose was Mickey Newman's "American Trilogy." Backed up by a trio of black harmony singers, Elvis began with a quiet, slow, elegiac rendition of "Dixie:" "I wish I was in the land of cotton. Old times there are not forgotten." Then he segued into a piece of traditional black folk music, singing "If religion was a thing that money could buy, the rich would live, and the poor would die . . . all my trials, Lord, soon be over." The last words of "American Trilogy" were from the "Battle Hymn of the Republic." The man who had combined black and white music to popularize rock and roll brought audiences to their feet with the final words: "Glory, glory hallelujah! His truth is marching on." "American Trilogy" had been composed to express in music how it felt to be southern in the 1960s.

Suggestions for Further Reading and Viewing

NUMAN BARTLEY, *The New South, 1945–1980* (1995)

TAYLOR BRANCH, *Parting the Waters: America in the King Years, 1954–63* (1989)

———, *Pillar of Fire: America in the King Years,* 1963–54 (1998)

DAN T. CARTER, *The Politics of Rage: George Wallace, the Origins of the New Conservatism, and the Transformation of American Politics* (1995)

DAVID CHAPPELL, *Inside Agitators: White Southerners in the Civil Rights Movement* (1994)

PETE DANIEL, *Lost Revolutions: The South in the 1950s* (2000)

JOHN DITTMER, *Local People: The Struggle for Civil Rights in Mississippi* (1994)

GLENN ESKEW, *But for Birmingham* (1997)

Eyes on the Prize (Video, Blackside Productions)

DAVID GARROW, *Bearing the Cross* (1986)

DEWEY GRANTHAM, *The South in Modern America* (1994)

HENRY HAMPTON AND STEVE FAYER, *Voices of Freedom: An Oral History of the Civil Rights Movement from the 1950s through the 1980s* (1990)

STEVEN F. LAWSON AND CHARLES PAYNE, *Debating the Civil Rights Movement* (1998)

CHARLES MARSH, *God's Long Summer: Stories of Faith and Civil Rights* (1997)

CHARLES M. PAYNE, *I've Got the Light of Freedom: The Organizing Tradition and the Mississippi Freedom Struggle* (1995)

HOWELL RAINES, *My Soul Is Rested: Movement Days in the Deep South Remembered* (1977)

BRUCE J. SCHULMAN, *From Cotton Belt to Sunbelt: Federal Policy, Economic Development and the Transformation of the South, 1938–1980* (1991)

TIMOTHY B. TYSON, *Radio Free Dixie: Robert F. Williams and the Roots of Black Power* (1999)

Rising Again: The South Since the 1960s

In the last thirty years the South has witnessed transformations in economics and politics that would have seemed unimaginable in 1900. In many ways the South now *is* the American mainstream, a phenomenon writer John Egerton referred to as the "Americanization of Dixie" and the "Southernization of America." Southern cultural products ranging from country music to pro wrestling to NASCAR now draw national audiences but in doing so have become less recognizably "southern" in quality. Southern political attitudes, including an abiding suspicion of government, have become common across the country.

Few southerners want to go back to the old days of poverty and white supremacy, yet many wish to maintain an identity as "southern." What follows are some sketches of the contemporary South, designed to raise the question, Is there really a distinctive South anymore, or has the region been melted into the nation?

The Climate-Controlled South

At the turn of the last century, southern historian U. B. Phillips began his book on the Old South with the sentence, "Let us begin by discussing the weather, for that has been the chief agency in making the South distinctive." Following Phillips's lead, historians, sociologists, and common southerners over the years have attributed everything from the region's high murder rate to its racial problems to the weather: it's hot, with average daily highs during the summer months always above 80 degrees, and frequently above 90. In a 1984 article, historian Raymond Arsenault suggested that the greatest social change in the South in the last thirty years has been the installation of air-conditioning.

Southerners used to build their houses for the climate, with wide porches and high ceilings. Despite all such efforts, the South used to be a very sweaty place. In the Deep South, many rural southerners developed a daily pattern rather like that of the Latin American tropics: rise early, work hard in the mornings, eat a big midday dinner, sleep a couple of hours, and work in the cool of the evening until it gets dark. People moved slowly, wore big hats, and drank lots of water. In southern cities, ceiling fans cooled stores, their ubiquitous, monotonous sound the background to commerce and conversation. Because it was so hot, southerners spent a great deal of time outdoors, sitting on front porches; it was easy to talk to neighbors.

All that is truly gone with the wind—the cooling wind roaring out of air conditioners throughout the region. Air-conditioning made possible the region's industrial, commercial and technological development after World War II and the rapid urbanization that accompanied it. Air conditioning made skyscrapers and shopping malls feasible.

Arsenault and other historians suggest that the impact of the technology has gone even deeper, transforming southern culture. Some of the more negative aspects of southern white folk culture have been undercut by the desire of bigots to stay in that cool living room, watch TV, and have one more beer. It is hard to imagine raising a lynch mob in an air-conditioned Wal-Mart. The flip side, according to regional sociologists, is that the South is losing its legendary character as the nation's friendliest region. No longer do southerners spend much of their time outside, talking to neighbors. The front porch has all but disappeared, as southerners (like other Americans) retreat to the backyard deck.

Wal-Mart

Founded in 1962 in Bentonville, Arkansas, by Sam Walton, Wal-Mart started out as a five-and-dime, a kind of store that no longer exists. Five-and-dime stores offered cheap essentials of everyday life, from T-shirts to pencils to soap. Walton turned the five-and-dime into the modern discount store. Starting with small stores in small rural market centers, Wal-Mart spread through the South in the 1960s and 1970s, then made a leap to the rest of the nation.

Using cutting-edge logistics, imported goods, and nonunion labor, Wal-Mart is able to offer the best bargains around. Known for ruthless cost cutting, the Wal-Mart chain is hated by small merchants throughout the nation but loved by consumers because it supplies an abundance of cheap goods. Today the Wal-Mart empire is worth about $200 billion.

Founder Sam Walton never lost his own enjoyment of a bargain. Although a multibillionaire, he drove around Arkansas in an old pick-up truck, often accompanied by a hound dog. Wal-Mart never moved its corporate headquarters out of Bentonville (where else could it operate so cheaply?) Currently, Wal-Mart's incessant attempts to cut costs require American manufacturers to do the same. The chain of stores from Arkansas is now the driving force in American retail.

In the days of their poverty, southerners prided themselves on their humanity, their sense of community and place. They knew their neighbors. Today, southerners walk from air-conditioned suburban houses to air-conditioned cars for lengthy commutes down interstates to jobs in air-conditioned buildings. (Southern workers have some of the longest commutes in the nation. It takes Atlanta residents on average thirty minutes to get to work daily—if they do not get caught in a traffic jam. Throughout the region, hour-long commutes are common.) Far from being leisurely, southern urban life is fast-paced and increasingly anonymous in quality.

The Multi-Ethnic South

After years of being the last place in the country immigrants in search of jobs would come to, the South is now experiencing an increase in immigration. Although the percentage of foreign-born residents in the old Confederate states is still low—only 5.8 percent, as compared with New York's 15.9 percent—the region now draws people from all over the world. Throughout the region, immigrants from Asia and Africa now find work in occupations ranging from running motels, restaurants, and other service businesses to staffing hospitals and engineering computer software.

The most important addition to the southern ethnic mix, however, comes from just a bit further south. During the last twenty years the region has received a transfusion of Hispanic immigrants from Mexico, Guatemala, Cuba, and other Central American and Caribbean countries. In 1990 the percentage of foreign-born residents in Florida was 12.9, and 12.2 percent of the state's population was Hispanic in ethnic origin. Since the early 1960s, when Communists took power in Cuba, refugees from that island have come to South Florida. More recently, immigrants from other Spanish-speaking countries have established their own communities in Miami. Today Miami is a bilingual city, and Floridians with aspirations to political office find it useful to learn Spanish. The same is true in Texas. Although only 9 percent of the state's population was born outside the United States, in 1990 25.5 percent of Texans were of Hispanic, primarily Mexican-American, ancestry.

Throughout the South, migrant workers from Mexico and the Caribbean do the agricultural stoop labor that southern whites and blacks used to do. While some southerners resent immigrant labor and others resent the fact that Spanish has become the dominant language in parts of

Table 1
Southern State Population by Race and Ethnicity, 2000

State	Population	White	Black	Native American	Asian/ Pacific	Other Race	Multiple Race	Hispanic
Alabama	4,447,100	3,162,808	1,155,930	22,430	32,755	28,998	44,179	75,830
Arkansas	2,673,400	2,138,598	418,950	17,808	21,888	40,412	35,744	86,866
Florida	15,982,378	12,465,029	2,335,505	53,541	274,881	477,107	376,315	2,682,715
Georgia	8,186,453	5,327,281	2,349,542	21,737	177,416	196,289	114,188	435,227
Louisiana	4,468,976	2,856,161	1,451,944	25,477	55,998	31,131	48,265	107,738
Mississippi	2,844,658	1,746,099	1,033,809	11,652	19,293	13,784	20,021	39,569
North Carolina	8,049,313	5,804,656	1,737,545	99,551	117,672	186,629	103,260	378,963
South Carolina	4,012,012	2,695,560	1,185,216	13,718	37,642	39,926	39,950	95,076
Tennessee	5,689,283	4,563,310	932,809	15,152	58,867	56,036	63,109	123,838
Texas	20,851,820	14,799,505	2,404,566	118,362	576,753	2,438,001	514,633	6,669,666
Virginia	7,078,515	5,120,110	1,390,293	21,172	264,971	138,900	143,069	329,540

Source: U.S. Census Bureau, 2000 Census (see http://factfinder.census.gov).

Note: Hispanics may be of any race. Therefore, the subtotals will not add up to the state population total. The category "Asian/Pacific" above includes the census categories of Asian, Native Hawaiian, and other Pacific Islanders. The category "Native American" above includes American Indian and Alaskan Natives. The category "Hispanic," above, is officially denoted "Hispanic and Latino" in the Census; similarly, "Black," above, appears in the Census as "Black or African-American." Multiple race means two or more races.

the region, still others respect the work ethic and the strong emphasis on family that immigrants usually exhibit.

Religion and Gender

Southern attitudes toward gender issues and feminism can be very confusing to outsiders. First, many southern men and women genuinely believe that in marriage, the man is supposed to be the head of the household, and women are supposed to be subordinate—concepts usually considered conservative. However, the same men and women who hold these ideas see nothing incongruous in encouraging their daughters to be strong, athletic, competitive, and outspoken. Nor do most southerners expect women to work only at home. In fact, southern women, even those with small children, work outside the home in greater percentages than typical in supposedly liberal northern states. Perhaps the key to understanding modern southern gender values lies in the region's religious and rural past.

Many southern Protestant churches, black and white, insist that the Bible mandates women's subordination to men. In the mid-1960s the Southern Baptist Convention (SBC), representative of the largest religious group in the region, issued a pamphlet urging Baptist women not to work outside the home. The pamphlet warned that if women had their own money, they might not be properly submissive to their husbands. In the late 1990s, the SBC issued as part of its "Faith and Message" a statement calling upon wives to be submissive to their husbands. In 2000 the SBC announced that it considered women pastors unbiblical.

Southern antifeminist attitudes have had national political consequences. Although scholars trace one source of the contemporary women's movement to female civil rights activists, structured, organized feminism has never been a strong force in the region. In the 1980s, the southern states were instrumental in defeating the Equal Rights Amendment, with Senator Sam Erwin of North Carolina and a cohort of right-wing Republicans and conservative Protestant ministers leading the charge against this perceived threat to the family. Historians who have researched the ERA debacle note that contemporary feminists' insistence that men and women should be equal in the family as in society struck a sour note with many southerners, who held the sexes to be inherently different, not just biologically, but in their assigned social roles, which many southerners assume to be God-given.

Yet the South also has a tradition of strong women, whose abilities to cope and keep the family going in tough times are commemorated in family legends by whites and blacks alike. White and black women in previous generations did farm labor to support their families. Today, they work outside the family circle. In 1980 the southern work force was about 40 percent female. In 1990, 55.9 percent of the region's women over age sixteen worked outside the home. The percentage was even higher among women with children under age six: 62.7 percent. (By contrast, the percentage of New York women with young children working outside the home is only 52.5.) While these women may be subordinate in home and church, anyone planning to do business in the South should be wary: southern women are not likely to be submissive in the workforce.

Religion and Politics

In the 1980s, the southern GOP began to draw support from an unexpected source: conservative Christians. For many years, evangelicals, fundamentalists, and holiness people had abjured any involvement in politics, which they saw as intrisically unholy and worldly. However, the countercultural movement of the 1960s, combined with rising rates of divorce, abortion, illegitmacy, drug use, extramarital sex, and crime of all kinds, convinced many conservative Christians that America was hell-bound. To turn it around, they would have to enter politics. Some were lured into the political arena by Jimmy Carter, a Southern Baptist, only to decide that he was too liberal on social issues, especially abortion and the Equal Rights Amendment.

In 1980 conservative Christians became a force in American politics when they turned out for Ronald Reagan, helping him win the presidency. Although their values were conservative, their methods were modern: mass computerized mailings and cable TV. During the 1970s southern preachers had taken advantage of the proliferation of cable stations to boost religious broadcasting. In Lynchburg, Virginia, the Reverend Jerry Falwell, a Baptist, put on the "Old Time Gospel Hour," while fellow Virginian Pat Robertson, a Pentecostal, created an entire Christian Broadcasting Network, complete with his own news-oriented talk show.

While lesser televangelists like Jim and Tammy Faye Bakker and Jimmy Swaggert confined their broadcasting mostly to preaching, both Falwell and Robertson got into politics in a big way in the 1980s. Falwell formed the "Moral Majority," a coalition of conservative Protestants, Catholics, and Jews, and used it to support Republicans and oppose feminists and liberals.

Politics in Religion

In a place where, as one writer noted, the Baptists are the center of gravity, changes in the Southern Baptist Convention can indicate changes in the region as a whole. The SBC is not a governing body, like a board of bishops or a synod. Southern Baptists elect delegates to the SBC and follow its proceedings with interest, but congregations are not required to do as the SBC suggests.

For the past several decades, conservative Baptists have warred with moderates for control of the SBC and especially of denominational seminaries and colleges. These battles have had secular political connotations, in that the conservative forces within the SBC were often also involved in conservative Republican politics and political campaigns. However, the struggle for the soul of the SBC should be understood primarily in religious terms, as a battle between what Knoxville Baptist pastor David Hull calls the forces of "purity" and the forces of "freedom." As of 2000, the conservatives were winning.

In October 2000, the most prominent Southern Baptist in the nation, former President Jimmy Carter, withdrew from the denomination. A Sunday school teacher for fifty years, Carter continues to attend his local Baptist church. He explained that he left the SBC over statements

in the 2000 Baptist Faith and Message, which condemned
women pastors as unbiblical and omitted a long-standing
statement that Baptists interpret the scriptures through
Jesus Christ. Carter and other moderate Baptists considered
the latter omission a major change in Baptist doctrine and
one that contradicts traditional Baptist concepts of "soul
freedom." By 2000, moderate Baptists had begun to
withdraw financial support for the SBC and to build their
own denominational structure.

In 1988 Pat Robertson ran for the presidency. His candidacy ultimately fizzled out, but it served to signify the growing political strength of conservative Christian voters. In 1989 Robertson and GOP political operative Ralph Reed formed the Christian Coalition, designed to educate conservative Christians for political activism. In addition to distributing voters' guides in church, the Christian Coalition has encouraged conservative Christians to run for office, starting on the local level. In parts of the South, conservative Christians control the GOP party apparatus, and they form a powerful voting block in general elections.

The Rich South

Since the 1960s, more people have moved into the South than out. Most strikingly, this is true for African-Americans. After decades of out-migration, in 1970 only about 40 percent of the nation's blacks lived in the South. By 1990, more than 50 percent did, and the region's population was just over 19 percent African-American. Blacks moved south for the same reason as whites and immigrants: to get good jobs.

In the 1970s, when the American economy languished under high inflation rates and high unemployment, the national media coined two new words: "Rustbelt," to describe the aged, deteriorating industrial cities of the Northeast and Midwest, and "Sunbelt," to describe the string of prosperous urban areas from the Southeast across the Southwest to California. The nickname stuck. Despite booms and recessions over the past three decades, the South is no longer stigmatized as the nation's number 1 economic problem. Today southerners work in high-tech industries ranging from computer manufacturing to General Motors and Nissan's new computerized auto plants in Tennessee. Millions more southerners have jobs in service industries and in retail. The nation's discount chain giant, Wal-Mart, got its start in rural Arkansas and has since spread across the region and the nation like kudzu. Only a small minority of southerners now farm but many are employed in agribusiness, such as the chicken factories created by Tyson, also of Arkansas.

For those who remember the impoverished South, the shiny new cities of the South, with their "shiny, happy people" (to quote REM, the Athens, Georgia, alternative rock band) look just fine. Yet economists have pointed out deep structural inequities in the Sunbelt economy. These are not related directly to race but to class. To summarize briefly: for the educated middle class, no matter what color or ethnic group, the Sunbelt holds great opportunity. Taking into consideration the lower cost of housing in the region, salaried workers in the South now make about the same as similar workers elsewhere in the nation. The economy is growing faster than that of the nation as a whole. Southerners whose parents made the right decisions in the 1950s and 1960s—stay in school, get that high school diploma, and make sure your children go to college—have no problem now finding well-paying jobs within the region. But the South is not a good place for the poor.

In the 1940s and 1950s northern businesses placed small-scale manufacturing plants in the rural South to capitalize on the region's low wages and the tax breaks that town and county governments typically offered as incentives. Though such plants still flourish in parts of the rural South, the decades since 1960 have not been kind to them. As business becomes more international in scope, other countries are doing to the South what the South did to New England a generation ago: they lure away factories with the promise of very low labor costs. As factories close, their laid-off workforces cannot usually find jobs with equivalent pay and benefits. Instead, many working-class southerners find jobs in service and retail, traditionally low-pay positions, or work two or three part-time jobs.

As always, economic change in the South is refracted through race. Although the rise of the black middle class is one of the region's great success stories, blacks in general are still poorer than whites, as they are throughout the nation.

Not Forgotten

We end this book as we began, with questions. If the South is now part of the American mainstream, is it still distinctive? In the next century, will there still be a South, or will the region come to be seen simply as a collection of states without collective identity? Does being a southerner mean anything anymore? Will the identity mean anything in 2050?

The Literature of Nostalgia

Southerners of the baby boom generation were born into the last days of the southern way of life that was based upon poverty and Jim Crow and came of age during the Civil Rights era. As southern baby boomers now approach midlife, the disparity between the world of their childhood and the Sunbelt South is productive of thought, meditation, and (for writers) a stream of highly interesting memoirs. Until World War II changed the southern scene, most poor whites and blacks did not get the educational and social chances that enable one to become a scholar, novelist or writer. As a result, southern autobiography has always been skewed toward the upper class—until now.

Many memoirs by black baby boomers focus on the Civil Rights Movement. In *Warriors Don't Cry*, Melba Patillo Beals describes her experience as one of the students integrating Little Rock Central High. *Coming of Age in Mississippi* by Anne Moody was actually written during the Civil Rights Movement by one of its participants. For insight into growing up in the Jim Crow era, see Clifton Taulbert, *When We Were Colored*, or view the film made from this memoir by BET Enterprises. *Colored People* by Harvard

professor Henry Louis Gates is a bittersweet account of life in a segregated West Virginia town that experienced the Civil Rights Movement from a distance, through television.
White plain folk memoirs include journalist Rick Bragg's *All Over But the Shoutin';* Bobbie Ann Mason's *Clear Springs,* which discusses growing up female on that disappearing artifact of southern life, the family farm; Harry Crews's *A Childhood,* about life in Bacon County, Georgia; and Mary Karr's *The Liar's Club,* a memoir of a rough-and-tumble girlhood in a East Texas refinery town.

The demise of the South and southern culture has been predicted for years, but the region and the people are still here and still think of themselves as southerners, as somehow different from the rest of Americans. In the new millennium, southerners continue to cling to their heritage, perhaps the more fiercely as it fades away.

Suggestions for Further Reading

PETER APPLEBOME, *Dixie Rising: How the South Is Shaping American Values, Politics and Culture* (1996)

RAMOND ARSENAULT, "The End of the Long, Hot Summer: The Air Conditioner and Southern Culture," *Journal of Southern History* (November 1984), 597–628.

DAN T. CARTER, *From George Wallace to Newt Gingrich: Race in the Conservative Counterrevolution, 1963–1994* (1996)

JOHN EGERTON, *The Americanization of Dixie* (1974)

FIFTEEN SOUTHERNERS, *Why the South Will Survive* (1981)

TONY HORWITZ, *Confederates in the Attic: Dispatches from the Unfinished Civil War* (1998)

ALEXANDER P. LAMIS, *The Two-Party South* (1990)

DONALD G. MATHEWS AND JANE SHERRON DE HART, *Sex, Gender and the Politics of ERA* (1990)

JOHN SHELTON REED, *My Tears Spoiled My Aim and Other Reflections on Southern Culture* (1994)

JOHN DAVID SMITH AND TOM APPLETON, EDS. *A Mythic Land Apart: Reassessing Southerners and Their History* (1997)

CAROL STACK, *Call to Home: African Americans Reclaim the Rural South* (1996)

With God on Our Side: The Rise of the Religious Right in America (PBS Video 1996)

Index